Vampires in Silent Cinema

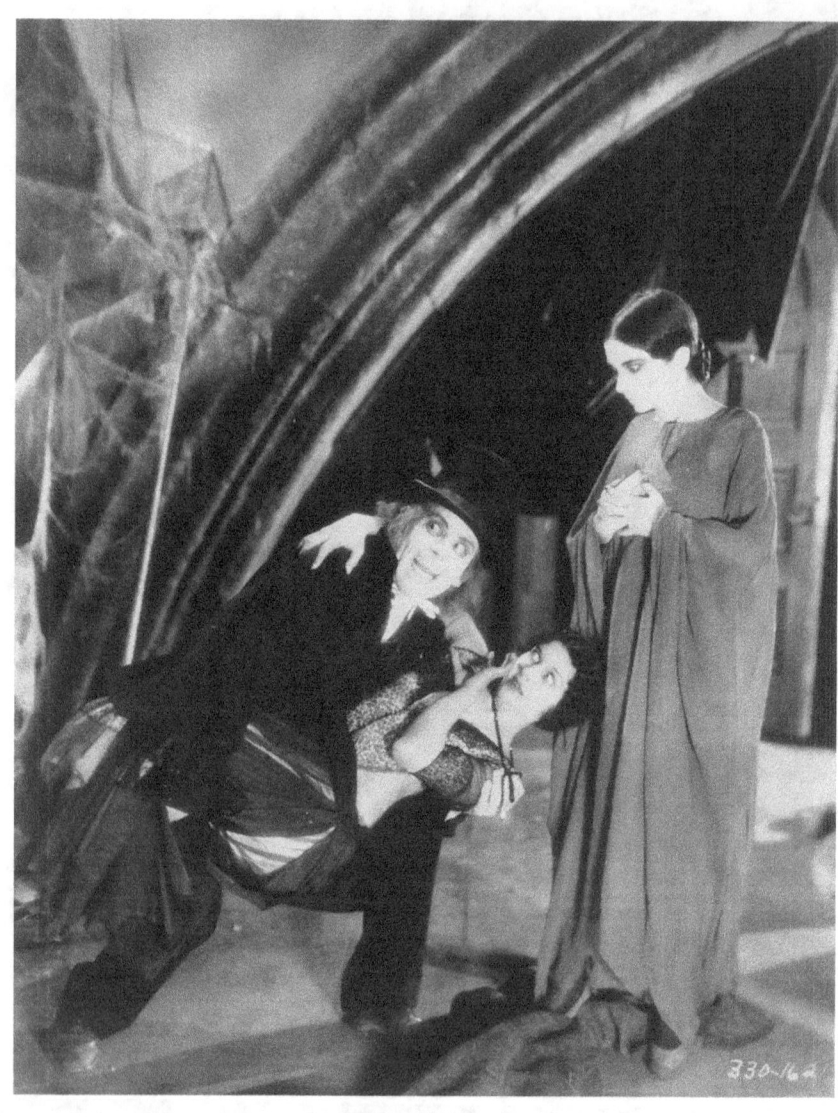

Frontispiece With the Bat Girl (Edna Tichenor) standing beside him, The Man in the Beaver Hat (Lon Chaney) holds the frightened Lucille (Marceline Day) in this publicity still for Tod Browning's *London after Midnight* (MGM, 1927). (Courtesy of Daniel Titley.)

Vampires in Silent Cinema

Gary D. Rhodes

EDINBURGH
University Press

Edinburgh University Press is one of the leading university presses in the UK. We publish academic books and journals in our selected subject areas across the humanities and social sciences, combining cutting-edge scholarship with high editorial and production values to produce academic works of lasting importance. For more information visit our website: edinburghuniversitypress.com

© Gary D. Rhodes, 2023, 2025

Grateful acknowledgement is made to the sources listed in the List of Illustrations for permission to reproduce material previously published elsewhere. Every effort has been made to trace the copyright holders, but if any have been inadvertently overlooked, the publisher will be pleased to make the necessary arrangements at the first opportunity.

Edinburgh University Press Ltd
13 Infirmary Street
Edinburgh EH1 1LT

First published in hardback by Edinburgh University Press 2023

Typeset in 11/13 Monotype Ehrhardt by
IDSUK (DataConnection) Ltd

A CIP record for this book is available from the British Library

ISBN 978 1 3995 2574 9 (hardback)
ISBN 978 1 3995 2575 6 (paperback)
ISBN 978 1 3995 2576 3 (webready PDF)
ISBN 978 1 3995 2577 0 (epub)

The right of Gary D. Rhodes to be identified as the author of this work has been asserted in accordance with the Copyright, Designs and Patents Act 1988, and the Copyright and Related Rights Regulations 2003 (SI No. 2498).

Contents

List of Figures vi
Acknowledgments x
Foreword by E. Elias Merhige xiii

Introduction 1

1 The First Vampire Films 8
2 Vamps 36
3 Criminals 60
4 Supernatural Vampires 80
5 *Drakula halála* 102
6 *Nosferatu, eine Symphonie des Grauens* 138
7 *London after Midnight* 156
8 Vampires at Home 175
9 Transformations 189

Index 205

Figures

Frontispiece. With the Bat Girl (Edna Tichenor) standing beside him, The Man in the Beaver Hat (Lon Chaney) holds the frightened Lucille (Marceline Day) in this publicity still for Tod Browning's *London after Midnight* (MGM, 1927). (Courtesy of Daniel Titley)   ii

F.1	Graf Orlok (Max Schreck) in F. W. Murnau's *Nosferatu, eine Symphonie des Grauens/Nosferatu, a Symphony of Horror* (Prana-Film, 1922). (Courtesy of the John Antosiewicz Collection)	xiii
I.1	Sheet music published in 1916	5
I.2	Albin Grau's publicity artwork for F. W. Murnau's *Nosferatu, eine Symphonie des Grauens/Nosferatu, a Symphony of Horror* (Prana-Film, 1922)	6
1.1	Philip Burne-Jones's painting *The Vampire* (1897)	13
1.2	The devil in bat form. A frame from *Le Manoir du diable/The Devil's Castle* (Georges Méliès, 1896)	17
1.3	As a Lubin catalogue explains, "Satan . . . vanishes immediately when the Cross [*sic*] is held before him." A frame from *Le Manoir du diable/The Devil's Castle* (Georges Méliès, 1896)	17
1.4–1.6	The title character's transformation in the film *Loïe Fuller* (Pathé Frères, 1905)	21
1.7	Published in the *Chicago Examiner* in 1910	22
1.8	A "Vampire Dance" from 1910	23
1.9	A vampire dance, *c*.1910–12	25
1.10	August Blom's *Vampyrdanserinden/The Vampire Dancer* (Nordisk, 1912, aka *Vampyr-danserinden*). (Courtesy of the Det Danske Filminstitut)	26
1.11	Alice Eis and Bert French in Kalem's *The Vampire* (1913)	27
1.12	Marfa Koutiloff (Stacia Napierkowska) in Louis Feuillade's serial *Les Vampires/The Vampires* (Gaumont, 1915–16)	28
2.1	Katharine Kaelred, the star of Porter Emerson Browne's play *A Fool There Was* (1909)	40

FIGURES

2.2	Publicity photograph of Virginia Pearson from 1917	42
2.3	Alice Eis and Bert French in *The Vampire* (Kalem, 1913)	43
2.4	Publicity photograph of Theda Bara from the mid-1910s	45
2.5	Photo montage of screen vamps created in 1919. Pictured are Louise Glaum, Theda Bara, Virginia Pearson, Clara Kimball Young, Olive Thomas, Dorothy Dalton, Olga Petrova, Pauline Frederick, Lina Cavalieri, and others	46
2.6	Movie poster for *Jerry and the Vampire* (Mutual, 1917) (Courtesy of Heritage Auctions)	48
2.7	Publicity photograph of Lew Cody	50
2.8	Sheet music published in 1917	52
2.9	Movie poster for *The Blonde Vampire* (F.B.O., 1922) (Courtesy of Heritage Auctions)	53
3.1	The cover of the dime novel *"Vampire," the Bravo: or, The Man of Many Disguises* (1891)	64
3.2	Movie poster for *Vasco the Vampire* (Universal, 1914) (Courtesy of Heritage Auctions)	65
3.3	*Vampires of the Night* (Aquila, 1913), originally titled *La belva della mezzanotte*	66
3.4	Theo Ortner's poster for *Der Vampyr* (Sport-Film, 1920), which starred Fred Stranz	67
3.5	Léonce Perret's *Le Mystère des roches de Kador*, released in the United States under the title *In the Grip of the Vampire* (Gaumont, 1912)	68
3.6	*La Tête coupée/The Severed Head*, Episode 1 of Louis Feuillade's *Les Vampires* (Gaumont, 1915–16)	70
3.7	*Le Cryptogramme rouge/The Red Codebook*, Episode 3 of Louis Feuillade's *Les Vampires* (Gaumont, 1915–16)	71
3.8	Trade advertisement from 1926	73
3.9	Roland West's *The Bat* (United Artists, 1926)	74
4.1	A frame from *Drakula (1920)*, a modern fake	86
4.2	Film poster for *Apakyna*, another modern fake	87
4.3	Viacheslav Turzhanskii's *Zagrobnaia skitalitsa/The Afterlife Wanderer* (1915) (Courtesy of *Daydreams Database: Cinema of the Russian Empire and Beyond*, edited by Anna Kovalova and developed by Alexander Grebenkov.)	89
4.4	Olga Baclanova in *Zagrobnaia skitalitsa/The Afterlife Wanderer* (1915) (Courtesy of *Daydreams Database: Cinema of the Russian Empire and Beyond*, edited by Anna Kovalova and developed by Alexander Grebenkov.)	90

4.5	Elga Beck as Lilith in Erich Kober's *Lilith und Ly/Lilith and Ly* (1919)	91
4.6	The scene in which Lilith (Elga Beck) drinks Landov's (Hans Marschall's) blood in *Lilith und Ly/Lilith and Ly* (1919)	93
4.7	*The Poet of the Peaks* (American Film Manufacturing, 1915)	94
4.8	Pictured on the right, Life-in-Death (Gladys Brockwell) rolls dice with Death (Robert Klein) in a scene from *The Ancient Mariner* (Fox, 1925)	95
4.9	Aleksandr Panteleev's *Derevo Smerti, ili Krovozhadnaia Susanna/The Death Tree, or Bloodthirsty Susanna* (1915)	96
5.1	*Lidércnyomás/Nightmare* (1920, aka *Jóslat/Prophecy*)	103
5.2	Károly Lajthay in *Vorrei morir* (Rex, 1919)	104
5.3	Paul Askonas as Mephistopheles in 1927 (Courtesy of George Chastain)	106
5.4	Autographed photo of Margit Lux	107
5.5	Paul Askonas (left) in *Drakula halála*. This scene likely depicts the wedding ceremony between Drakula and Mary Land	108
5.6	Paul Askonas and Margit Lux in *Drakula halála*	109
5.7	Paul Askonas in a publicity still for *Drakula halála*	111
5.8	Advertisement published in *Mozi és film* on March 23, 1923	112
5.9	The cover of the *Drakula halála* novella	115
5.10	The title page for the *Drakula halála* novella	116
6.1	Albin Grau's publicity artwork for F. W. Murnau's *Nosferatu, eine Symphonie des Grauens/Nosferatu, a Symphony of Horror* (Prana-Film, 1922)	139
6.2	Published in *8 Uhr-Abendblatt* on February 28, 1922	141
6.3	Published in *BZ am Mittag* on March 3, 1922	143
6.4	The cover of *Tanz und Welt* celebrated the Berlin premiere of *Nosferatu*. (Courtesy of Kantonsbibliothek Appenzell Ausserrhoden Ausserrhoden (CH), CMO-59-01-D-17-01-03-02)	144
6.5	The Marmorsaal Theater in Berlin, as photographed c.1910. (Courtesy of the Deutsche Kinemathek)	146
6.6	The program for Das Fest des Nosferatu. (Courtesy of Kantonsbibliothek Appenzell Ausserrhoden Ausserrhoden (CH), CMO-59-01-D-17-01-03-02)	147
6.7	Artwork of Das Fest des Nosferatu, as published in *Berliner Lokal-Anzeiger* on March 6, 1922	150

FIGURES

7.1	The Man in the Beaver Hat (Lon Chaney) in Tod Browning's *London after Midnight* (MGM, 1927) (Courtesy of Daniel Titley)	157
7.2	Max and Dave Fleischer's *Swing You Sinners!* (Paramount, 1930)	160
7.3	The November 1962 issue of *Famous Monsters of Filmland*. (Courtesy of George Chastain)	162
7.4	Fake film frame created by Jack Theakston. (Courtesy of Jack Theakston)	165
7.5	Faked footage of *London after Midnight* featuring the Man in the Beaver Hat doll produced by Sideshow Toys	168
7.6	Film frame discovered in the Canary Islands	170
7.7	Daniel Titley's book featuring the film frames that he rediscovered	171
8.1	Film frame from *F-0343*	178
8.2	Film frame from *F-0343*	179
8.3	Film frame from *F-0332*	181
8.4	Film frame from *F-0332*	182
8.5	The cover of *Le Film Complet* for December 3, 1925	185
9.1	The title lobby card for *Exit the Vamp* (Paramount, 1921) (Courtesy of Heritage Auctions)	191
9.2	Published in the New Orleans *Times-Picayune* on December 7, 1924	192
9.3	Published in the *Detroit Times* on May 18, 1927	193
9.4	Artwork depicting Hamilton Deane's adaptation of *Dracula* during its successful run in London	194
9.5	This artwork, published on the cover of *The Film Daily* on November 9, 1930, uses the tagline, "The Story of the Strangest Passion the World Has Ever Known"	198
9.6	Published in *Motion Picture Herald* on January 31, 1931	199
9.7	Dracula (Bela Lugosi) and Mina (Helen Chandler) in a publicity still for Tod Browning's *Dracula* (Universal, 1931)	201

Acknowledgments

Gary D. Rhodes would like to extend his gratitude to the various archives, libraries, organizations, and universities that offered assistance during the research phase of this project: the Alexander Library of Rutgers University of New Brunswick, New Jersey, the American Heritage Center at the University of Wyoming, the Andover-Harvard Theological Library of Massachusetts, Wisconsin, the Ardmore Public Library of Oklahoma, the Bancroft Library at the University of California at Berkeley, the Berkshire County Historical Society in Pittsfield, Massachusetts; the Billy Rose Theater Division of the New York Public Library, the British Film Institute, the Bundesarchiv in Berlin, the Crossley Motors Automobile Club, Inc., the Chicago History Museum Research Center of Chicago, Illinois, the Cleveland Public Library of Ohio, the DC Public Library of Washington, D. C., the Department of Special Collections at the University of California at Santa Barbara, the Deutsche Kinemathek, the Free Library of Philadelphia, the Harry Ransom Center at the University of Texas at Austin, the Howard Gottlieb Archival Research Center at Boston University in Massachusetts, the Hungarian Film Institute, the Kiplinger Research Library of Washington, D. C., the Library of Congress of Washington, D. C., the Los Angeles Public Library, the Margaret Herrick Library of the Academy of Motion Picture Arts and Sciences, the Media History Digital Library, the National Archives of the United States, the New York State Historical Association, the Research Service of the Budapest City Archives of Hungary, the San Diego Public Library of California, the San Francisco Public Library, the University of Oklahoma, the University of Pennsylvania Penn State Special Collections Library, and the University of Washington Libraries/Special Collections.

In addition, Rhodes would like to express his appreciation to the following individuals: Leonardo D'Aurizio, Marty Baumann, Tom Brannan, Olaf Brill, John Brunas, Michael Brunas, Bob Burns, Joe Busam, Bart Bush, Mario Chacon, Richard Daub, the late Robert Ray Edgington, Ruth Edgington, Scott Essman, the late Philip R. Evans, the late William K. Everson, Lawrence Fultz, Jr., the late Gordon R. Guy, Steve Haberman, G. D. Hamann, David J. Hogan, Roger Hurlburt, the late Steve

Jochsberger, Steve Kaplan, Anthony Kerr, Nancy Kersey, Eugene Kirschenbaum, Frank Liquori, the late Linda Miller, D'Arcy More, Peter Michaels, Jean-Claude Michel, Mark A. Miller, the late Lynn Naron, the late Randy Nesseler, the late Ted Newsom, John Norris, Jim Nye, Chris O'Brien, Dennis Payne, Victor Pierce, William Pirola, Mike Ravnitzky, Robert Rees, Jeffrey Roberts, Bruce Scivally, Samuel M. Sherman, Zoran Sinobad, Don G. Smith, Graham Sutton, László Tábori, the late Brian Taves, Al Taylor, Maurice Terenzio, Mario Toland, John Ulakovic, Judit Katalin Ulrich, Jon Wang, Leo Wiltshire.

Rhodes would also like to offer his deepest thanks to the following persons who have helped greatly in making this book possible: the late Forrest J Ackerman, Malcolm Asquith, Cristiana Astori, Matthew E. Banks, Buddy Barnett, Jr., Ivo Blom, the late Margaret Brannan, Tom Brannan, Olaf Brill, Kevin Brownlow, Mario Chacon, Bill Chase, Ned Comstock, Michael Copner, Michael J. David, Jack Dowler, Kristin Dewey, the late Edward "Eric" Eaton, Theodore Estes, Michael Ferguson, the late Phillip Fortune, Beau Foutz, Fritz Frising, Christopher R. Gauthier, Robert Guffey, Cortlundt Hull, Erin Hunt, Roger Hurlburt, Bill Kaffenberger, Richard Koszarski, Murray Leeder, Mark Martucci, Charles Musser, David Nahmod, Henry Nicolella, Donald Rhodes, Phyllis Rhodes, William Rosar, the late Richard Sheffield, Robert Singer, Anthony Slide, Carter Smith, Billy Stagner, Yuri Tsivian, David Stenn, David Wentink, Glenn P. White, and Kristopher Woofter.

Special recognition goes to the following: John Antosiewicz for sharing important publicity stills; RoseMary Appelkvist and the Svenska Filminstitutet for sharing research on Swedish silent films; Jannie Dahl Astrup and Madeleine Schlawitz at the Det Danske Filminstitut for sharing research and film frames; Gyöngyi Balogh for her crucial assistance with Hungarian silent cinema; Giorgio Bertellini for his advice and assistance on Italian silent films; Mariona Bruzzo and Rosa Cardona for sharing important research on Segundo de Chomón; George Chastain for sharing research and images; Robert Cremer for translating so many documents from German to English; Debora Demontis and the Fondazione Centro Sperimentale di Cinematografia for assistance with Italian silent films; Ulrich Döge for research assistance with German silent films; Amandine Dongois and Rachel Guyan at the La Cinémathèque française for assistance with my research into French silent films; Donald F. Glut for our regular messages about silent film vampires; Anika Goetz for searching for court records related to *Nosferatu* (1922); Argyle Goolsby and Blitzkid for providing the soundtrack for so much of my time writing this book; Anna Kovalova for sharing invaluable research and images of Russian silent films, as well as for her Russian-to-English translations; Michael Lee for helping me borrow and examine so many interlibrary loan items, as well as his help with French-to-English translations; Péter Litván and Tamás Gyurkovics for help with Hungarian-to-English translations; Barbara Tepa Lupack and Eric Stedman for sharing their thoughts on *The Mysteries of Myra* (1916); Elif Rongen and the Eye Filmmuseum for assistance with *Eclair Bulletins*; Brigitte Mayr for sharing research on *Lilith und Ly* (1919); Bob Murawski for his analysis of the fake Russian *Dracula* silent films; Lisa Roth and the Deutsche Kinemathek for helping with silent German films; Sabine Schwientek for her amazing assistance with research on *Nosferatu* and other German films; Elisabeth Streit and the Österreichische Filmmuseum for assistance with research on Austrian silent films; Daniel Titley for sharing important research and images of *London after Midnight* (1927); and Denise J. Youngblood for her invaluable help with my research into the fake Russian *Dracula* silent films, as well as her help with Russian-to-English translations.

And of course to John Soister and Tom Weaver for carefully proofreading book chapters and providing invaluable feedback; Robert Singer for his extensive support of this project and our regular discussions about its progress, E. Elias Merhige for his wonderful foreword; and Edward Clark, Sam Johnson, and Gillian Leslie at Edinburgh University Press for their kind support and assistance.

Gary D. Rhodes, Ph.D.
Oklahoma City, Oklahoma
2022
Dedicated to my friend and colleague Tom Weaver

Foreword

By E. Elias Merhige

Figure F.1 Graf Orlok (Max Schreck) in F. W. Murnau's *Nosferatu, eine Symphonie des Grauens/Nosferatu, a Symphony of Horror* (Prana-Film, 1922). (Courtesy of the John Antosiewicz Collection.)

A century has passed since the birth of *Nosferatu* (1922), and as we stand in the shadows of this haunting milestone, we find ourselves reflecting upon the metamorphosis of cinema – a peculiar process that I propose is a devolution, rather than an evolution. The 1920s was an era of cinematic innocence when the moving image was a force unto itself, eloquently conveying stories and emotions with an otherworldly, hypnotic majesty.

Throughout the vast expanse of human history, the image has been our ultimate storyteller, transcending time and culture. It has spoken to us through the ancient inscriptions of Hammurabi, the hieroglyphs of Egypt, and the enduring masterpieces of the Renaissance. However, as the curtains closed on the 1920s, so too did the silent era of cinema. The arrival of sound and dialogue initiated an insidious transformation – a vampiric assault on the lifeblood of the moving image.

In my eyes, the true vampire of cinema is the very sound and dialogue that has drained the image of its profound, hypnotic power. *Nosferatu*, then, serves as a dark harbinger of the changes to come. These ruminations laid the foundation for my film, *Shadow of the Vampire* (2000), a lamentation of the silenced image and its lost power to evoke the unconscious and the contemplative.

Over time, dialogue has relegated the moving image to a lowly servant of rational thought, robbing it of its enigmatic essence. Gary Rhodes's book revisits the haunting world of *Nosferatu*, celebrating the uncanny dread and beauty that still echoes through its images. In doing so, it draws us back to the primordial allure of the vampire, an ancient symbol embodying the cyclical, devouring nature of life itself.

The vampire, in all its seductive and horrifying forms, has ensnared our collective imagination like no other mythic creature. It serves as a vessel to explore our deepest desires, fears, and moral quandaries. In this book, we delve into the murky depths of the vampire's cinematic history, shedding light on the cultural significance and undying allure of these enigmatic beings. Embrace the darkness and join us on this exploration of the vampire's eternal grip on the silver screen, as we rediscover the evocative power of the moving image that once held us in a state of mesmerized wonder.

Introduction

"I woke; it was the midnight hour,
The clock was echoing in the tower;
But though my slumber was gone by,
This dream it would not pass away–
It seems to live upon my eye."
– Samuel Taylor Coleridge
Christabel (1816)

"All was dark and silent, the
black shadows thrown by the
moonlight seeming full of a
silent mystery of their own."
– Bram Stoker
Dracula (1897)

In *Bram Stoker's Dracula* (Francis Ford Coppola, 1992), the vampire count (Gary Oldman) strolls through London, depicted in grainy footage that appears to have been shot at 16 or 18 frames per second. The sound of a projector clicks in the background while a street barker invites everyone to experience the "Amazing Cinématographe." Dracula and Mina (Winona Ryder) attend the exhibition, the images quickly arousing the vampire's passions. On two occasions, a phantom-like train appears on the screen.

Coppola created these images for his film, inspired by such early moving pictures as *L'Arrivée d'un train en gare de La Ciotat/The Arrival of a Train* (Lumière Brothers, 1895) and *The Ghost Train* (American Mutoscope and Biograph, 1901).[1] *Bram Stoker's Dracula* thus links vampirism and the cinema. Indeed, Stoker's novel first appeared in print in 1897, at approximately the same time that public film screenings became commonplace. As he wrote, "It is nineteenth century up-to-date with a vengeance."

Connections between vampirism and silent cinema resonate loudly. E. Elias Merhige's *Shadow of the Vampire* (2000) stars Willem Dafoe as actor Max Schreck. In this fantastical alternate history about the production of *Nosferatu* (1922), Schreck is an authentic vampire, hired by director F. W. Murnau (John Malkovich) to add realism to his film. Murnau confidently declares, "If it's not in frame, it doesn't exist." In one scene, Schreck becomes fascinated by a film projector, peering into its lens without speaking, the light flickering on his face. The project has become the projected.

We need only consider the question of where cinema resides to understand the potency of these metaphors. Film is archived on a film reel or on a DVD or in hard drives, but that is not where the audience sees it. Rather, light pulses temporally and temporarily on a screen. And yet the screen is not a film's permanent home, certainly not in the same way that a frame provides to a painting. The location of a film is always in motion, ever in flux. A film is most alive while it is being projected, materialized in the darkness, and that is when it exists between two worlds, illuminated between the moving projector and the static screen. The same is true of a vampire: its status is difficult to locate, let alone comprehend.[2] To be undead is to be neither alive nor dead, but rather to exist in a twilight between the two.

The poem *The Vampyre* (1837) warns us, "For a sound from the Vampyre's lips would start, A chill of fear in the strongest heart."[3] But what of those occasions when the lips do not start, when the vampire remains quiet? Let us recall an even older poem, *The Vampire* (1826), in which William Brent writes, "Conjecture is silent, and wonders alone."[4] And then there is the "strange horror," the truly "dreadful horror" that creeps over the narrator of Amelia B. Edwards's short story *The Phantom Coach* (1864), originating not from a sound, but rather from silence:

> He moved his head slowly, and looked me in the face, without speaking a word. I shall never forget that look while I live. I turned cold at heart under it. I turn cold at heart even now when I recall it. His eyes glowed with a fiery unnatural lustre. His face was livid as the face of a corpse. His bloodless lips were drawn back as if in the agony of death, and showed the gleaming teeth between.[5]

We find ourselves in, to borrow a phrase from Reginald Hodder's 1914 essay on the subject, "the "vampyr condition," one in which the site of horror is sight rather than sound.[6]

The vampire of silent cinema is complicated, enigmatic, and manifold, though generally understood through only two films: Murnau's *Nosferatu* and Tod Browning's *London after Midnight* (1927), the latter as instantly recognizable (thanks to surviving film stills) as it is unknown (thanks to the lack of surviving prints). Being undead in reel life might be as paradoxical as being undead in real life. Those two films were certainly not alone, but most of their kith and kin are long forgotten. They ache to be remembered. They yearn for new blood. As Professor Van Helsing says to Harker in Stoker's *Dracula*, "You have kept diary of all these so strange things; is it not so? Yes! Then we shall go through all these together when we meet." Thus, our present meeting, now, amid these archaic images, in these new pages chronicling old films: *Vampires in Silent Cinema*.

In 1895, Maxim Gorky famously referred to the moving pictures exhibited by the Lumière Brothers' Cinématographe as the "Kingdom of Shadows." For him, they were "not life, but its shadow," the figures depicted in them "condemned... unto eternity." There was "not motion, but its soundless spectre," ominously "fraught with a vague but sinister meaning that makes your heart grow faint."[7] At roughly the same time, Edvard Munch exhibited his oil painting *Love and Pain*.[8] For him, the painting depicted a woman embracing a man and kissing his neck. But Munch's friend Stanisław Przybyszewski interpreted it quite differently:

> She bit into the man's neck with razor-sharp teeth, she smeared his face with the blood of her scarlet hair, she grasped his head with her powerful hand of unbridled lust and suffocates him and bites – and bites. And in the background, a chaotic scene of bloody-hued thunderbolts, toxic green – an angry chaos of assorted blotches, colors, spots – yet like delicate crystals such as one sees on a frosted windowpane.[9]

Thereafter *Love and Pain* became known as *Vampire*. Munch himself eventually adopted the title.[10] The woman in the painting was not a vampire, but she became one, much as the human who returns from the grave with newfound bloodlust.[11]

In the Kingdom of Shadows live many denizens. Some are vampires; some are not. As a journalist warned in 1919, "the word 'vampire' is in danger of becoming one of the most abused or misused words in the English language."[12] That danger remains. As this book will explain, vampire-hunting historians have at times perceived the undead in films where they do not reside, just as modern pranksters have produced fakes to entrap audiences not versed in silent cinema. For example, some writers wrongly supposed the footage screened at the Cinématographe in *Bram Stoker's Dracula* dated to the early cinema period, when it was simulacra created by Coppola, new footage made to look old, not authenticity but its soundless specter.

Chapter 1, "The First Vampire Films," investigates these concerns at length. Building on my prior research, I return to Georges Méliès's *Le Manoir du diable/The Devil's Castle* (1896), which modern critics have repeatedly mistaken for featuring a vampire, and to Segundo de Chomón's *La Légende du fantôme/Legend of a Ghost* (1908, aka *The Black Pearl*), which a writer in 1908 incorrectly cited as including a vampire.[13] And then there is the largely unknown Pathé Frères' film *Loïe Fuller* (1905), with its depiction of a vampire dance.

Some vampires are supernatural; the dancer in *Loïe Fuller* certainly seems to be, making her probably the first supernatural vampire in film history. Other vampires are not supernatural, but instead metaphorical, residing in a cinematic netherworld, a strange place between the normal and the supernormal. During the silent film era, they carried the weight of the term "vampire" and were thus tainted by folklore and superstition. And so, we must raise our lantern and open its slide, shining light on their dark deeds, recording them in our diary of strange things. As the *Los Angeles Times* told readers in 1913, "A vampire, allegorical or otherwise, arouses attention."[14]

Chapter 2, "Vamps," chronicles the lusty human vampire popularized by artist Philip Burne-Jones and poet Rudyard Kipling, a creation that largely displaced the supernatural vampire in the early twentieth century, a creation best understood in the plural, as it evolved into a non-gender specific character, one obsessed with mental and sexual power instead of blood. As film star Alice Hollister once said, the vamp was "the vampire of the soul rather than of the body."[15] Similarly, Chapter 3, "Criminals," explores other vampire metaphors of the nineteenth and early twentieth centuries, concentrating on the brigands, pirates, thieves, and gang members who fed off the wealth of others. In the cinema, these vampire criminals achieved lasting fame thanks to Louis Feuillade's *Les Vampires* (1915–16) and Roland West's *The Bat* (1926).

By contrast, Chapter 4, "Supernatural Vampires," excavates the little-remembered heirs of *Loïe Fuller*, the earliest known films featuring the undead, specifically Viacheslav Turzhanskii's Russian film *Zagrobnaia skitalitsa/The Afterlife Wanderer* (1915), starring Olga Baclanova, and Erich Kober's German film *Lilith und Ly/Lilith and Ly* (1919), written by Fritz Lang. It also investigates their cinematic relatives and imposters. Chapter 5, "*Drakula halála*," examines the first film to feature Stoker's character, a little-known 1921 Hungarian movie also inspired by Robert Wiene's *Das Cabinet des Dr. Caligari/The Cabinet of Dr. Caligari* (1920). *Drakula halála* depicted not a supernatural vampire, but a madman who believes himself to be Stoker's bloodthirsty character, its narrative requiring audiences to be aware of the fictional Dracula in order to understand an appropriation of him. And Chapter 6, "*Nosferatu*," revisits Murnau's 1922 vampire film by focusing on its premiere in Berlin, a subject largely

Figure I.1 Sheet music published in 1916.

ignored in previous literature, thus pondering a world that now seems so hard to conceive, a world before the pestilence known as Count Orlok.

Chapter 7 covers "*London after Midnight*" by examining how the lost film survives as a type of undead cinema, thanks to its subsequent incarnations and reincarnations over the decades. It is so well remembered, and yet none of us have seen it. Chapter 8, "Vampires at Home," investigates

Figure I.2 Albin Grau's publicity artwork for F. W. Murnau's *Nosferatu, eine Symphonie des Grauens/Nosferatu, a Symphony of Horror* (Prana-Film, 1922).

two American home movies featuring supernatural vampires, both shot in the mid- to late twenties. They are as enigmatic as they are unknown, and they probably represent the first supernatural vampires in American film history. And then Chapter 9, "Transformations," concludes the book by illustrating how the metaphorical vampire – so very common in silent cinema – was finally consumed by the supernatural vampire, the result of Stoker's novel being adapted for the stage and then for the screen, in the form of Tod Browning's sound film *Dracula* (1931).

Here then are the vampires of silent cinema, some metaphorical, some supernatural, all citizens of a shadow kingdom materialized on the screen, at least until the light from the projection booth extinguishes. As Stoker wrote, "They simply seemed to fade into the rays of the moonlight and pass out through the window, for I could see outside the dim, shadowy forms for a moment before they entirely faded away."

The silence of vampire silents reverberates loudly. It is time again for those vampires to speak, even to shriek, if only as words on the screen, in the form of intertitles, and as words on the page, in the form of this book.

Gary D. Rhodes, Ph.D.
2022

Notes

1. Sigrid Anderson Cordell, "Sex, Terror, and *Bram Stoker's Dracula*: Coppola's Reinvention of Film History," *Neo-Victorian Studies* 6, no. 1 (2013): 1.
2. I have previously made these observations in Gary D. Rhodes, "The First Vampire Films in America," *Palgrave Communications* 3, no. 1 (December 2017): 1–10.

3. A. T. L., "*The Vampyre*," *Ithaca Herald* (Ithaca, NY), September 20, 1837, 1.
4. William Brent, *Sturry, and Other Poems* (Canterbury: Henry Ward, 1826), 133.
5. Amelia B. Edwards, *The Phantom Coach*, in *The Phantom Coach and Other Stories* (New York: T. R. Dawley, 1865).
6. Reginald Hodder, "The Vampire," *Occult Review* (April 1914): 226.
7. Maxim Gorky, "The Kingdom of Shadows" (1895), accessed July 2, 2022, https://publish.iupress.indiana.edu/read/authors-on-film/section/c5672b46-7193-41d1-9a75-2e96b10d22de.
8. Munch created six different versions of *Love and Pain* between 1893 and 1895.
9. Quoted in Piotr Policht, "Sex, Art & Vampires: The Friendship of Stanisław Przybyszewski & Edvard Munch," Culture.pl, June 18, 2020, accessed April 12, 2022, https://culture.pl/en/article/sex-art-vampires-the-friendship-of-stanislaw-przybyszewski-edvard-munch.
10. Sue Prideaux, *Edvard Munch: Behind the Scream* (New Haven, CT: Yale University Press, 2019), 209.
11. Ibid., 209.
12. "Term 'Vampire' Is Much Abused in Common Use," *Rapid City Journal* (Rapid City, SD), October 5, 1919, 8.
13. Rhodes, 1–10.
14. Hector Addict, "*The Vampire*, An Allegory," *Los Angeles Times*, May 21, 1913, III4.
15. Elizabeth Seales, "A Vampire Off Guard," *Film Fun*, September 1916, unpaginated.

CHAPTER 1

The First Vampire Films

"Have you seen that awful den of hellish infamy, with the very moonlight alive with grisly shapes, and every speck of dust that whirls in the wind a devouring monster in embryo?"

– Bram Stoker
Dracula, 1897

Phantoms form out of aerial dust and celluloid grain, but are their grisly shapes real or imaginary? Are they possible to identify with certainty, or are we left to grasp at the gossamer, to remember what never really was? In Stoker's *Dracula*, Jonathan Harker's journal explains, "Let me begin with facts – bare, meagre facts, verified by books and figures, and of which there can be no doubt. I must not confuse them with experiences which will have to rest on my own observation, or my memory of them." In the awful den of hellish infamy, such is not an easy task.

During the late nineteenth and early twentieth centuries, cinema and vampirism underwent various evolutions that impacted heavily on the ability of audiences to comprehend them, to make sense of them. The two invariably pose questions, but those questions are particularly pronounced when considering the first two decades of film exhibition. To explore this issue, the United States serves as an important case study, as it represents a geographical location in which these issues converge, collide, and even collapse. The protean vampire was never more unstable than in America during the early cinema period.

Consider the following account from Rhode Island, published in March 1896, only days before Edison's Vitascope premiered at Koster and Bial's in New York City:

> It gives one a creeping sensation of horror to think that in enlightened New England, during the final decade of the nineteenth century, the corpse of a young

woman buried eight weeks was dug out of the ground, the heart and liver cut out and burned, and all this that the dead might cease to be nourished at the expense of living relatives.[1]

In this case, the understanding of and belief in supernatural vampires was so strong that a suspected corpse was exhumed. The incident stems from longstanding folkloric superstitions.

But only one year later, Philip Burne-Jones's painting *The Vampire* (1897), and Rudyard Kipling's companion poem of the same name, depicted the creature as a mortal woman who metaphorically bleeds men of their lives. The impact on popular culture was so robust that many persons were no longer certain as to what a vampire was. For some, the term became plural, indicative of old superstitions and recent art. For others, the new definition replaced the old.

Questions of meaning and legibility are also important in the viewing of early cinema, its film content striking some later viewers as so distinct from the classical Hollywood style as to be avant-garde. For example, the Bruce Posner-curated DVD collection *Unseen Cinema: Early American Avant-Garde Film, 1894–1941* features many moving pictures produced before 1915, including by such mainstream companies as the Edison Manufacturing Company and American Mutoscope & Biograph.[2] Kristin Thompson has argued that it is "only after the formulation of classical Hollywood norms was well advanced that we can speak of an avant-garde alternative."[3] But whether we view a term like "avant-garde" to be a modern imposition on early cinema, or whether we might concentrate on – as Bart Testa sees it – the "back and forth" interactions between early cinema and later avant-garde films that appropriated footage from the period, the discussion leads us to realize that some early film narratives are opaque, if not obscure.[4] Their "codes of intelligibility," as Thomas Elsaesser called them, pose challenges for modern audiences, just as they did for some of their original viewers.[5]

Tom Gunning, André Gaudreault, Charles Musser, and others who have analyzed early cinema narratives have appropriately complicated the period, observing different and evolving narrative patterns. Gunning believes the earliest films represented a "cinema of attractions," meaning not only that film exhibitions were themselves attractions (including in terms of the demonstration of projection equipment), but also that, during its early years, the cinema focused on the presentational and the spectacular in order to incite "visual curiosity" and supply visual "pleasure."[6] As Gunning explains, "this cinema differs from later narrative cinema through its fascination in the thrill of display rather than its construction of a story."[7] Narrative storylines were minimal, and so the possibility for them to be misread was very real.

Gunning originally suggested that the period from 1907 to approximately 1911 "represents the true *narrativization* of the cinema."[8] In his later work, he augmented that view by noting the cinema of attractions predominated until circa 1903, followed by a period of transition that lasted until circa 1908.[9] At no other time during the history of American film did greater change occur, unfolding, as Elsaesser observed, not as a linear progression, but "in leaps; not on a single front, but in more jagged lines and waves: this history of film form emerges as a complicated transformational process involving shifts in several dimensions."[10]

As the early cinema period advanced, film narratives became simultaneously more complicated and more legible. For example, Gunning's monograph on D. W. Griffith includes a chapter entitled "Complete and Coherent Films, Self-Contained Commodities," which argues the "narrator system . . . came into focus" by the end of 1908.[11] Nevertheless, audiences still experienced occasional difficulty in comprehending given film narratives. In 1911, a journalist for the *Moving Picture World* observed:

> Ambiguity in pictures is one of the chief failures of the day in moving picture subjects; this is evident to the critic and the public. If only the critic experienced this ambiguity, it might become a matter of opinion between keen minds, but when the student of moving pictures finds it difficult sufficiently to grasp the "plot" or see the "point," there is further evidence of this weakness . . . the public is full of inquiries so that when sitting in the theaters one overhears a constant stream of queries – especially the exclamation at the sudden abrupt or ambiguous ending of a subject.[12]

The same journalist also recounted such "audible exclamations" from viewers as "What does it mean?" and "Could you understand it?"

For Gunning, early cinema represents a "paradox" in that it is "simultaneously different from later practices – an alternate cinema – and yet profoundly related to the cinema that followed it."[13] It is an evolving cinema, and its relationship to later film practices might well be one of the reasons it can be so hard to read properly. Anyone in the twenty-first century struggles to avoid seeing these moving pictures through the lens of post-1915 filmmaking. Put another way, it is at times difficult even for film theorists and historians to read given films from the early cinema period.

The vampires that appeared during the early cinema period also represent a paradox, one in which distinctive characters emerged in jagged lines and waves, some supernatural and some not, all as part of a complex transformational process in which – despite their differences – alternate vampires were profoundly related to those that came before and those that would appear after. The result was a complicated and overlapping set of vampire depictions that are also difficult to read, to analyze, to fathom.

As John Edgar Browning and Karen Picart have noted, "The vampire is a construction that is under continuous development, an assemblage of words, images, and places especially that almost resembles a Frankensteinian creature."[14]

The question is whether or not the undead walked onscreen in early cinema. Consider Stacey Abbott's monograph *Celluloid Vampires: Life after Death in the Modern World* (2007), in which she writes the "vampire was absent from the early days of cinema," after having already announced, "French magician and filmmaker Georges Méliès brought forth the first celluloid vampire in his [1896] film *Le Manoir du diable*," but prior to describing the character in that same film as a "satanic figure."[15] It is not the apparent contradiction in these comments that is important, but instead the reasons for the confusion that exist in the archive and in the scholarship.

Nowhere are these issues more pronounced than in three specific moving pictures, all of them screened in the United States: *Le Manoir du diable/The Devil's Castle* (Georges Méliès, 1896), which modern critics have sometimes mistaken as featuring a supernatural vampire; *La Légende du fantôme/Legend of a Ghost* (Pathé Frères, 1908, aka *The Black Pearl*), which an American writer in 1908 mistook as featuring a supernatural vampire; and *Loïe Fuller* (Pathé Frères, 1905), a film featuring a character probably meant to be a supernatural vampire.

This investigation allows us to consider what the earliest vampire films were, or at least might have been, an important pursuit given scholarly interest in early cinema and horror studies. The trio of moving pictures also allow us to explore the paradoxical nature of vampires and early cinema. At times, both are murky, their images fleeting and indistinct, their stories needing to be read, but always at the risk of being misread.

The Supernatural Vampire in America

As early as June 15, 1732, the *American Weekly Mercury* published a nonfiction account about Hungary that claimed "certain Dead Bodies (called here Vampyres) killed several persons by sucking out all their blood."[16]

During the nineteenth century, Americans learned about vampires from the increasing role that they played in fictional literature and entertainment. For example, in 1819, the American press excitedly announced the publication of the short story *The Vampyre, A Tale*, initially attributed to Lord Byron before the real author, John Polidori, was revealed.[17] The *Rhode Island American* told readers in April 1819, "It is said to be of a most horrifick [sic] nature."[18] The description was apt. In the story, the mysterious Lord Ruthven appears in London and befriends a young

Englishman named Aubrey, who later suffers a nervous breakdown. Ruthven marries Aubrey's sister, but leaves her for dead on their wedding night. As the final line of the story explains: "Lord Ruthven had disappeared, and Aubrey's sister had glutted the thirst of a *Vampyre!*"

By October of 1820, theatrical producers staged an adaptation of the story in such cities as New York and Washington, D. C. Entitled *The Vampyre; or, The Bride of the Isles* (aka *The Vampire, or the Bride of the Isles*), James Robinson Planché had written it for the London stage. *The Vampire; or, The Bride of the Isles* was revived time and again, making it the most important vampire play in America during the nineteenth century.[19] As an article in the *New York Literary Journal* reported in 1821, "Since the appearance of the story of the Vampire, the conversation of private parties has frequently turned to the subject, and the discussion has been prolonged and invigorated by the pieces brought at the theatres...."[20]

The subject's popularity resulted in subsequent vampire plays, notably Dion Boucicault's two-act play *The Phantom* (originally titled *The Vampire* when a different, three-act version premiered in England).[21] At its debut at Wallack's Theater in New York in 1856, Boucicault assumed the title role, a vampire named Alan Raby, whose family castle is in Wales. As one character explains, within the castle "dwells a terrible thing – man or fiend." Immediately after he speaks those words, a clap of thunder shakes the theater. Then the same character describes travelers who wander into the ruins after nightfall. All are later found dead, "each with a wound in his throat in the right side, from which they have evidently bled to death – but no blood is spilt around, the face is white and fixed, as if it had died of horror."

Announcements of Bram Stoker's *Dracula* appeared in the American press in 1897, but it was not until 1899 – when Doubleday and McClure published the novel in New York – that it received widespread attention. Thereafter, when American journalists discussed Stoker, they generally cited *Dracula* as being his most famous work.[22] In 1908, one writer even declared that *Dracula* placed Stoker "on a par" with Edgar Allan Poe.[23] The novel remained in print throughout the early cinema period and beyond.[24]

In the United States, *Dracula* soon played a role in other kinds of entertainment.[25] A European acrobat performed under the name "Dracula, the Frolicsome Demon" in American vaudeville theaters as early as 1902 and as late as 1916.[26] The name Dracula also became attached to at least one real-life villain. In 1906, a "wild man" lurked in the woods near a village in Long Island, causing residents to shudder in a "state bordering on terror." According to a newspaper article, the local "watchword" became "Dracula, alive or dead."[27]

Figure 1.1 Philip Burne-Jones's painting *The Vampire* (1897).

This brief overview indicates the endurance supernatural vampires had for American readers and theatergoers, particularly until the end of the nineteenth century, but it does not take into account the surprising malleability of the term "vampire," which splintered rather than solidified at roughly the same time Stoker's novel was initially published.

The Vamp

In May 1897, American newspapers announced the "sensational" London exhibition of Philip Burne-Jones's painting *The Vampire*. Some newspapers printed line art drawings of the painting, while others were left to describe it as best they could with words. Cleveland's *Plain Dealer* told readers that *The Vampire* "shows a room flooded with moonlight, in which a dying man, with a wound in his breast, lies sleeping. Over him lies a beautiful woman – who has just drained him of his life blood." The newspaper also mentioned that Rudyard Kipling had written a poem of the same name: "Kipling has seen in the female vampire an allegory of the worthless woman who loves a man . . . until at last he finds she has stolen all or the better part of his life."[28]

While some members of the press drew allusions to supernatural vampires, Kipling's poem makes clear that he conjured a different kind of character. As Burne-Jones recalled in an interview published in America in 1898, "I intended to paint one of those women who . . . drain the life blood of a man and Kipling's verses just hit the idea."[29] Though born out of supernatural vampires, Burne-Jones and Kipling had dispatched a very different creation. Here was a particular kind of powerful woman, one with dominance over male conquests. As Janet Staiger has written, "Motifs of the supernatural or diabolical are sometimes used to explain how a woman could have such unnatural power over the man. The vampire or spider image of sucking away the man's blood was a powerful metaphor for the threat she represented."[30]

The impact of the Burne-Jones painting and Kipling poem on the term "vampire" had an immediate and profound effect. In 1899, a journalist in the *New York Times* reported:

> People nowadays carelessly use the word "vampire" as a stronger and trifle more loathsome term than "parasite." Burne-Jones once painted a picture called the *Vampire*. It was a very beautiful woman leaning over a man she had just slain. And Kipling wrote some symbolic verses about it.[31]

The journalist added, "Probably few persons know what the real vampire is," the Burne-Jones depiction having so quickly displaced the supernatural character in much of popular culture.

And so, despite the success of Stoker's novel, the foremost understanding of vampirism in America in the early twentieth century remained the Burne-Jones and Kipling character. Consider this article published in the *Chicago Tribune* in 1903:

> "What is a vampire, anyway?" asked a young woman looking at the Burne-Jones picture now on exhibition.
>
> "A vampire," [replied] her companion. "A vampire is the rag and a bone and a hank of hair that Kipling talks about."

> They probably had not spent a portion of their youthful lives in a small town visited occasionally by the "greatest show on earth" with its sideshow. If they had they would have known all about the "blood sucking vampire." They would have dreamed about it....[32]

Exasperated by cultural confusion over the term, the journalist felt compelled to describe supernatural vampires in great detail, both in their folkloric roots and in Stoker's novel, all in an effort to (re-)educate at least some Americans.

Nevertheless, the Burne-Jones and Kipling vampire continued to flourish. Not surprisingly, when David McKay published the American edition of Dudley Wright's book *Vampires and Vampirism* in 1914, it was necessary to begin with the question: "What is a vampire?"[33]

Le Manoir du diable/The Devil's Castle (1896)

Georges Méliès' *Le Manoir du diable* is a key example of the horror-themed film in early cinema. Its tone is more serious than most of his subsequent moving pictures, which generally emphasized humor, and its visual content includes tropes later associated with the horror film genre, including devils, ghosts, and witches cavorting inside a haunted castle. Believed lost for decades, a copy resurfaced in 1988 at the Ngā Taonga Sound & Vision archive, and then appeared on the Flicker Alley DVD *Georges Méliès Encore* in 2010.[34]

In America, Siegmund Lubin distributed *Le Manoir du diable* as *The Devil's Castle*; Edison released it as *The Infernal Palace*.[35] When American audiences first saw it is difficult to determine. The film appears in a 1900 catalog for American Vitagraph, which offered it in three lengths, meaning 50, 100, or 200 feet.[36] However, newspaper advertisements as early as 1899 include Lubin's title at moving picture exhibits. For example, in April 1899, the Ninth and Arch Museum in Philadelphia featured a vaudeville show that ended with the "Cineograph" moving pictures. Foremost among the group were two Méliès films, *L'Lune à un mètre/The Astronomer's Dream* (1898) and *The Devil's Castle*, the duo being presented as the most important on the bill, "the most striking moving pictures ever taken."[37] That same month, an advertisement for Huber's Museum publicized the "Historiograph" on a bill with live entertainment made up of: "Royal Japanese Wrestlers and Acrobats, Great Success of Allini's Monkeys, Boxing Bouts, Wire Walking, and Trapeze Performance."[38] The Historiograph was to present twenty-five minutes of moving pictures, but *The Devil's Castle* – which would be screened "complete in every detail" – was the only one mentioned by name.[39]

In May 1899, the Beach Park of Galveston, Texas, presented a "Grand Cinematograph" program of "25 Different Pictures," the films ranging from nonfiction to fiction, from serpentine dances to comedies. *The Devil's Castle* appeared by "special request," according to an advertisement that listed the moving picture as the last to be screened, as if it was the pinnacle of the program.[40] In yet another indication of its apparent popularity, an American newspaper article on film piracy published in 1901 specifically cited *The Devil's Castle* as being one of six Méliès films that had been illegally duped.[41] The culprits included Lubin, who continued to offer the film in his catalogs until as late as 1908.[42]

In addition to Stacey Abbott, numerous writers in the modern era have referred to *The Devil's Castle* as – to use the words of J. Gordon Melton – the "very first vampire film."[43] Such a judgment appears in books, academic papers, and vampire-related websites.[44] It appeared in early histories of the horror film, including Denis Gifford's *Movie Monsters* (1969), as well as in such children books as Thomas G. Aylesworth's *The Story of Vampires* (1977).[45] Nowhere is this trajectory more evident than in the title of John L. Flynn's book *Cinematic Vampires: The Living Dead on Film and Television, from* The Devil's Castle *(1896) to* Bram Stoker's Dracula *(1992)*.[46] And yet, however crucial Méliès's moving picture was, with all the many horror tropes it introduced to cinema, no supernatural vampires appear during its running time. There are ghosts and witches, a devil and an imp, but absolutely no vampires. None whatsoever. As early as 1970, Ron Borst published an article that corrected Gifford, clarifying that the film did not feature a vampire.[47] Similarly, in 1972, Raymond T. McNally and Radu Florescu stated the character was Mephistopheles and "not a real vampire."[48] Unfortunately, Gifford's book had the greater influence.

To begin, *Le Manoir du diable*'s French title and most common period English translation indicate that the key villain is a devil, not a vampire.[49] Méliès reiterates this point through the character's appearance: the devil's costume features fabric horns, much as stage productions of *Faust* had used throughout the nineteenth century. Film catalogs reinforce this interpretation. In 1900, an Edison synopsis describes its climax as follows: "Finally one of the cavaliers produces a cross, and Mephistopheles throws up his hands and disappears in a cloud of smoke."[50] Three years later, a Lubin synopsis said much the same: "Satan ... vanishes immediately when the Cross [sic] is held before him."[51]

During the era of sound cinema, the use of a cross to dispel vampires became so common as to obscure the fact that the same religious iconography had been used in an earlier age to dispel devils. Consider the short story *A Ghost*, published in the *Connecticut Gazette* in August 1797,

Figure 1.2 The devil in bat form. A frame from *Le Manoir du diable/The Devil's Castle* (Georges Méliès, 1896).

Figure 1.3 As a Lubin catalogue explains, "Satan . . . vanishes immediately when the Cross [sic] is held before him." A frame from *Le Manoir du diable/The Devil's Castle* (Georges Méliès, 1896).

in which the narrator tells us: "At length I concluded, if it be a demon, he will fly at the sign of the cross."[52] This was also true in Domenico Ronzani's ballet *Uriella* (1854), which was staged in New York in 1870. It was also the case in early cinema. In *Le Fils du diable/Mephisto's Son* (Pathé Frères, 1906), the son of Satan cowers before a priest carrying a cross.[53] In Vitagraph's *The Gambler and the Devil* (1908), the female lead "holds up a cross before him. The devil covers his eyes with his hands, there is a puff of smoke, and he disappears."[54] Then, in *La Défaite de Satan/Satan Defeated* (Pathé Frères, 1910), a character "holds up the crucifix and Satan disappears forever."[55]

If the use of the cross is one reason that modern viewers have mistaken the devil in *The Devil's Castle* for a vampire, the other is the film's opening, in which a large bat transforms into Mephistopheles. Here again, vampire literature and films of the post-1896 era have clouded the ability for modern viewers to read *The Devil's Castle* as it was intended. Indeed, even though he acknowledges the character is Mephistopheles and not a vampire, Stephen Prince still refers to the prop as a "vampire bat," when there is no historical or textual reason to suggest the bat was specifically meant to be a vampire bat.[56]

Satan is not a vampire, but prior to 1896 there is a lengthy history that gives him demonic wings or likens him to a bat. It is important to recall Ephesians 2:2, which describes Satan as the "prince of the power of the air." To enumerate the sheer volume of artwork over the following centuries that depicts devils and demons as having bat-like wings would be difficult. Famous examples include Botticelli's and Doré's illustrations for Dante's *Inferno*, as well as Doré's engravings for Milton's *Paradise Lost*.[57] Many more examples appear in late nineteenth-century visual culture, including in numerous French "diablerie" stereographs.[58]

Similar imagery can be seen in early cinema, including in Méliès's *Le Diable au couvent/The Devil in the Convent* (Méliès, 1900, aka *The Sign of the Cross; or the Devil in a Convent*), in which Satan flies into the convent, in Méliès's *Le Puits fantastique/The Enchanted Well* (1903), in which a devil transforms into a bat, and in Méliès's *Le Chevalier des Neiges/The Knight of the Snow* (1912), in which a bat emblem appears on the devil's shirt, as well as on a large banner behind him. But the imagery was hardly unique to Méliès. American trade advertisements for the Italian-made *Satana, ovvero il dramma dell'umanità/ Satan, or, The Drama of Humanity* (Ambrosio, 1912) used artwork of a bat to promote a film about the devil's negative impact on humankind.[59] No narrative or visual cues in these cases suggest the wings or bats have any affiliation with vampirism or vampire bats.

Given that *Le Manoir du diable* was hardly unique in its treatment of Satan, the film's meaning was probably unambiguous to many of its original audiences. But that has not proven true of modern viewers, who have imposed their understanding of later vampire cinema onto Méliès, seeing a vampire where one definitely does not exist. A key way to understand and correct this error is to consider Charles Musser's research on Edwin S. Porter's *The Great Train Robbery* (Edison, 1903), a film regularly cited as the first, or one of the first, westerns. Perceiving this to be a "retrospective reading," one that positions *The Great Train Robbery* within a film genre that did not yet exist, Musser examines it in relation to moving pictures that preceded it, specifically in "its ability to incorporate so many trends, genres and strategies fundamental to the institution of cinema at the time."[60] These included the travel genre (specifically the railway subgenre), the genre of re-enacted news events, and the crime genre.⁶¹ *Le Manoir du diable* likewise integrated characters and narrative concerns that preceded it, none of them involving supernatural vampires.

La Légende du fantôme/Legend of a Ghost (1908)

If one person proved to be Méliès's immediate heir, it was Segundo de Chomón, a Spanish filmmaker whose expertise with coloring moving pictures gained him employment at Pathé Frères in 1905. He became "one of the main supervisors (and shortly after, the manager) of the company's trick film section."⁶² In many ways, Chomón's narrative and aesthetic approach intentionally mimicked Méliès; in 1908, for example, he remade Méliès's *Le Voyage dans la Lune/A Trip to the Moon* (1902) as *Excursion dans la lune/An Excursion to the Moon* (Pathé Frères, aka *Excursion to Moon*).⁶³ But in other respects, Chomón advanced the trick picture, including in his expert use of color and animation, and to be fair, Chomón's overall filmography reveals he was capable of far more than special effects.

Of particular importance is the fact that Chomón at times used tricks to construct dramatic, horror-themed storylines, most notably in the hand-colored *La Légende du fantôme/Legend of a Ghost* (Pathé Frères, 1908).⁶⁴ Here is a key link in the evolution of the horror-themed moving picture, with the attraction of cinematic tricks logically embedded into a dramatic narrative, one inspired by Dante's *Inferno* and the Greek myth of Orpheus. How American audiences reacted at the time is hard to determine, but *Variety* praised the film's "curious, mystic light effects," which were "well handled to heighten the weirdness of the scenes."⁶⁵

For one American in 1908, *Legend of a Ghost* depicted a supernatural vampire. According to a plot synopsis published in *Moving Picture World*:

> Arriving at the gate of Satan's kingdom, they mount a chariot of fire and, arriving at the devil's palace, give fight to the demons mounting guard over their king, and after having defeated them, rush into the palace. Now Satan, seeing his life in peril, disappears in a cloud of smoke and thunder, and is seen again as he dashes through his vast domains gathering together his people, and while they await the conquering chariot another fight ensues. The devil is beaten again and the bottle of life is stolen by the leader of the victorious army, and they are all about to depart when a terrible explosion takes place and the chariot and its occupants are dashed to the ground. All are killed but the brave woman who undertook the expedition, and she goes forth alone. . . .⁶⁶

The synopsis – which was also printed in *Views and Film Index* – continues with explicit mention that "dragons and vampires" attempt "to stop her progress towards earth."⁶⁷

Here seems to be the earliest reference in the American press of a moving picture featuring a supernatural vampire, the synopsis writer presumably being someone working for Pathé Frères in the United States. But viewing the surviving film indicates why synopses published in other countries did not mention vampires. Nor did the aforementioned review published in *Variety*. The young lady's difficult journey back to the surface shows characters that appear similar to dragons, but an examination of the mise-en-scène indicates they might be sea creatures.

This case seems to be the reverse of *Le Manoir du diable*, in that a period viewer (presuming the synopsis writer actually viewed the film) mistook onscreen characters for vampires when no one else has, either at the time (so far as can be determined) or in the modern era (other than those recapitulating the 1908 English-language text). However, the error is potentially more complicated than what amounts to retrospective misreadings of *Le Manoir du diable*. The synopsis writer might well have found *La Légende du fantôme* ambiguous (particularly insofar as not understanding scenes that appear to be underwater), and also found vampires to be ambiguous, not understanding what they looked like or how they should appear, whether in a film or otherwise. The ambiguity of vampirism and early cinema thus converged.

Loïe Fuller (1905)

In 1905, Pathé Frères released the moving picture *Loïe Fuller* in the United States. The director is unknown, although it seems that Segundo de Chomón oversaw its hand-coloring. This French-made film showcased Loïe Fuller, the American artist who helped pioneer modern dance. Lynda Nead explains that "astronomy, illumination, cinematography, and the gendered allegorical body" had "come together, finally, in the figure of Loïe Fuller."[68] Fuller invented the serpentine dance in 1892 for a New York play about hypnotism, although the dance achieved its greatest fame soon thereafter at the Folies-Bergère in Paris.[69] Gunning describes her performances as "visual pyrotechnics created by colored and sharply focused electric light and shadows using the swirling surface of Fuller's fabric as a screen for the projection of an equally protean succession of colors."[70] The result was an ethereal, even otherworldly performance.

In the film *Loïe Fuller*, a large bat flies onto the terrace of a country home (or even a castle, perhaps, as we do not see its exterior). A clever transition occurs in which a woman – who is not actually the real Fuller, but rather an imitator – appears for a moment with the bat on her head. When the bat disappears, the woman spreads her costume in bat-wing style, her

Figure 1.4 The title character's transformation in the film *Loïe Fuller* (Pathé Frères, 1905).

Figure 1.5 [shared with 1.4]

Figure 1.6 [shared with 1.4]

feet balanced on the terrace ledge. With the bat-to-woman transformation complete, the Fuller imitator steps down to the terrace, performs her dance, and then dematerializes thanks to a dissolve, another cinematic sign of her apparent supernaturalism.

Why might this character have been understood as a vampire when the character in *Le Manoir du diable* was not, even though both change from bat to human form? Cultural context provides the answer. Though largely forgotten, vampire dance acts became somewhat popular in the *fin de siècle* period.[71] As early as 1890, the Famous Hi Henry's Minstrels presented the "Grand Vampire Transformation Dance" in America.[72] Whether its transformation involved a bat is unknown, but it's clear that other vampire dances soon followed. Nellie Navette first performed her "Vampire Dance" in London in December 1892.[73] In it, she costumed "as a bat."[74] Then, in Springfield, Massachusetts, in 1896, women at a variety show performed a "vampire" dance by wearing "black gowns with loose skirts, which were ornamented by gilt stars and spangles."[75] Being staged prior to the creation of the Burne-Jones painting and the Kipling poem, these dances intended to invoke the supernatural creature.

Vampire dances became popular again in 1909, but these later performances were inspired by Burne-Jones, Kipling, and – perhaps most specifically – Porter Emerson Browne's stage adaptation of their work, *A Fool There Was* (1909), which brought increased attention to the "vamp." Fuji-ko's *Vampire Dance* was probably the first of those staged in 1909.[76] More famously, Burt French and Alice Eis premiered their *Vampire Dance* in July 1909.[77] It was accompanied by tarantella music.[78] French explained:

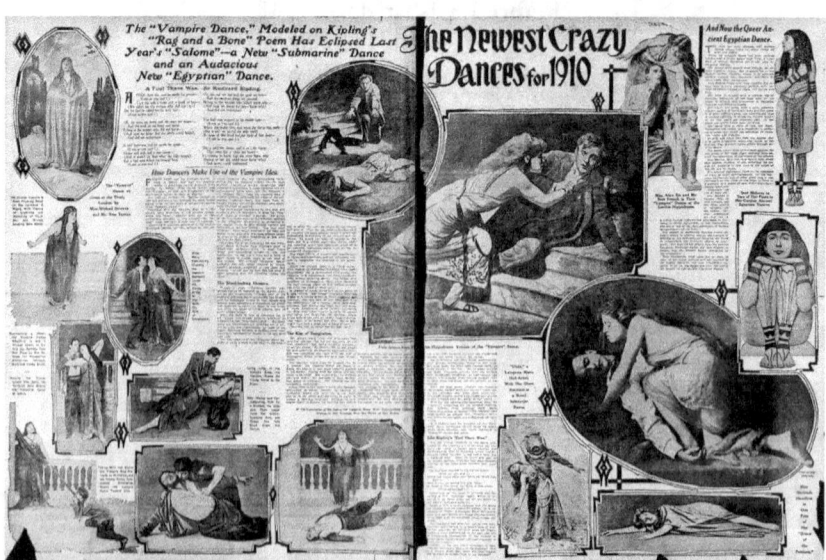

Figure 1.7 Published in the *Chicago Examiner* in 1910.

With Miss Eis, I had been performing the Apache Dance, and I was anxious to find some artistic and unconventional to follow it. I wanted something totally unlike anything which had been done before. Enquiries, study, and thought had provided me with several ideas, but none of them wholly pleased me. Then one morning I received from a friend a hurried note scribbled upon a picture postcard. That card bore a reproduction of the famous Burne-Jones painting *The Vampire*, and Rudyard Kipling's verses *A Fool There Was*. In a flash I saw that this was what I wanted. Here was *The Vampire Dance*, and, with Miss Eis, I began the invention of a pantomime drama.[79]

During the dance, Eis appeared in a "cloth of gold that conceal[ed] little of her womanly charms," with one photograph showing her holding out a cape in bat-like fashion.[80] She was "wild-eyed," the dance "calculated to make [viewers] gasp." A critic at the *San Francisco Chronicle* reported that an audience "shuddered even while they applauded."[81]

Figure 1.8 A "Vampire Dance" from 1910.

French and Eis's *The Vampire Dance* was successful, enough so that they performed it in England. Despite their overt use of Burne-Jones and Kipling, the London *Morning Post* remarked, "It is, in fact, rather more reminiscent of Mr. Bram Stoker's novel *Dracula*."[82] That response may have been prompted by the dance's climax, in which Eis "deliberately stoop[ed] down, Vampire like, and gnaw[ed] his throat, sucking his life blood."[83]

Joseph C. Smith developed a different *Vampire Dance* in 1909, which Vera Michelena (and, later, Violet Dale and Eulalie Jansen) performed in the "musical comedy" *The Flirting Princess*. In it, the vampire and victim appeared on a "darkened stage, with a black background, green spotlights and bars of red light coming from the depths under stage." The male dancer wore black; the vampire wore a "greenish, snake-like clinging gown."[84] Funeral music accompanied the "startling" performance.[85] At the climax, the vampire smiled wickedly and "suck[ed] the blood from the throat of her victim."[86] Similar to French and Eis, Smith's dance merged the supernatural vampire with the vamp, so much so that one review in 1911 argued it would be "vastly improved by the omission of the inexcusable and revolting ghoulishness of the final tableau."[87]

Tom Terriss and Mildred Deverez performed their own *Vampire Dance* in 1909. An article in the *San Francisco Examiner* described their act as follows:

> Though it seems sufficiently horrible that woman should be accepted as the modern symbol for the bloodsucking "chimere dire" of the ancients, this new dance can hardly fail to conjure up nightmare visions of that clawed winged beast resembling a monstrous bat which was supposed to fasten its fangs in the throat and drink the blood of living infants, even of adult human beings.
>
> More and more of late, in literature and in art works, the alleged vampire attribute of womankind has been accentuated. Novelists, poets and playwrights are picturing her in colors as vivid and unmistakable as those of the classic Succubus, perhaps in modern times most startingly portrayed by Balzac in his tale with that title.
>
> The lady of the "Vampire" dance appears to claim a more literal right to the title – she is after the real life blood of her victim and gets it. Thus far the deed is accomplished in virtually the same general series of poses and pantomimic expressions of the vampire and her victim. To sound the note of tragedy at the start, she is a typical siren – fair, daring, alluring, exhaling power and assurance, while he is an innocent, ingenous youth with all the illusions of inexperience.
>
> The stage effects of scenery and management of lights are important, and are cunningly utilized to emphasis the meaning of the pantomime.
>
> When a curtain rises on a "dark scene," with flashes of lightning revealing what looks suspiciously like a churchyard with graves, the vampire, in a voluminous, but semi-transparent robe, is seen prowling about. You realize with shudders of anticipation that, while haunting the last resting place of her lifeless victims, she feels the need of fresh prey.
>
> A change of scene shows her on the scent of a new victim. She creeps stealthily into the studio of a young artist – a youth romantic and innocent. She has cast off her robe and is in the habiliments of a typical siren, her long abundant hair falling over bare bust and arms, a loose, diaphanous gown hardly concealing her body and lower limbs. A smile of unholy joy lights her face – but the innocent young artist sees in her only an ideally beautiful creature ready to be wooed and won. She is Kipling's "rag and a bone and a hank of hair."
>
> ... The innocent youth does not suspect that he is doomed. The Vampire begins her dance of death ... Toying with her victim, she pretends to be timid. She eludes him. She pretends to have no further power of resistance. The Vampire has him completely enthralled.[88]

At the end of the dance, Deverez's vampire "glories in her triumph over the death of her victim" after drawing "his life blood from his throat." A surviving photograph depicts her biting the victim's neck.[89] The supernatural element was quite pronounced in the Terriss and Deverez dance.

Theodora Gerard created her vampire dance, which she performed in Russia and France.[90] "Business was tremendous" in Paris in 1909.[91] Julian

THE FIRST VAMPIRE FILMS

Figure 1.9 A vampire dance, c.1910–12.

Mitchell and Louise Alexander presented their vampire dance in 1910.[92] Emile Lessard developed a "Vampire Walk" dance in 1915, its "peculiar carriage" being an "effort to embody into rhythmic and almost seductive form of locomotion revealed by Miss Theda Bara in her screen portrayals."[93] In 1917, "Princess Ka, the only and original vampire dancer," performed

Figure 1.10 August Blom's *Vampyrdanserinden/The Vampire Dancer* (Nordisk, 1912, aka *Vampyr-danserinden*). (Courtesy of the Det Danske Filminstitut.)

in vaudeville.[94] Three years later, the comedy team of Gildea and Phillips included a vampire dance in their vaudeville sketch *All in Fun*.[95] By that time, filmmakers had long been aware of the dance's ability to attract audiences.

This type of vampire dance appeared onscreen as early as 1912, in August Blom's *Vampyrdanserinden/The Vampire Dancer* (aka *Vampyr-danserinden*), a Nordisk moving picture released in America by the International Feature Film Co.[96] The film was salacious enough to be banned in San Francisco and in Harrisburg, Pennsylvania.[97] As one critic noted, the film was provocative and "weird," its dancing vampire Silvia played by Clara Wieth, aka Clara Pontoppidian, who had earlier starred in *Dorian Grays Portræt/The Picture of Dorian Gray* (Alex Strøm, 1910) and would later appear in *Häxan* (Benjamin Christensen, 1922).[98] A studio synopsis for *Vampyrdanserinden* explained:

> Now comes a presentation of the Vampire Dance, mystic and thrilling, and laid in the underground haunt of the blood sucker, whose beauty, syren like, holds her victims fascinated. The Vampire is roused out of her sleep by the noise of a human being approaching her lair. It is a young man who has stumbled unawares into a passage that leads from the outer world to her haunt. When he reaches the level he is surprised to see what appears to be the form of a beautiful woman but in whose eyes lurk the spirit of the devil. She dances backwards and forwards keeping her eyes

upon him until, hypnotised, he has temporarily lost control of his will. Again and again he is enslaved by her charms. Thus the dance proceeds until the dénouement when the human heart ceases to beat and the Vampire, like some loathsome and nauseating beast, crouches over her prey.[99]

Within the context of a stage performance danced by a human character, the vampire is meant to be supernatural. As a surviving print reveals, the vampire bites her victim's hand, his facial expression becoming one of pain, before she bites him twice on the neck, the second time as he in lying on the ground. Here are likely the first vampire bites in the history of cinema.[100]

The following year, Kalem released *The Vampire* (1913). A period synopsis notes, the lead character "goes to a theatre where Bert French and Alice Eis are presenting their famous *Vampire Dance*."[101] As one newspaper wrote, "Gliding out from the threshold of the forest trees, the lithe form of [the title character] allures, recoils, challenges, only repeatedly to repulse her artist victim."[102] The *New York Clipper* told readers that the film depicted a "woman, youthful and voluptuous, tempting the man, and his final capitulation and death." The dance was, in other words, "taken from Kipling's poem."[103] Whether Eis bit French in the film, as she pretended to do onstage, is unknown. While *The Vampire* appended a happy ending, it received complaints in Atlanta for being too salacious.[104] Nevertheless, the film proved popular enough that Kalem produced a follow-up entitled *The Dance of Death* (1914).[105]

Figure 1.11 Alice Eis and Bert French in Kalem's *The Vampire* (1913).

Colonia released the two-reel German film *Hiawatha* (1913), which starred Joe Biller and Hild Hadges. It also featured a vampire dance.[106] Here was a tale of a love triangle and a woman's desire for revenge. Its dancer's movements were "bewitching, sensuous [and] beguiling." At the film's climax, the seething dancer kisses her partner tightly before her "predator teeth dig into his throat," allowing her vengeance and his destiny "to be fulfilled."[107] Her partner dies. Ads promised the "sensational film" would keep audiences "in breathtaking suspense until the last scene."[108]

In 1914, Yakov Protazanov directed the short Russian film *Tanets Vampira/Vampire's Dance*, produced by Russkaia zolotaia seriia and starring V. Laskina and Richard Boleslavsky.[109] Little is known of the film, other than the claim it featured a "new dance."[110] *Sine-Fono* added, "Obviously, the tango dance has finally found a worthy rival in the new 'dance of the Vampire,' which surpasses other dances in beauty. The viewer will get to know more in the film."[111]

Far more enduring is the vampire dance that appears in *La Bague qui tue/The Deadly Ring* (aka, *The Ring That Kills*), Episode 2 of Louis Feuillade's serial *Les Vampires/The Vampires* (Gaumont, 1915–16). Marfa Koutiloff (Stacia Napierkowska) costumes as a vampire bat for her ballet *The Vampires*, flying down to the stage and outstretching her wings before approaching a sleeping woman. Koutiloff's dance remains forever incomplete, though, because she collapses, having been poisoned by the leader of a criminal gang known as Les Vampires. Here is an inversion of prior vampire dances; the vampire dies and the victim survives. Given the serial's success upon its original release and its continued fame and accessibility, Koutiloff's vampire dance remains the most famous of them.

Figure 1.12 Marfa Koutiloff (Stacia Napierkowska) in Louis Feuillade's serial *Les Vampires/The Vampires* (Gaumont, 1915–16).

It must be said that Koutiloff's dance, as well as vampire dances on the stage from 1909 and in the cinema from 1912, occurred after the production of *Loïe Fuller*. However, all of these films, including *Loïe Fuller*, come after Burne-Jones and Kipling, with the vampire dances on the stage from 1909 to 1912 illustrating a range of possibilities, their inspiration either coming predominantly from the vamp tradition, or predominantly from the supernatural vampire tradition, or some relatively equal proportion of the two.

In terms of the larger issue of vampire cinema, it does seem clear that the Loïe Fuller imitator – who is in no way garbed as a devil or described as such in the film's title or in catalog synopses – was performing her own version of a vampire dance. Her bat transformation and dematerialization at the end of the film suggests that she is not merely a female vampire, but a supernatural vampire, which some viewers in 1905 might have understood. Other viewers might even have understood the Fuller imitator to mark the convergence of two traditions, the supernatural vampire and the Burne-Jones/Kipling creation. Those watching the film in 1909 or the years that followed might well have read the film in a similar manner, but with the additional context of Browne's *A Fool There Was* and the later vampire dances.

Loïe Fuller probably features the first supernatural vampire in cinema history. How is it that scholars looking for early examples of screen vampires have not recognized one in *Loïe Fuller*? The answer likely resides in the film's title, which simultaneously headlines a celebrity and yet obscures specific content. Rather than being a misreading of a film, here is a surviving film that has not been analyzed, at least in the context of horror and vampirism.[112]

Conclusion

In Stoker's *Dracula*, Van Helsing asks Dr. Seward to "believe in things that you cannot." The undead are not inscrutable, but they are difficult to comprehend and challenging to understand, much in the same way that narratives in early moving pictures have at times seemed ambiguous and even elusive to viewers, not only at the time, but also to the present day. In terms of vampires onscreen, it seems apparent that *La Légende du fantôme* simply fooled one viewer in 1908, just as *Le Manoir du diable* has fooled many viewers in the modern era. Neither features a vampire. To say they do constitutes misreadings of them. And yet, to rephrase Van Helsing, audiences sometimes wish to believe in things they should not.

To the extent that a supernatural vampire appeared in any moving picture produced before 1915, *Loïe Fuller* is one of the most likely examples. The film's title character possesses supernatural powers and very much appears to be part of a vampire dance tradition that predates the metaphorical worlds of Burne-Jones and Kipling. That said, the intentionality of the filmmakers remain unknown. And no period responses to the film have survived, making commentary about how audiences viewed it in 1905 at best informed speculation.

We should also strongly consider *Vampyrdanserinden* to be a necessary inclusion in any filmography of supernatural vampires. Certainly a hypnotic "blood sucker" appears during the course of the onstage dance in in the film, even though it is performed by a human character. Fortunately, a print of *Vampyrdanserinden* survives in the archives of the Library of Congress and Det Danske Filminstitut. Similar qualities may have been true of *Hiawatha* and Kalem's *The Vampire*, though limited details in plot synopses and the lack of surviving prints makes the case for them far more difficult to make.

Such ambiguities mark early cinema, to be sure, as well as all of film history. Daniel Frampton rightly reminds us, "Everything in a film may be well interpretable, but not every formal moment has meaning, arbitrariness is always possible."[113] Vampires and films remain elusive in the years after the early cinema period, at least on occasion. Viewers would generally agree that the character Ellen (Greta Schröder) collapses at the end of Murnau's *Nosferatu* (Prana-Film, 1922), but not all perceive that she has died.

In Stoker's novel, Mina Harker records the destruction of Dracula: "the whole body crumbled into dust and passed from our sight." Written accounts of the vampire are all that remain, as Jonathan Harker observes at the end of the novel:

> We were struck with the fact that, in all the mass of material of which the record is composed, there is hardly one authentic document! Nothing but a mass of typewriting, except the later note-books of Mina and Seward and myself, and Van Helsing's memorandum. We could hardly ask anyone, even did we wish to, to accept these as proofs of so wild a story.

Vampires are not ineffable, but their codes of intelligibility are shifting and amorphous. Like early cinema, vampires onscreen and off are shadowy, nebulous, and crepuscular. Every speck of dust that whirls in the wind, and every grain that swirls on screen, is not a devouring monster, though some of them might be.

Notes

1. V. J. Briggs, "Vampires in Exeter," *Tacoma News* (Tacoma, WA), March 28, 1896.
2. Bruce Posner, curator, *Unseen Cinema: Early American Avant-Garde Film, 1894–1941*, DVD boxed set (Image Entertainment, 2005).
3. Kristin Thompson, "The Limits of Experimentation in Hollywood," in *Lovers of Cinema: The First American Film Avant-Garde, 1919-1945*, edited by Jan-Christopher Horak (Madison: University of Wisconsin Press, 1995), 68.
4. Bart Testa, *Back and Forth: Early Cinema and the Avant-Garde* (Toronto: Art Gallery of Toronto, 1992).
5. "Introduction," in *Early Cinema: Space, Frame, Narrative*, edited by Thomas Elsaesser with Adam Barker (London: British Film Institute, 1990), 11.

6. Tom Gunning, "The Cinema of Attractions: Early Film, Its Spectator and the Avant-Garde," in *Early Cinema: Space, Frame, Narrative*, 56.
7. Gunning, "Primitive Cinema: A Frame-Up? Or the Trick's on Us," in *Early Cinema: Space, Frame, Narrative*, 100.
8. Gunning, "The Cinema of Attractions," 60.
9. Tom Gunning, "'Now You See It, Now You Don't': The Temporality of the Cinema of Attractions," *Velvet Light Trap*, no. 32 (1993): 10–11.
10. Thomas Elsaesser, "Afterword," in *Early Cinema: Space, Frame, Narrative*, 408.
11. Tom Gunning, *D. W. Griffith and the Origins of American Narrative Film: The Early Years at Biograph* (Urbana, IL: University of Illinois Press, 1991), 130.
12. "The Ambiguous Picture – Some Causes," *Moving Picture World*, January 7, 1911, 14.
13. Gunning, "Primitive Cinema," 102.
14. John Edgar Browning and Caroline Joan (Kay) Picart, "Introduction: Documenting Dracula and Global Identities in Film, Literature, and Anime," in *Draculas, Vampires, and Other Undead Forms: Essays on Gender, Race, and Culture*, edited by John Edgar Browning and Caroline Joan (Kay) Picart (Lanham, MD: Scarecrow Press, 2009), xvii.
15. Stacey Abbott, *Celluloid Vampires: Life after Death in the Modern World* (Austin, TX: University of Texas Press, 2007), 44, 1, 50.
16. "Medreyga in Hungary," *American Weekly Mercury* (Philadelphia, Pennsylvania), June 15, 1732, 2.
17. "Byron's Vampyre," *Rhode-Island American, and General Advertiser* (Providence, RI), June 25, 1819, 2.
18. Untitled, *Rhode-Island American, and General Advertiser*, April 27, 1819, 2.
19. See, for example: Advertisement, *Charleston Courier* (Charleston, SC), January 14, 1825, 2.
20. "On Vampires and Vampirism," *New York Literary Journal* 4, no. 3 (January 1, 1821).
21. Roxana Stuart, *Stage Blood: Vampires of the 19th Century Stage* (Bowling Green, OH: Bowling Green State University Press, 1994), 148.
22. See, for example: "Men and Women Who Make Books," *New York Times*, September 15, 1906, BR566.
23. "A Remarkable Story," *The Evening Post* (Charleston, SC), May 4, 1908, 4.
24. Fictional vampire literature continued to appear in the 1910s as well, with F. Marion Crawford's short story *For the Blood is the Life* (published by Macmillan in the 1911 short story collection *Wandering Ghosts*) being perhaps the most notable.
25. See, for example: "The Common Vampire," *Washington Post*, August 21, 1904, A5.
26. "At the Theatres," *The Daily People* (New York, NY), August 18, 1902; "Donnelly and Hatfield's Minstrels," *Fort Wayne Journal-Gazette* (Fort Wayne, IN), August 11, 1907, 4.
27. "Wild Man Roosts in Tree Tops," *Pawtucket Times* (Pawtucket, RI), June 14, 1906, 11.
28. "The Vampire," *The Plain Dealer* (Cleveland, OH), May 23, 1897, 23.

29. "Creation of the Vampire," *Galveston Daily News* (Galveston, TX), June 26, 1898, 20.
30. Janet Staiger, *Bad Women: Regulating Sexuality in Early American Cinema* (Minneapolis: University of Minnesota Press, 1995), 150.
31. "Without Prejudice," *New York Times*, March 5, 1899, IMS2.
32. "Vampires," *Chicago Tribune*, January 25, 1903, 40.
33. Dudley Wright, *Vampires and Vampirism* (Maple Shade, NJ: Lethe Press, 2001), 1.
34. *Georges Méliès Encore – New Discoveries (1896–1911)* (Los Angeles: Flicker Alley, 2010).
35. *Complete Catalogue No. 94, Edison Films*, March 1900, 39–40.
36. *List of New Films, American and Imported*, K-0002 (New York: American Vitagraph, 1900), 2.
37. "Ninth and Arch Museum," *Philadelphia Inquirer*, April 30, 1899, 12.
38. Advertisement, *New York Times*, April 2, 1899, 17.
39. Ibid., 17.
40. Advertisement, *Galveston Daily News* (Galveston, TX), May 28, 1899, 1.
41. "Two Governments in Picture Suit," *Davenport Weekly Leader* (Davenport, IA), June 7, 1901, 1.
42. Lubin's Films (Philadelphia: S. Lubin, 1908), 56. Available in *A Guide to Motion Picture Catalogs by American Producers and Distributors, 1894–1908: A Microfilm Edition* (New Brunswick: Rutgers University Press, 1985), Reel 3.
43. J. Gordon Melton, *The Vampire Book: The Encyclopedia of the Undead* (Canton, MI: Visible Ink Press, 2011), 448.
44. Books include David J. Skal, *V is for Vampire: An A–Z Guide to Everything Undead* (New York: Plume, 1996), 231. Academic papers include Lyz Reblin, "Trio of Terror," *e-Research: A Journal of Undergraduate Research* 2, no. 1 (2011), http://digitalcommons.chapman.edu/e-Research/vol2/iss1/6; websites include the South African Vampyre Culture Center, accessed October 10, 2016, https://vampyreculturecenter.wordpress.com/vampyre-culture/vampyre-art-literature-music/the-celluloid-vampiyre/. Another example would be House of Horrors.com, accessed October 10, 2016. See "Fangs for the Memories: 13 Ghastly Films," http://www.houseofhorrors.com/vampires.htm. Yet another example would be The Vampire Project, accessed October 10, 2016. See "Introduction to Cinematic Vampires," http://thevampireproject.blogspot.co.uk/2009/01/introduction-to-cinematic-vampires.html.
45. Denis Gifford, *Movie Monsters* (New York: E. P. Dutton, 1969), 62; Thomas G. Aylesworth, *The Story of Vampires* (New York: McGraw-Hill, 1977), 12.
46. John L. Flynn, *Cinematic Vampires: The Living Dead on Film and Television, from The Devil's Castle (1896) to Bram Stoker's Dracula (1992)* (Jefferson, NC: McFarland and Company, 1992).
47. Ron Borst, "Vampire Film Checklist," *Photon*, no. 19 (1970): 26. Borst also addressed the issue of *Le Manoir du diable* in "The Vampire in the Cinema: Additions and Corrections," *Photon*, no. 21 (1971): 25.
48. Raymond T. McNally and Radu Florescu, *In Search of Dracula: The History of Dracula and Vampires* (Greenwich, CT: New York Graphic Society, 1972), 216.

49. In *The Vampire Film: Undead Cinema* (London: Wallflower Press, 2012), Jeffrey Weinstock notes that *The Devil's Castle* "has been described as the cinema's first vampire," but opts to refer to the character as a "devilish figure" (79).
50. *Edison Films, No. 94* (Orange, NJ: Edison Manufacturing Company, March 1900), 40. Available in *A Guide to Motion Picture Catalogs by American Producers and Distributors, 1894–1908: A Microfilm Edition* (New Brunswick: Rutgers University Press, 1985), Reel 1.
51. *Complete Catalogue of Lubin's Films* (Philadelphia: Lubin, January 1903), 20. Available in *A Guide to Motion Picture Catalogs by American Producers and Distributors, 1894–1908: A Microfilm Edition* (New Brunswick: Rutgers University Press, 1985), Reel 3.
52. "A Ghost," *Connecticut Gazette* (New London, CT), August 30, 1797, 1.
53. "*Mephisto's Son* at Nickelo," *The Daily Democrat* (Shelbyville, IN), December 14, 1906, 5.
54. "*The Gambler and the Devil*," *Moving Picture World*, October 3, 1908, 267.
55. "*Satan Defeated*," *Moving Picture World*, March 18, 1911, 602.
56. Stephen Prince, "Introduction," in *The Horror Film*, edited by Stephen Prince (New Brunswick: Rutgers University Press, 2004), 1.
57. Arturo Graf, *Art of the Devil* (New York: Parkstone Press International, 2009).
58. Terry Borton and Deborah Borton, *Before the Movies: American Magic-Lantern Entertainment and the Nation's First Green Screen Artist, Joseph Boggs Beale* (New Barnet, Herts.: John Libbey, 2014), 139.
59. Advertisement, *Moving Picture World*, January 11, 1913, unpaginated.
60. Charles Musser, "The Travel Genre in 1903–1904: Moving Towards Fictional Narrative," in *Early Cinema: Space, Frame, Narrative*, edited by Thomas Elsaesser with Adam Barker (London: British Film Institute, 1990), 130.
61. Ibid., 131.
62. Joan M. Minguet Batllori, "Segundo de Chomón and the Fascination for Colour," *Film History* 21, no. 1 (2009): 97.
63. *An Excursion to the Moon* is available on the DVD *Saved from the Flames: 54 Rare and Restored Films, 1896–1944* (Los Angeles: Flicker Alley, 2007).
64. A copy of *Legend of a Ghost* under the title *The Black Pearl* is available on the DVD *Fairy Tales: Early Colour Stencil Films from Pathé* (London: British Film Institute, 2012).
65. Rush, "*Legend of a Ghost* (Spectacular)," *Variety*, May 23, 1908, 12.
66. "*Legend of a Ghost*," *Moving Picture World*, May 23, 1908, 463.
67. "Latest Films of All Makers," *Views and Film Index*, May 23, 1908, 10.
68. Lynda Nead, *The Haunted Gallery: Painting, Photography, Film c. 1900* (New Haven, CT: Yale University Press, 2007), 241.
69. Loïe Fuller, Fifteen Years of a Dancer's Life, with Some Account of Her Distinguished Friends (Boston: Small, Maynard & Company, 1913), 25–40.
70. Tom Gunning, "Loïe Fuller and the Art of Motion: Body, Light, Electricity, and the Origins of Cinema," in *Camera Obscura, Camera Lucida: Essays in Honor of Annette Michelson*, edited by Richard Allen and Malcolm Turvey (Amsterdam: Amsterdam University Press, 2003), 79.

71. The earliest mention of a vampire dance act in the United States likely came with the English-language translation of Hans Christian Anderson's *Lykke-Per* (1870) as *Lucky Peer* in *Scribner's Monthly* in March 1871. Making reference to a vampire ballet, Christian writes: "He whirled about, as in the memorable vampire dance, but he thought not of that, he thought not at all of aught more, but was enveloped in the wondrous beauty he saw around him" (510).
72. "The Minstrels," *Charlotte News* (Charlotte, NC), October 29, 1890, 4.
73. "London Variety Stage," *The Stage* (London), December 22, 1892, 15.
74. "The Royal," *The Era* (London), December 24, 1892, 16.
75. "Holiday Festival in City Hall," *Springfield Republican* (Springfield, MA), February 12, 1896, 4.
76. See "Vaudeville," *New York Times*, May 30, 1909, X8; Dixie Hines and Prescott Hanaford, *Who's Who in Music and Drama* (New York: H. P. Hanaford, 1914), 129.
77. "The Vaudeville Profession," *The Billboard*, July 24, 1909, 8.
78. "The 'Vampire' Dance," *Columbus Dispatch* (Columbus, OH), August 8, 1909, 4.
79. "Shepherd's Bush Empire," *Ealing Gazette and West Middlesex Observer* (Ealing, England), February 19, 1910, 3.
80. "The Vampire Dance," *Columbus Dispatch*, August 29, 1909, 4.
81. "Old Folks and Little Orphans Share Honors of Day at Mechanics' Fair," *San Francisco Chronicle*, October 2, 1913, 7.
82. "The Hippodrome," *The Morning Post* (London), December 2, 1909, 10.
83. "Amusements," *Pensacola Journal* (Pensacola, FL), April 23, 1911, 20.
84. "*The Vampire Dance* in *The Flirting Princess*, at the Syndicate Theatre, April 27," *Evening Waterloo Courier* (Waterloo, IA), April 23, 1910, 12.
85. "Something about the Vampire Dance in *The Flirting Princess*," *Colorado Springs Gazette*, Feburary 26, 1911, 22; "Colonial," *Columbus Dispatch*, December 11, 1910, 3.
86. "Amusements," *Houston Post*, April 6, 1911, 11.
87. "Lyric," *Cincinnati Post*, January 30, 1911, 3.
88. "The *Vampire Dance*, Modeled on Kipling's *Rag and a Bone* Poem Has Eclipsed Last Year's *Salome* – a New *Submarine* Dance and an Audacious New *Egyptian* Dance," *San Francisco Examiner*, January 23, 1910, 62.
89. "The Sketch," *Illustrated London News*, December 1, 1909, 225.
90. "Theodora Girard [sic] Returns," *The Commercial Appeal* (Memphis, TN), March 6, 1911, 4; "Vampire Dancer Here," *The Commercial Appeal*, September 4, 1909, 16.
91. Edward G. Kendrew, "Paris Notes," 1909, *Variety*, 11.
92. "Follies of 1910," *Variety*, 1910, 15.
93. "The Vampire Walk!", *The Oregonian* (Portland, OR), December 26, 1915, 5.
94. "Walters and Walters and Eiler's Animal Circus and Princess Ka Headline Big Vaudeville at Hippodrome," *The Morning Echo* (Bakersfield, CA), July 22, 1917, 10.
95. "It's a Double Feature Pan Bill at Burns This Week," *Colorado Springs Gazette*, May 2, 1920, 13.

96. Advertisement, *Moving Picture World*, September 21, 1912, 1209. *Vampyrdanserinden* was released in France as *La Danse vampiresque* and in Germany as *Die Vampir-Tänzerin*.
97. See, for example: "Lid Clamped on the Picture Shows," *Harrisburg Telegraph* (Harrisburg, PA), October 24, 1912, 8; "Film Exchanges Resent Proposed Censorship Tax," *San Francisco Call*, January 21, 1913, unpaginated.
98. The term "weird" appears in Nordisk Films, Co., 24 Cecil Court, W.C., *Supplement to the Kinematograph and Lantern Weekly*, February 29, 1912, 41.
99. I am grateful to the Danske Filminstitut for sharing the original programs for *Vampyrdanserinden*, from which this text is quoted.
100. The film ends in tragedy. Silvia's partner Oscar dies onstage, which she realizes when he fails to stand for their applause.
101. "*The Vampire*," *Kalem Kalendar*, October 1, 1913, 15.
102. "Vampire Dance Is an Exceptional Picture," *Alaska Daily Empire* (Juneau, AK), November 5, 1915, 2.
103. "New York City," *New York Clipper*, July 31, 1909, 637. Two years later, in *The Dream Dance* (1915), a man visits the Moulin Rouge and dreams a picture of a woman "comes to life and lures him into a wild vampire dance." See "*The Dream Dance*," *Moving Picture World*, June 19, 1915, 1986.
104. "The Vampire Dance," *Asbury Park Press* (Asbury Park, NJ), October 22, 1913, 8; "Movies' Censor Calls His Job Thankless," *Atlanta Georgian and News*, October 17, 1913, 4; "Members of Vice Squad Shocked by the Awful Vampire Dance, but It Will Go on All the Same," *The Constitution* (Atlanta, GA), October 17, 1913, 2.
105. "*The Dance of Death*," *Washington Post*, April 19, 1914, SP6. *The Dance of Death* starred Alice Joyce and Tom Moore.
106. It is important to note that Colonia-Films' *Hiawatha* is a different film than Edgar Lewis's film of the same name, which was also released in 1913. Based on Henry Wadsworth Longfellow's poem *Hiawatha* (1855), Lewis's film starred Jesse Cornplanter and Soon-goot.
107. "*Hiawatha*," *Kinematographische Rundschau*, October 26, 1913, 116. Though sometimes rendered as "Hilde Hadges," I have opted for "Hild Hadges," the spelling that appears in German reviews and advertisements for *Hiawatha* (1913).
108. Advertisement, *Der Kinematograph*, July 30, 1913, unpaginated.
109. Some modern sources, such as the Internet Movie Database (IMDb) incorrectly refer to this film by the title *Tanets s vampirom*.
110. V. E. Vishnevskii, *Khudozhestvennyie fil'my dorevoliutsionnoi Rossii* (Moscow, Goskinoizdat, 1945), 49. I am grateful to Anna Kovalova for the primary sources on this film and the translation of them.
111. "Novye lenty," *Sine-Fono*, no. 11 (1914): 68.
112. I have previously made these observations in Gary D. Rhodes, "The First Vampire Films in America," *Palgrave Communications* 3, no. 1 (December 2017): 1–10. That article provided the basis for this chapter.
113. Daniel Frampton, *Filmosophy* (London: Wallflower Press, 2006), 180.

CHAPTER 2

Vamps

"She cast a dark shadow on my fancy."
— Robert Louis Stevenson
Olalla, 1885

"No one . . . has won a more prominent niche in the hall of film fame than the vampire."[1]
— *Motography*, 1916

"The 1914–1918 dame was something out of a Bram Stoker thriller."[2]
— *Photoplay*, 1930

Life involves change, from youth to old age. Death, too, is a transformative state, the cadaver decomposing into dust. But to be undead is to never grow old. It is to be static and unchanging. A supernatural vampire does not evolve. A "vamp," on the other hand, can change, and did, frequently, during the first two decades of the twentieth century.

In 1920, as the "vamp" film craze was on the wane, a newspaper reporter observed, "So many misleading things have been written about these often gentle and inoffensive creatures, and there is so much popular ignorance on the subject, it would seem high time that they be given a hearing."[3] That comment had great merit. Only one year earlier another journalist asked readers, "Do you really know what a vamp is?" To help readers, he clarified, "we are not talking about honest-to-goodness vampires, but rather of the vamp, who is shown in a variety of ways to be different. Just what the difference – and how much the difference – is hard to figure out."[4]

Such questions were easier to ask than to answer, in part because the vamp was arguably as chimerical as she was vampirical. She developed, and she transformed, so much so that even her origins are difficult to pinpoint. In the early twentieth century, some writers cited Salome and Cleopatra as early examples of vamps, and yet they were much further from folkloric vampires than some of their early twentieth-century counterparts. A definition published in 1920 explained, "Vamp is an abbreviation of the word 'vampire,' which means a person who preys on others . . . The term has been popularized by Kipling's famous poem, *The Vampire*."[5]

Along with Rudyard Kipling, it is crucial to mention Philip Burne-Jones and his painting *The Vampire* (1897). The resulting vamp became the most notable of the metaphorical vampires of the nineteenth and early twentieth centuries, due not only to its popularity but also its ability to invoke the uncanny, even the supernatural, through visual and thematic means. An American journalist believed Kipling's poem to be as "weird as Poe's *The Raven*."[6] When a gallery in Washington, D. C. exhibited *The Vampire* in 1902, its curator displayed the painting in "darkened room beneath a brilliant electric light, shielded and shaded." One reporter called *The Vampire* "gruesome."[7] Another called it "ghoulish."[8]

Burne-Jones and Kipling were certainly not the first to apply the term vampire to an immoral or amoral woman. Consider the following description in John Mackie's novel *The Devil's Playground*, published in 1894:

> She was in his eyes a species of human vampire, whose thirst for the blood of man would never be satiated. She played a part in order to consummate the utter destruction of his already wrecked life. And she was still the wife of another man . . . He cursed her for her heartlessness, and he cursed himself for his folly, in that he could not break the spell that bound him to her, and which was ever more surely weaving its invisible toils around him.[9]

Regardless of any predecessors, though, it was the popularity of Burne-Jones and Kipling' creation that crystallized the vamp into a recognizable character and a cultural phenomenon.

Their inspirations are as obvious as they are obscure. The press claimed that actress Beatrice Rose Stella Tanner ("Mrs. Patrick Campbell") was Burne-Jones's model; he countered that his muse was actually a woman who lived in Brussels.[10] Kipling once described the San Francisco man on whom he based his poem's victim.[11] As for the vampire character, it is possible that the duo had read nonfiction accounts from the 1870s, accounts about women in New York City who allegedly drank blood obtained from abattoirs or even from their lovers (the "champagne of bloods") as part of an effort to improve their health.[12] It is also possible they were familiar with such paintings as Albert Joseph Pénot's *La Femme Chauve-Souris/ The Bat-Woman* (c.1890) and Eugène Samuel Grasset's *Vitrioleuse/The Acid Thrower* (1894).

Perhaps fiction inspired Burne-Jones and Kipling, including such poetry as John Keats's *La Belle Dame sans Merci* (1819), the ballad of a woman without mercy, a supernatural femme fatale. They might also have been influenced by George Du Maurier's novel *Trilby* (1894), which was extremely successful onstage and in popular culture. Its villain Svengali became the embodiment of the nineteenth century's longstanding fascination with mesmerism and hypnotism.[13]

However much Burne-Jones and Kipling did or did not know about previous vampire literature, it certainly served as an important context for them. Consider the following verses from Henry Liddell's poem *The Vampire Bride* (1833):

> He lay like a corse [sic] 'neath the Demon's force,
> And she wrapp'd him in a shroud;
> And she fixed her teeth his heart beneath,
> And she drank of the warm life-blood![14]

That same year, *Literary Tablet* published *Louisa: A Fragment*, in which the narrator pointedly declares, "Like the loathsome vampire, she had marked thee for her victim, and while one drop of purple blood coursed through thy veins, she would not resign thee!" A few years later, Théophile Gautier's short story *La Morte amoureuse/The Dead Woman in Love* (1836) featured the vampire Clarimonde, who wields mental power over a young priest.

William H. G. Kingston's *The Vampire; or, Pedro Pacheco and the Bruxa* (1863), a "Legend of Portugal," includes the following text:

> Many a poor wretch has thus been led across the country, over rough rocks and through brambles and briars, which have scratched his face and torn his clothes, till, almost worn to death, wet, weary, and bloody, he has at length returned home, complaining that the horrible Bruxas have thus led him astray and maltreated him, and that the wine shops are in no way to blame.

The bruxas – female vampires in bat-like form – led males astray geographically and perhaps morally as well.

Vampire literature of the nineteenth century also contain descriptions of characters that culminated in Burne-Jones's painting. Geraldine is pale in Coleridge's *Christabel* (1797–1800), as are Clarimonde in *La Morte amoureuse* and Miss Penclosa in Arthur Conan Doyle's *The Parasite* (1894). In *La Belle Dame sans Merci*, Keats describes the title character's hair as long and her eyes as "wild." In Charlotte Brontë's *Jane Eyre* (1847), Bertha has "thick and dark hair hanging long down her back," as well as "black eyebrows" and "fiery eyes." The title character of J. Sheridan Le Fanu's *Carmilla* (1872) has "very dark brown" hair and "dark eyes." Miss Penclosa has "dark hollows under her eyes." And in Florence Marryat's *The Blood of the Vampire* (1897), Harriet Brandt has "colourless but clear skin," "blue-black hair," "black lashes," and "slumbrous black eyes."

Similar descriptions appeared in Stoker's *Dracula* (1897), which was published shortly after Burne-Jones's painting had been unveiled, their respective release dates meaning neither could have influenced the other, though both emerged from similar contexts. Two of Dracula's brides in Stoker are "dark," and the undead Lucy has "eyes unclean and full of hellfire." Similar descriptions occur in literature published soon thereafter. The vampire in Hume Nisbet's *Vampire Maid* (1900) shares most of these traits, from her "black tresses" to her "savage eyes, glowing white face, and blood-stained red lips." And the title character of Mary Wilkins Freeman's *Luella Miller* (1902) has "black hair" and "dark eyes."[15]

Such physical attributes are hardly surprising. The undead vampire was a reanimated corpse; that it would be pale is logical. However unfairly, dark features in the nineteenth century visually evoked dark deeds and dark souls; they were also indicative of foreign origins that to many in Great Britain and the United States seemed exotic, mysterious, and dangerous. As a result, male vampires shared many traits with their female counterparts. The title character of James Malcolm Rymer's *Varney the Vampire* (1845–7) has a "sallow face" with "dark" eyes. Dom Antoine Augustin Calmet's *The Phantom World* (1850) includes a story about a "pale man with very black eyes."[16] Stoker's Dracula is at times "deathly pale," his eyes "blazing" with "red light." And then of course there was sex appeal. In John Polidori's *The Vampyre* (1819), Lord Ruthven practices the "seductive arts"; Janet Staiger has notably referred to the silent film vamp as a "seductress."[17]

In 1903, the *Washington Post* reported that the Burne-Jones painting had the effect of "awakening interest" in the "subject of vampirism as it exists in the Orient," adding that, "prior to appearance of a recent article in the *Post*, a great many people had never heard of the vampire superstition."[18] Perhaps that was true to an extent, but Burne-Jones and Kipling's major influence on popular culture was the metaphorical vamp, which became the dominant vampire of the silent film era, certainly in terms of numbers. The character held America's imagination tightly in its grasp, not just in exhibitions of the painting and reprints of the poem, but also in popular entertainment. As early as 1898, Harry Morris's *Twentieth Century Maids* displayed a "living reproduction of Philip Burne-Jones' great painting" onstage under the title *The Human Vampire*.[19] And in 1901, Killayni's *Living Pictures* presented "Nature's Choicest Models in Correct Posing of Celebrated Paintings." *The Vampire* became the company's most prominently advertised reproduction.[20]

Literary characters inspired by Burne-Jones and Kipling were many, including Dazaar, the beautiful and hypnotic nemesis of detective Nick Carter. The two characters battled each other in six separate stories. In

Figure 2.1 Katharine Kaelred, the star of Porter Emerson Browne's play *A Fool There Was* (1909).

July 1904, the *New Nick Carter Weekly* featured *In the Shadow of Dazaar, or, At the Mercy of Vampires*.[21] Her cult worshipped Satan, and "honor[ed] vampires."[22] She was herself a "human vampire," with "brilliant, red lips which suggested the vampire of legend. . . ."[23] To be a captive in her fiendish hands "meant torture and death."[24]

Porter Emerson Browne relied on Burne-Jones and Kipling for his novel *A Fool There Was* (1909), its title taken directly from a verse in Kipling's poem. Browne wrote:

> Coming down the deck was a woman, a woman darkly beautiful, tall, lithe, sinuous. Great masses of dead black hair were coiled about her head. Her cheeks were white; her lips very red. Eyes heavy lidded looked out in cold, inscrutable hauteur upon the confusion about her. She wore a gown that clung to her perfectly-modelled figure– that seemed almost a part of her being.[25]

Elsewhere Browne describes the character as wearing a "shimmering black gown," furthering the connection between dark appearance and dark soul. Such clothing also had literary antecedents. The title character of Mary E. Braddon's *Good Lady Ducayne* (1896) wears a "gorgeous garment of black and crimson brocade."

Browne adapted his novel for the stage, the play opening in New York City in 1909. *A Fool There Was* featured Robert Hilliard as the title character and Katharine Kaelred as – to quote the synopsis published in the *New York Times* – the "Vampire Lady."[26] One critic described Kaelred as a "sinuous, dark type" who approached her victim like a "famished vampire from her grave."[27] She was "terrifying and monstrous."[28] For a touring version of *A Fool There Was*, Virginia Pearson played the vamp. The *Cincinnati Post* described one scene as follows:

> In the green light that streams in through the window the uncanny, white-faced siren stands over the prostrate body of a man.
> "Kiss me, my fool, kiss me."
> She bends down, seizes the arm thrown across his chest, but it slips from her nervous fingers and drops lifeless to the floor.
> "Kiss me, my fool, kiss me."
> The Vampire's lips are pressed to the lips of the dead man. There is a crash of thunder followed by a mechanical shriek.
> The curtain falls. The audience shudders. Will the house lights never go up and dissolve the spell?[29]

The vamp onstage could be eerie, but, as one critic observed, "you will not be afraid to go home in the dark after seeing it."[30]

Most audiences responded favorably to *A Fool There Was*, even though many critics did not. As the *Baltimore American* observed in 1910, "The vampire woman is the latest and most spectacular of stage characterizations."[31] The following year, Victor Records released a 78 rpm of Robert Hilliard performing *Scenes from A Fool There Was*, which included his recitation of Kipling's poem.[32] By 1911, newspapers touted vampire fashions in ladies' clothing. The vamp seemed to be everywhere, with a journalist

Figure 2.2 Publicity photograph of Virginia Pearson from 1917.

warning readers, "The vampire girl will get you if you don't watch out!"[33] That was particularly true at the movie theater, her favored den of iniquity.

The Cinematic Vamp

In 1917, actress Dorothy Dalton wrote, "Film history recordeth not the name of the inventor, the discoverer, the designer of the film vamp, but once she was introduced to the public her name was legion."[34] Dalton was correct, as it is difficult to determine which filmmaker first considered translating the character to the screen, but it certainly occurred as a direct result of Browne's play. The first vamp film was likely Selig Polyscope's *The Vampire* (1910), which featured Margarita Fischer in the title role. The moving picture attempted to bring the Burne-Jones painting to life and quoted Kipling in its intertitles.[35] According to the *Nickelodeon*, "This is the latest embodiment of Kipling's famous poem, and probably the last, for the vampire's vogue is on the wane. We have had her in poetry, in painting, in drama, in the dance, and now in the photoplay."[36]

Such predictions were dramatically premature, as the vamp quickly advanced on other countries. In the German film *Der Vampyr/The Vampire* (Messters Projektion, 1911), a character becomes a "sensible man" after having a nightmare about a "vampire woman."[37] Two years later, Mauritz Stiller directed the Swedish film *Vampyren/The Vampire* (Phoenix/Svenska Biografteatern, 1913), which bore the subtitle *En kvinnas slav/A*

Woman's Slave. In it, Theresa (Lili Beck) seduces Lieutenant Roberts (Victor Sjöström) and encourages him to commit a crime.³⁸ Then, in Georgii Azagarov's Russian film *Zhenshchina vampir'/The Vampire Woman* (T-vo "I. N. Ermoliev," 1917, aka *Zhensh'ina-vampir/The Vampire Woman*), the title character tries to murder her husband through intense sexual intercourse.³⁹ A synopsis explained,

> her ecstatic lovemaking, unhealthy passion, and wild kisses, like a fast-acting poison, began to destroy Victor's weak organism. Sometimes, in the delirium of his illness, it seemed to him that his favorite painting *The Vampire Woman* came to life, and he saw Alla [his wife] in this image.⁴⁰

While she was a world traveler, the vamp made the bulk of her conquests in America. Eclipse released *A Woman's Slave* in 1911; *Moving Picture World* called it a "fair representation of Kipling's famous poem, *The Vampire*."⁴¹ *The Inventor's Secret* (George Kleine, 1912) featured a "naval officer" who "invents a new explosive" before falling "victim to the wiles of a fascinating vampire, who betrays him and wins the secret."⁴² The title character finally detonates his own invention to kill the vamp. In 1913, Vitagraph promoted its moving picture *The Vampire of the Desert* as a "dramatic adaptation of Kipling's well-known poem."⁴³ That same year, as Chapter 1 noted, Kalem produced its version of *The Vampire*. Alice Hollister played Sybil, an "adventuress." *Moving Picture World*

Figure 2.3 Alice Eis and Bert French in *The Vampire* (Kalem, 1913).

declared it to be "one of the most powerful features" that Kalem had ever released.[44] The publication incorrectly noted, "When the writer of screen history comes to a chapter dealing with the vampire craze, he will have to give special mention to Alice Hollister as 'the original vampire of the photoplay.'"[45] Hollister was not the first, but she was became notable for vamp roles. In 1914, for example, Kalem released *The Vampire's Trail*, in which a cabaret singer (Hollister) seduces a young married man (Tom Moore) until her "spell is broken."[46]

Lubin produced *A Fool There Was* in 1914, its title drawing on Browne's play and, by extension, on Browne's novel and Kipling's poem.[47] But it would be a movie of the same title released in 1915 that transformed the vamp into a screen phenomenon. Produced by William Fox, *A Fool There Was* starred Theda Bara as "The Vampire."[48] The *New York Dramatic Mirror* wrote:

> It is bold and relentless; it is filled with passion and tragedy; it is right in harmony with the poem. For a few moments during the last reel we had fearful premonitions of the approach of a happy ending – the Fool turned into a repentant wise man – but fortunately there is no such inartistic claptrap. He is a wreck, he dies, and the Vampire continues on her path, red with the blood of men. The film, then, remains true to its theme, for which the producers are to be thanked.
>
> ... The Vampire is a neurotic woman gone mad. She has enough sex attraction to supply a town of normally pleasing women, and she uses it with prodigal freedom. To come into contact with her is like touching the third rail, and all along the track we see, or hear about her victims.[49]

The film's impact on vampire cinema is hard to overestimate. Bara soon appeared in numerous other vamp movies for the Fox Film Corporation, among them *Destruction* (1915), *The Devil's Daughter* (1915), *The Rose of Blood* (1917), *The Tiger Woman* (1917), and *The She-Devil* (1918). Publicity for her movie *The Clemenceau Case* (1915) declared it to be the "greatest vampire play."[50]

More than any other actress, Theda Bara – whose first name was an anagram for "death" – became the very epitome of the screen vamp. As *Film Fun* declared in 1916, "Other vampires may vamp and go, but Theda vamps on forever."[51] Her dark makeup, hair, and attire drew upon Burne-Jones and Kipling, as well as on the literary vampires who preceded them. Like her forebears, including Dracula, Bara was exotic and foreign, or so Fox publicity claimed. Instead of being Theodosia Goodman from Cincinnati, Ohio, Bara was allegedly born in the Sahara, a daughter of the Sphinx, a reincarnation of Cleopatra. She posed in photographs with male skeletons; some artwork depicted her with bats.[52] "I became famous for the vampire-woman I am not," she once wrote.[53]

Figure 2.4 Publicity photograph of Theda Bara from the mid-1910s.

Bara's success did not go unnoticed by producers who hired other actresses to appear in similar roles. For example, Olga Petrova (real name Muriel Harding) portrayed the title role in the feature film *The Vampire* (Metro, 1915). Intertitles referred to Petrova's character as a "vampire" and "spider."[54] Other films with titles heralding their vamps included *Tricked by a Vampire* (Warner's Features, 1914), *Was She a Vampire?* (Powers, 1915), and *The Vamp* (Paramount Pictures, 1918).[55] Ford Tarpley even shot a low-budget, independent film *Veda the Vampire* (1916), in Portland, Oregon.[56]

Vamps were becoming ubiquitous, turning the screen from shiny silver to seductive black. As Theda Bara observed in 1916, "scarcely a week goes by that a big vampire picture is not released."[57] That same year, a journalist reported, "Film-makers apparently are going 'vampire mad' in their deluded convictions that the picture public just loves to see vampire picture after vampire picture."[58] Some viewers loved the films; others did not. An exhibitor made the following complaint in 1916, "Last week I had a vampire every night, and we are being vampired, vampired, and vampired until we are sick of vampire pictures."[59]

The sheer number of actresses portraying vamps also continued to grow, their ranks including Charlotte Burton, Lina Cavalieri, Dorothy Dalton, Lillian Drew, Pauline Frederick, Louise Glaum, Maria Hesperia, Nita Naldi, Dora Rogers, Valeska Suratt, Iva Shepard, Olive Thomas, and Clara Kimball Young. And films about vamps did not necessarily require the word

Figure 2.5 Photo montage of screen vamps created in 1919. Pictured are Louise Glaum, Theda Bara, Virginia Pearson, Clara Kimball Young, Olive Thomas, Dorothy Dalton, Olga Petrova, Pauline Frederick, Lina Cavalieri, and others.

"vampire" in their titles. Examples include *The Forbidden Way* (Essanay, 1913), *When a Woman Loves* (George Kleine, 1913), *The Eternal City* (Famous Players, 1915), *The Soul of Broadway* (Fox, 1915), *Ashes of Embers* (Famous Players, 1916), *The Female of the Species* (Kay-Bee, 1916), *The Lotus Woman* (Kalem, 1916), *The Straight Way* (Fox, 1916), *The Price Mark* (Thomas H. Ince, 1917), and *The Devil's Playground* (Fraternity, 1918).

The vampires in these films shared the very traits that inspired Burne-Jones and Kipling, sexual power unleashed, the return of the unrepressed. In 1918, the *Los Angeles Times* wrote, "When you see your pet vampire on the screen, you see her in 'atmosphere.'"[60] Film vamps usually lived in luxurious city apartments or homes, the décor featuring animal prints and other "exotic" motifs. The vamp herself had black hair, "like the raven's wing, unless it is red like a flame."[61] She had a "vampire face," which was pale and "alabaster white," featuring "red lips and very dark eyebrows over darkened eyelids."[62] The eyelids featured "vampire black" makeup.[63] She was an "almond-eyed, carmine lipped woman of subtlety and mystery."[64] Theda Bara believed, "I think most vampires are dark women, though some have blood-red hair and green, snakelike eyes."[65] Comparisons of the screen vamp to snakes and serpents was not uncommon, dating contextually at least to Keats's word "serpent" to describe the title character of *Lamia* (1820). In Marryat's *The Blood of the Vampire*, Harriet Brandt resembles a "coiling snake." Similarly, in Stoker's *Dracula*, the vampiric Lucy has brows that "were wrinkled as though the folds of the flesh were the coils of Medusa's snakes. . . ."

Again borrowing from her literary forebears, the screen vamp's clothing was usually dark. As one would-be vamp wrote, "We used to have great arguments as to which was the most dangerous looking – scarlet or jet black."[66] The *Baltimore American* stated that the "vampire gown":

> must be made of clinging material unlined so that it hug[s] closely to the form, the same as a woman entwines her arms around her victim. It must have a train that clutches the floor. It must expose just enough of the shoulder and arm so that it could not be termed immodest, and it should show enough of the ankle to be tantalizing at both the top and bottom.[67]

Some of these gowns featured spiderweb patterns.[68] And the vampire's "undulations" in them were regularly described with words like "sinuous," "writhe," and "wriggle."

Screen parodies of vamps appeared almost as frequently as their dramatic counterparts. In 1914, even before Theda Bara starred in *A Fool There Was*, Universal released the comedy *Universal Ike, Jr., and the Vampire*, which features a man who bests a group of cowboys ("fools there was") for the affections of a "vampire" (Louise Glaum).[69] Other comedies included *An Innocent Vampire* (Kalem, 1916), *The Latest in Vampires* (Victor, 1916), *Love Will Conquer* (Keystone, 1916), *She Was Some Vampire* (Universal, 1916), *A Vampire Out of Work* (Vitagraph, 1916), *A Comedy Vampire* (L-KO, 1917), *Jerry and the Vampire* (Mutual, 1917), *A Milk-Fed Vamp* (Fox, 1917), *To Oblige a Vampire* (Universal, 1917), *The Vamp of the Camp* (Universal, 1917), *Vamping Reuben's Millions* (L-KO, 1917), *Vamping the Vamp* (Universal, 1918), *The Vamp Cure* (1918), *The Calico Vampire* (Triangle, 1920), *Vamps and Scamps* (Universal, 1921), and *Vamped* (Universal, 1923).[70]

In 1917, one journalist complained, "It was [the Burne-Jones] portrait and Kipling's poem that started all of this modern vampire business that has become such a pest on stage and screen."[71]

Figure 2.6 Movie poster for *Jerry and the Vampire* (Mutual, 1917). (Courtesy of Heritage Auctions.)

The He-Vamp

Numerous poets wrote variations on and responses to Kipling's *The Vampire*, among them Felicia Blake Rees in 1911:

> A fool there was, and she lowered her pride
>   (Even as you and I).
> To a bunch of conceit in a masculine hide–
> We saw the faults that could not be denied;
> But the fool saw only his manly side.
>   (Even as you and I).[72]

As another writer explained in 1917, "*the male vampire is just as old as the female of the species – and he's just as deadly.*"[73] According to a analysis, "history teems" with vampire men who "used all the powers of mesmerism that a vampire employs."[74] The language recalls a character in *Trilby*, who declares, "He's a bad fellow, Svengali – I'm sure of it! He mesmerized you; that's what it is – mesmerism! . . . They get you into their power and just make you do any blessed thing they please. . . ."

The male vamp had deep roots in nineteenth-century literature, being the immediate offspring of Polidori's *The Vampyre*. In August 1819, *The Ladies' Literary Cabinet* published a short story called *The Modern Vampyre*, its author credited only as "Anna."[75] Her choice of terminology was metaphorical. A woman named Louisa comes under the spell of Stanley Darling: "he passed his hand across his brow, a shade darkened his countenance, it rolled over like an April shower." When the clock strikes twelve, Stanley leaves Louisa's company without "declaring himself." She is crestfallen. "How many are there of the present day who may be classed with Stanley!", Anna inquired:

> who, without any settled principle of depravity, gain the esteem of artless innocence, and when the poor girl has anticipated ideal felicity with her bosom's choice, *he*, on whom she had fixed every fondest thought, forgets all moral obligations, and devotes his attention to the next novelty.[76]

As early as 1910, Katharine Kaelred had observed, "Wherever you find a vampire woman you will find a man vampire first."[77] By 1917, *Film Fun* announced, "At last a male form of the word 'vampire' has been found."[78] That term was "he-vampire," which, along with "male vampire," had already been in use for a few years. A newspaper article in 1920 told readers:

> Heigh-ho for the masculine vampire! May his tribe decrease! This life is tough enough without the male hussies blocking traffic in front of the corset shop windows. Still, the census shows there's one he-lily born every hour. That's a lot slower than suckers are born, but still it's plenty.
> . . . You know the male vampire, with a form like a figure 8 and a dome like 6 below zero. He has patent leather hair and a shoe-laced torso. Nature has blessed him with teeth like pearls, lips like coral and ears like pink seashells. All of 'em attached to solid rock . . . Life is just one hand-picked eyebrow after another to this guy.[79]

Here was one of the most pronounced of the vamp's evolutions, the cinema's acknowledgment and embrace of the male vampire.

George S. Viereck's novel *The House of the Vampire* (1907) provides an important context. Reginald Clarke, the story's vampire, psychically feeds off others. As one character observes, "your vampires suck blood; but Reginald, if vampire he be, preys upon the soul. How can a man suck from another man's brain a thing as intangible, as quintessential as thought?" Together with Edgar Allan Woolf, Viereck adapted his tale into a three-act stage play called *The Vampire* (1909). Its villain, as portrayed by Warner Oland, was capable of "robbing" men of their thoughts. As the *Chicago Tribune* explained, "This theft he accomplishes by a mesmeric control he exercises over certain gifted young people."[80]

Though it took a few years, he-vamps soon brought their mesmeric control to the cinema, usually for the purpose of dominating women. In *Mr. Vampire* (Rex, 1916), the son of an unfaithful husband (played by Francis Ford) is known as the:

> Vampire because of his hatred of women. Born while his mother was embittered by her experience, his hatred of women is almost uncanny. The Vampire attends a house party, and is shunned by the men, but much sought after by the women. It is strange that though he hates women they invariably seek him out. One of the married women at the party takes a violent fancy for Mr. Vampire, which causes comment.[81]

At the conclusion of the film, "The Vampire Man sardonically smiles at the ways of women and reiterates his hatred for them."

The "He Vampire" appeared onscreen in such comedies as *Saved from the Vampire* (Biograph, 1915), *Vampire Ambrose* (Keystone, 1916), *His Vampy Ways* (Pathé, 1919), and *A He Male Vamp* (1920), as well as in such dramas as *The Heritage of Hate* (Red Feather, 1916), *Reputation* (Mutual, 1917), and *Modern Husbands* (National Film Corporation of America, 1919).[82] Publicity touted the "Male Vampire" in Erich von Stroheim's *Blind Husbands* (Universal, 1919).[83] *The Devil's Claim* (Robertson Cole, 1920) starred Sessue Hayakawa as a "mental vampire" who mistreats the young woman who loves him.[84] And *Moving Picture World* drew attention to the unique feature of *The Forbidden Path* (Fox, 1918), in which Theda Bara was not the vampire, but rather "the victim of a vampire."[85]

Figure 2.7 Publicity photograph of Lew Cody.

A limerick published in 1917 included verses about Stuart Holmes, referring to him as "that debonair devil of filum."[86] Holmes portrayed the "he-vamp" in such films as *Love and Hate* (Fox, 1916) and *The Other Man's Wife* (Carl Harbaugh Productions, 1919). But it was Lew Cody who became the most notable male vampire of the screen.[87] He vamped in films like *The Butterfly Man* (Robertson-Cole, 1920) and *Occasionally Yours* (Robertson-Cole, 1920).[88] Adela Rogers St. John characterized him as a "sort of chocolate-coated cave man."[89] Cody himself said:

> The real male vampire is essentially a bachelor. His freedom is his most cherished possession. He desires wide fields in which to rove, and he doesn't care to cheat. His heaven is anticipation. His hell is a woman he is tired of.
>
> The male vampire is necessarily frivolous – at heart. The moment a man becomes earnest he bores a woman to tears. You cannot harness most men. That is why marriage as an institution is too often a failure.
>
> There is only one really bad man – the man who desires innocence. That is why the male vampire is not bad – he is only a little humanly wicked. He doesn't really care to waste his time on inexperience. The battle of wits is more engrossing when played with a skilled opponent.[90]

As of 1919, *Photoplay* informed film fans that "the change that has swept the face of the world seems to have switched the vampire's sex. Mr. Cody, and others, are invading Theda Bara's business."[91]

Conclusion

Moving Picture World's synopsis of *Billie Van Deusen and the Vampire* (Mutual, 1916) described its denouement as follows:

> Johnny arrives on the minute, quickly followed by Carol. The vampire's charm "works like a charm" and Johnny falls under her spell to the great sorrow of Carol and the boundless joy of Billy, who rushes out to commend the vampire. She straightway works the charm on him. This is too much for Carol, who denounces the vampire and calls her a cat. But the vampire professes violent love for Carol, tears off a wig and before Carol stands a man. Billy and Johnny fall into dead faint and the "vampire" embraces the surprise-loving Carol.[92]

A screen vamp could thus be a woman, a man, or one gender dressed as another. They shared the same term, "vampire," as well as the same qualities. As early as 1898, a journalist remarked, "A human vampire is always an incarnation of selfishness. His or her (it is usually her) trials and discomforts blot out the sun in heaven, spreading over the skies like a pall of blackness – or grayness at the very least."[93]

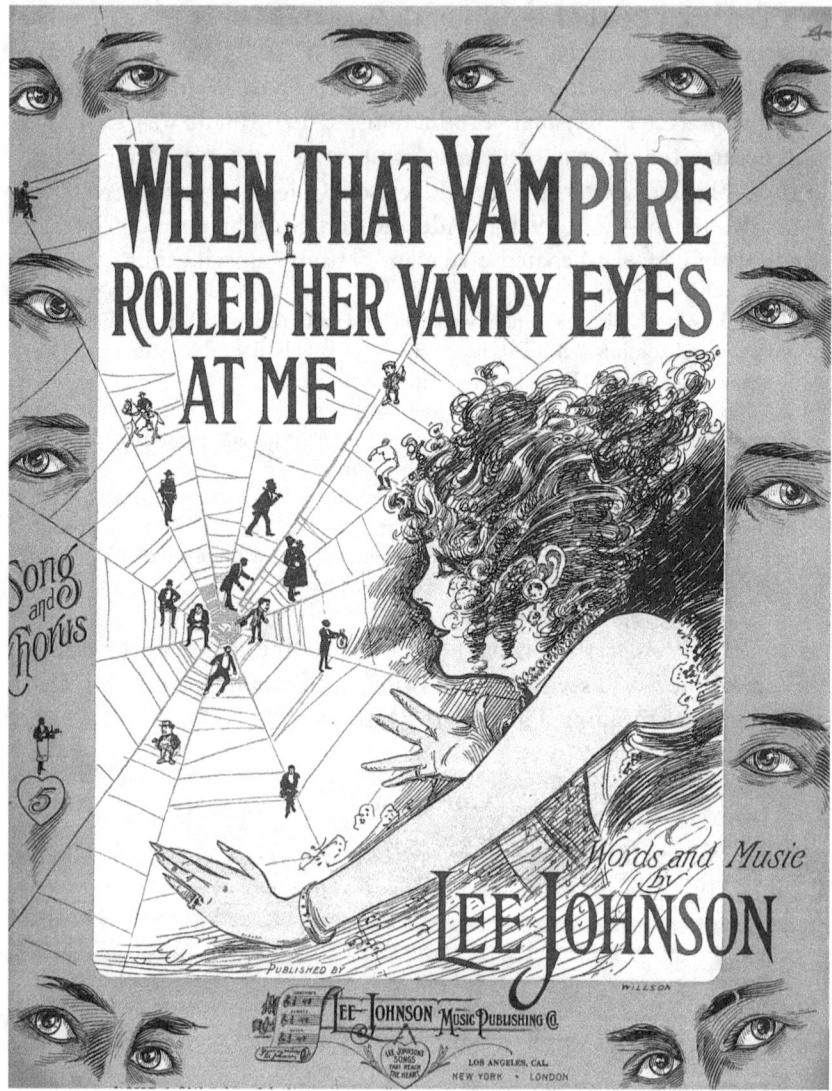

Figure 2.8 Sheet music published in 1917.

In 1916, the *Los Angeles Times* attributed the vamp's popularity to public interest in "morbidity and the love of mysticism."[94] Lee Johnson's song *When That Vampire Rolled Her Vampy Eyes at Me* (1917) featured lyrics about a vamp who "hypnotized" and "mesmerized" her "caveman." By that time, a critique of Porter Emerson Browne's play had already noted, "Over it all was the spell of the vampire, the weird mystery of occult power, the spectacle of a man struggling with the invisible meshes which bound him and unseen forces which dragged him inevitably to his doom . . . it is a gruesome story, uncanny and creepy. . . ."[95] And yet, the gruesomeness and weirdness diminished over time. Expanding the gender identification of the vamp was only one of the transformations that occurred.

The perceived need for change may have stemmed from the vamp's obviousness in dress and demeanor. In 1917, the *Chicago Tribune* derisively commented:

> The vampire as conceived by some of our largest moving picture corporations is a queer freak from whom the tired businessman would retire at a gallop. She would scare the crows away from any field, and to promenade the sidewalks of a well-regulated city would require a permit from the mayor . . . her intentions stick out on her like horns.[96]

"Of course, there is no such thing as a vampire," Theda Bara added in 1920. "No women are like that. That is why you can't get good stories for vampire pictures."[97]

Thus, evolutions proved necessary. In October of 1916, *Motion Picture News* realized that Alice Hollister's character in *The Lotus Woman* (Kalem, 1916) was a "vampire who depends upon her mental appeal to entice her victims, "thus making her a "novelty in this day and age."[98] The title character in *The Beloved Vampire* (Knickerbocker Star Features, 1917) was notable due to her character's redemption.[99] The title character of *A Virtuous Vamp* (First National, 1919, aka *The Virtuous Vamp*), which starred Constance Talmadge, is interested in wooing only one man, whom she actually loves.[100] And *A Homespun Vamp* (Paramount, 1922), starring May McAvoy, featured no vamp at all, just a woman who falls for a handsome stranger.[101]

Other vamp variations involved age. In 1919, *Photoplay* stated, "[I]n the celluloid they are generally known as 'Baby Vamps'–or 'Vampettes.'" Such a woman was a "youngish little rascal, with big innocent blue orbs – or eyes to that effect – who knows naught of your city ways, but always

Figure 2.9 Movie poster for *The Blonde Vampire* (F.B.O., 1922). (Courtesy of Heritage Auctions.)

managed to dress well without any visible means of support."[102] The "Baby Vamp" spawned such popular songs as Milton E. Schwarzwald, Gus Kahn, and Edward Beck's *Baby Vampire* (1917) and Grace Doro's *I'll Be Your Baby Vamp If You'll Be the Fool There Was* (1919).

And so, the screen vamp was no longer singular, thanks in some measure to the intrinsic multivalence of the term "vampire." In 1919, *Photoplay* observed the changes:

> We have come far since the day of "a rag and a bone and a hank of hair." That lady is now considered a rank amateur. She has been followed by the baby vamp, the intellectual vamp, and the person who slings slightly obese charms in your face with a freedom ridiculous or disgusting according to your sex and disposition.[103]

In 1922, F.B.O. released Wray Physioc's *The Blonde Vampire*, which attempted to distinguish itself through its title character's hair color.[104] And film director Hobart Henley predicted the arrival of another "new vampire," one who would be "interested in outdoor sports," even being successful at golf and tennis.[105]

Many screen vamps might have seemed like "something out of a Bram Stoker novel," but some others did not, especially as the 1910s progressed, with the gulf between vamp and vampire expanding. Consider what Virginia Pearson, one of the earliest stage and screen vamps, said in 1919:

> I have an idea, though, that I should like to play a real vampire role. And by that, I mean that the vampire, according to my understanding of it, has never been attempted. The so-called vampires are only representations of more or less immoral and unscrupulous women. My idea of the vampire is the Oriental conception – that of an unworldly creature whose only human characteristic is that it takes the form of a woman.[106]

What a wonderfully original idea: for an actor to portray a vampire, a "real vampire," a supernatural vampire, on the screen.

Notes

1. Thomas C. Kennedy, "*The Wolf Woman*," September 9, 1916, 610.
2. Marquis Busby, "The 'Other Woman,'" *Photoplay*, March 1930, 36.
3. Thomas L. Masson, "The Truth About Vampires," *Kansas City Star*, July 25, 1920, 20.
4. Clive Marshall, "What Is a Vamp?", *The Plain Dealer* (Cleveland, OH), January 19, 1919, unpaginated.
5. "Answers to Questions," *Greensboro Record* (Greensboro, NC), February 17, 1920, 6.
6. "Popular Plays by Popular Players," *Philadelphia Inquirer*, March 3, 1914, 16.
7. "Art Notes," *The Evening Star* (Washington, D. C.), June 14, 1902, 26.

8. "Burne-Jones's *Vampire*," *New York Times*, January 16, 1903, 1.
9. John Mackie, *The Devil's Playground: A Story of the Wild Northwest* (New York: Frederick A. Stokes Company, 1894), 130.
10. "Burne-Jones's *Vampire*," 1.
11. "Man Who Inspired *The Vampire*," *Illinois State Journal* (Springfield, IL), October 28, 1906, 9.
12. "Female Vampires," *St. Louis Globe-Democrat*, April 29, 1876, 10.
13. With regard to mesmerism and hypnotism in American popular culture, see Gary D. Rhodes, *The Birth of the American Horror Film* (Edinburgh: Edinburgh University Press, 2018).
14. Henry Liddell, *The Wizard of the North; The Vampire Bride; and Other Poems* (Edinburgh: William Blackwood, 1833), 45–6.
15. To these examples, we can consider that the title character of Honoré de Balzac's *Le Succube/The Succubus* (1837) has "flaming" eyes, "from which gleamed forth a fire of hell" and teeth which can draw one "to the bottom of hell."
16. Calmet's work was originally published in 1746 as *Dissertations sur les apparitions des anges, des démons et des esprits, et sur les revenants et vampires de Hongrie, de Bohême, de Moravie et de Silésie* and then in revised and expanded form in 1751 as *Traité sur les apparitions des esprits et sur les vampires ou les revenans de Hongrie, de Moravie, &c.*
17. Janet Staiger, *Bad Women: Regulating Sexuality in Early American Cinema* (Minneapolis: University of Minnesota Press, 1995), 150.
18. Reprinted in "Myth of a Vampire," *The State Sentinel* (Indianapolis, IN), February 18, 1903, 8.
19. "Theatrical Gossip," *Philadelphia Inquirer*, March 31, 1898, 5.
20. Advertisement, *The Times-Picayune* (New Orleans, LA), March 10, 1901, 7.
21. "*In the Shadow of Dazaar, or, At the Mercy of Vampires*," *New Nick Carter Weekly*, July 30, 1904.
22. Ibid., 6.
23. Ibid., 8.
24. Ibid., 11.
25. Porter Emerson Browne, *A Fool There Was* (New York: H. K. Fly Company, 1909), 111.
26. "*A Fool There Was*; No Doubt of That," *New York Times*, March 25, 1909, 9.
27. "Trio of Feminine Vampires Obsess the New York Stage," *Washington Post*, April 4, 1909, SM2.
28. "The Theatre," *The Sunday Star* (Washington, D. C.), January 30, 1910, 6.
29. "Woman Who Is Creepy Vampire in Play Does Not Believe That Men Need Have Fear of Finding Her Kind in Real Life," *Cincinnati Post*, October 29, 1910, 4.
30. "Stage News of Chicago," *Indianapolis Sun*, February 22, 1909, 3.
31. "The Vampire Woman," *Baltimore American*, January 16, 1910, 9.
32. Porter Emerson Browne and Robert Hilliard, *Scenes from A Fool There Was* (Camden, NJ: Victor, 1911), accessed May 4, 2022, https://www.loc.gov/item/jukebox-130245/.

33. "Oof! The Vampire Girl Will Get You If You Don't Watch Out!", *San Francisco Chronicle*, September 3, 1911, 18.
34. "The Vampire Role a Thing of the Past," *Montgomery Advertiser* (Montgomery, Alabama), November 18, 1917, 29.
35. "*The Vampire*," *Moving Picture World*, November 12, 1910, 1127.
36. "*The Vampire*," *The Nickelodeon*, November 15, 1910, 280.
37. "Der Filmeinkäufer," *Lichtbild-Bühne*, May 27, 1911, 12; "*The Vampire*," *Moving Picture World*, January 20, 1912, 338.
38. Here I am grateful to the Swedish Film Institute for providing me with a copy of the original script to *Vampyren*. Additional details regarding the film may be found at the Institute's website, https://www.svenskfilmdatabas.se/en/item/?type=film&itemid=3301.
39. *Zhenshchina vampir'* – as rendered with the apostrophe – is the correct transliteration. However, it is commonly transliterated as *Zhensh'ina-vampir*.
40. "Novye lenty," *Sine-Fono*, nos 1–2 (1918): 34. I am deeply grateful to Anna Kovalova for this primary source and the translation of it.
41. "*A Woman's Slave*," *Moving Picture World*, November 11, 1911, 468.
42. Advertisement, *Moving Picture World*, 313.
43. Advertisement, *Moving Picture World*, May 10, 1913, 564.
44. "*The Vampire* (Kalem)," *Moving Picture World*, October 4, 1913, 51.
45. "Alice Hollister, First Vampire," *Moving Picture World*, June 24, 1916, 2246.
46. "*The Vampire's Trail*," *New York Dramatic Mirror*, July 29, 1914, 26.
47. "A New Movie Vamp," *Pictures*, April 23, 1921, 416.
48. For more information on Theda Bara, see: Ronald Genini, *Theda Bara: A Biography of the Silent Screen Vamp, with a Filmography* (Jefferson, NC: McFarland, 1996); Eve Golden, *Vamp: The Rise and Fall of Theda Bara* (Vestal, NY: Emprise Publishing, 1996).
49. "*A Fool There Was*," *New York Dramatic Mirror*, January 20, 1915.
50. "Greatest Vampire Play Is *The Clemenceau Case*," *Anaconda Standard* (Anaconda, MT), May 9, 1915, 11.
51. "Vamps – and How to Be Them," *Film Fun*, December 1916, unpaginated.
52. For more information, see Ronald Genini, *Theda Bara: A Biography of the Silver Screen Vamp, with a Filmography* (Jefferson, NC: McFarland and Company, 1996) and Eve Golden, *Vamp: The Rise and Fall of Theda Bara* (New York: Vestal Press, 1996).
53. Theda Bara, "How I Became a Film Vampire: The Self-Revelations of a Moving-Picture Star," *Forum*, June 1919, 715.
54. Kitty Kelly, "Flickerings from Filmland," *Chicago Tribune*, August 11, 1915, 10.
55. "*Was She a Vampire?*," *Moving Picture World*, July 10, 1915, 384; *The Vamp* Press Book, Paramount Pictures, 1918, accessed May 8, 2022, https://archive.org/details/paramountpressbo05unse/page/n545/mode/2up?view=theater.
56. "Society's Elect to Appear in Movies," *The Oregonian* (Portland, OR), June 2, 1916, 1; Edith Knight Holmes, "Veda the Vampire Has Monopoly on Local Society," *The Oregonian*, June 18, 1916, 4.

57. Theda Bara, "Poor Vampire Can Lure No More," *Duluth News-Tribune* (Duluth, MN), September 3, 1916, unpaginated.
58. "Screenings," *Jersey Journal* (Jersey City, NJ), March 24, 1916, 6.
59. Frank J. Rembusch, "Misleading Publicity and Suitable Programs," *Motography*, June 15, 1916, 120.
60. Truman B. Handy, "Re-Enter the Vampire," *Los Angeles Times*, November 24, 1918, III14.
61. Marthe Troly-Curtain, "Vamps – or Witches?," *Film Weekly*, January 21, 1929, 17.
62. "Vampire Make-ups for Fall," *Trenton Evening Times*, August 16, 1911, 7; Gaby Deslys, "Don't Affect Vampire Type Says Gaby," *Denver Post*, January 18, 1913, 8.
63. Warren Reed, "The Beautiful Brute," *Picture-Play Magazine*, May 1917, 105.
64. "To Be or Not to Be a Vampire," *Anaconda Standard*, May 16, 1916, 6.
65. Quoted in "Theda Bara Says a Vampire Can't Have Real Lover," *Cleburne Morning Review* (Cleburne, TX), August 12, 1915, 7.
66. Winifred Black, "Passing of the Vampire," *Bridgeport Evening Farmer* (Bridgeport, CT), July 6, 1918, 8.
67. "A Vampire Gown," *Baltimore American*, May 29, 1917, 3.
68. "Will You Buy Your Wifie a Vampire Gown?," *Tacoma Times* (Tacoma, WA), December 28, 1912, 1.
69. "*Universal Ike, Jr., and the Vampire*," *Motion Picture News*, July 11, 1914, 92.
70. "*An Innocent Vampire*," *Moving Picture World*, May 20, 1916, 1354; "*The Latest in Vampires* – Victor," *Moving Picture Weekly*, July 22, 1916, 26; "*Love Will Conquer*," *Moving Picture World*, February 19, 1916, 1192; "*A Vampire Out of Work*," *Motography*, October 14, 1916, 897; Peter Milne, "Three Christie Comedies," *Motion Picture News*, December 23, 1916, 4041; "*She Was Some Vampire*," *Moving Picture Weekly*, July 15, 1916, 18; "October Program of L-KO Comedies," *Motion Picture News*, September 29, 1917, 2177; "*Jerry and the Vam*pire," *Moving Picture World*, November 24, 1917, 1191; "*A Milk Fed Vamp*," *Moving Picture World*, December 15, 1917, 1643; "*Vamping Reuben's Millions*," *Moving Picture World*, November 3, 1917, 713; "*To Oblige a Vampire*," *Moving Picture World*, May 19, 1917, 1145; "*The Vamp of the Camp*," *Moving Picture Weekly*, July 28, 1917, 47; "*Vamping the Vamp*," *Moving Picture Weekly*, January 19, 1918, 38; "*The Vamp Cure*," *Moving Picture Weekly*, July 13, 1918, 34; "*Vamps and Scamps*," *Moving Picture Weekly*, January 22, 1921, 38; "*Vamped*," *Moving Picture Weekly*, March 31, 1923, 40.
71. "Playhouse Paragraphs," *Brooklyn Eagle*, May 13, 1917, 2.
72. "Women Victims; Men 'Vampires,'" *Chicago Tribune*, January 9, 1911, 8.
73. Shirley Burns, "Male Vampires," *Forum*, February 1917, 183. Emphasis in the original.
74. Harlowe R. Hoyt, "He Vamps of History," *Washington Post*, February 26, 1922, 80.

75. Anna, "*The Modern Vampyre*," *The Ladies' Literary Cabinet* (August 1819), 107.
76. Emphasis in original.
77. "Men Make the Vampire Women," *Grand Rapids Press* (Grand Rapids, MI), April 20, 1910, 12.
78. "Who's Who and Where," *Film Fun*, May 1917, unpaginated.
79. Neal R. O'Hara, "Male Vampires," *The News-Tribune* (Tacoma, WA), October 1, 1920, 26.
80. "News of the Theaters," *Chicago Tribune*, February 9, 1909, 10.
81. "*Mr. Vampire*," *Moving Picture World*, December 30, 1916, 2005.
82. "*Saved from the Vampire*," *Moving Picture World*, May 27, 1915, 1970; "*Vampire Ambrose* Is a Triangle-Keystone," *Motion Picture News*, November 18, 1916, 3143; "*A He Male Vamp*," *Moving Picture Weekly*, June 26, 1920, 38; "*The Heritage of Hate*," *Wid's*, November 9, 1916, 1088; "*Modern Husbands*," *Wid's Daily*, June 1, 1919, 15.
83. "Male Vampire Comes on Screen," *Wyoming State Tribune* (Cheyenne, WY), February 13, 1920, 5.
84. "*The Devil's Claim*," *Motion Picture News*, May 22, 1920, 4404.
85. "Male 'Vampire' Plays Opposite Miss Bara," *Moving Picture World*, February 9, 1918, 841.
86. Frank M. Wollen, *The He-Male Vampire-Man*, *Motion Picture Magazine*, May 1917, 94.
87. Photo Caption, *Motion Picture Classic*, March 1920, unpaginated.
88. "Inside Dope on the Movie Stars," *Chicago Tribune*, August 21, 1924, D7. See also "*The Butterfly Man*," *Motion Picture News*, May 29, 1920, 4543; "*Occasionally Yours*," *Motion Picture News*, October 2, 1920, 2713.
89. Adela Rogers St. John, "The Confessions of a Male Vampire," *Photoplay*, March 1919, 28.
90. Ibid., 29.
91. "The Ambisextrous Vampire," *Photoplay*, June 1919, 66.
92. "*Billie Van Deusen and the Vampire*," *Moving Picture World*, February 12, 1916, 1020.
93. "The Human Vampire," *Trenton Evening Times* (Trenton, New Jersey), December 19, 1898, 3.
94. Henry Christeen Warnack, "The Fashion of Vampires," *Los Angeles Times*, December 10, 1916, III21.
95. "Weird and Gruesome, but of Great Compelling Interest," *The Advocate* (Charleston, WV), April 21, 1910, 6.
96. Mae Tinée, "A New Style Vampire Is in Our Midst," *Chicago Tribune*, August 26, 1917, 16.
97. Agnes Smith, "The Confessions of Theda Bara," *Photoplay*, June 1920, 57.
98. Edward Weitzel, "*The Lotus Woman*," *Moving Picture World*, June 17, 1916, 2055.
99. "*The Beloved Vampire*," *Moving Picture World*, February 17, 1917, 1075.

100. "Current Productions," *Moving Picture World*, November 29, 1919, 536.
101. Fritz Tidden, "*A Homespun Vamp*," March 4, 1922, 84.
102. Kenneth McGaffrey, "Introducing the 'Vampette,'" *Photoplay*, March 1919, 47.
103. St. John, "The Confessions of a Male Vampire," 28.
104. "*The Blond [sic] Vampire*," *Variety*, September 15, 1922, 42.
105. "Modern Vamp Combination of Old Types, Says Henley," *Washington Post*, July 11, 1926, SM8.
106. Jean Francis, "Virginia of the Many Roles," *Picture-Play Magazine*, February 1919, 221.

CHAPTER 3

Criminals

And the hideous vampires were busy now; there were long, lean, lank fellows, moving with ophidian measure, and reminding one somewhat of the Italian bandit."[1]
— *The Mystery of Ravenswald*, 1878

"Salt-water pirate! Red-handed highwayman! Plunderer! Caitiff! Ingrate! Vampire! I loathe and scorn thee!"[2]
— *New York Dispatch*, 1878

Supernatural vampires are criminals. Their dark deeds range from sexual harassment to rape and murder. And they are imposters, not just of other people, as when Dracula pretends to be Count de Ville in Bram Stoker's 1897 novel, but they also imposters *of* people, impersonating the living as they wine and dine with and on victims, whether in Transylvania or London or anywhere the undead might journey, which they also do illegally, travelling in crates of dirt without passport or stamped visa. Though they may not feel guilt, vampires are guilty, and guilty of so very many sins. Here are crimes against the law, as well as crimes against humanity.

Robbing, looting, purloining: how very often vampires participate in those felonies, their misconduct transgressing social norms and expectations. As Charles A. Kinkaid's *The Vampire's Treasure* (1922) explains, "Even a vampire would give up its riches, if it were given human blood to drink."[3] But as the title character in Stoker's *Dracula* proves, a vampire need not deplete its wealth to obtain blood. Stealing blood is a relatively easy task, even if it unlawful and immoral. Horrid abomination or minor infraction, the vampire is nothing if not a scofflaw.

Staged in London in 1823, *The Three Vampires; or, Maids Beware of Moonshine* depicted a trio of shady humans thought to be vampires. One is a "Practitioner of Medicine," the second a "Pork Butcher," and the third an "Undertaker," their combined professions potentially helpful to so many malefactions. The maids guzzling their illicit homebrew are members of the same family, aptly named "Swallow-all." A playbill described the play as a "New Operatic, Melo-Dramatic, Terrific Vampiric, Monstrous, Frankensteinish, Horrific Romantic Burletta, comprising much *Moonshine*, and more Mirth, written under the *Lunar* influence, but not by a lunatic. . . ."[4] One did not necessarily need to be crazy to perceive the value of vampirism as a dynamic and compelling metaphor for criminality.

Over two decades later, the play *Invisible Prince! Or, the Island of Tranquil Delights* appeared in Boston in 1854. It featured not one, not two or even three, but four vampires: Ruffino, Desperado, Stiletto, and Sanguino, the latter name being very suggestive of blood, red and ruddy.[5] While this quartet may have shared bloodlust, they did not share blood because they were not supernatural. By contrast, they were "vampire robbers," bandits who engaged in "terrific combat," or so the playbill promised. Here were thieves in the night, characters leeching off the innocent.

By that time, various types of metaphorical vampires had thrived in literature. Consider an 1844 poem by "John Jones of New-London," which reads as follows:

> Vampyre! Spare that skin –
> Pierce not that ivory neck;
> Oh! Pause and let its purity
> Thy horrid purpose check.
> Know, monster, that the blood
> Thou seekest to engorge,
> I will defend from the
> The Dragon, or St. George.[6]

The poem clearly evokes the supernatural. But its title explains the villain's natural, even mundane, origin: *Lines to a Mosquito Upon My Wife's Bosom.*

Vampire metaphors became as common as they were potent. Examples appeared in print at least as early as 1763, when a letter published in the *Newport Mercury* compared a "mercenary magistrate" to a "Human Hyena" who "sucks blood like a Vampyre."[7] Joel Barlow's poem *The Conspiracy of Kings* (1792) decried "Courts and Kings" as "vampires nurs'd on nature's spoils."[8] A newspaper published a speech in 1798 decrying England as a "vampyre" that wanted to "suck the blood" of the Irish.[9] For the *Buffalo Advertiser* of 1863, the Confederate States of America were nothing more than a "vampyre from its cave."[10] Others perceived world war to be vampiric, including Count Ernst zu Reventlow in his book *The Vampire of the Continent* (1916).[11]

Advertisers in the nineteenth and early twentieth centuries relied on vampire metaphors to sell black leather oil, pharmaceuticals (including pills to ward off the "merciless vampire of iron-starvation"), and medical devices (including an electric belt to dispel "weakness and disease" that fastened on the sick "like a vampire").[12] Racehorses, sailing vessels, and locomotives bore the name Vampire, as did more than one acrobat.[13] An astronomer declared Venus to be the "vampire of the skies."[14] In 1891, Anthony Comstock even dismissed a "spicy book" about sex for being nothing more than "vampire literature."[15]

Such metaphors served helpfully against dangers to our moral and physical well-being. Published in London in 1858, *The Vampyre* (written "by the Wife of a Medical Man") compared alcoholism to vampirism.[16] At a sermon in 1906, a reverend in New York recounted vampire folklore to his congregation before explaining:

> Of course the word 'vampire' has come to have a metaphorical meaning, and you frequently hear it used, as, such and such person 'is a vampire,' that is, one who sucks the blood of others or who lives upon the vitality and resources of others . . .
> There are two classes of metaphorical vampires, the voluntary and involuntary ones . . . the voluntary vampire, the one who rejoices in his nature, takes advantage of his opportunities and increases his power to the full extent of his ability.[17]

By 1909, an advertisement in the industry trade publication *Show World* even characterized the "duper" – a bootlegger who made illegal copies of moving pictures – as a "blood-sucking vampire, absorbing the life, poisoning the very arteries after they are sucked dry, stifling what would grow to be the healthiest infant industry the old world or new has ever known."[18] And the serial *Beatrice Fairfax* (International Film Service, 1916) features a scandalous weekly newspaper called *The Vampire*.[19] Vampires were among us, everywhere it seemed.

As Chapters 1 and 2 explained, the vamp of Philip Burne-Jones and Rudyard Kipling was a particularly successful metaphor, one that coincided with the rise of cinema. In Essanay's film *The Forbidden Way* (1913), Cora (Lillian Drew) was not just a vamp, she was a "vampire of the underworld."[20] And *Exhibitors Trade Review* referred to Barbara La Marr's character in Fred Niblo's *Strangers of the Night* (1923) as a "vampire crook."[21] Most vamps were crooks, swindling their victims out of their money and even their free will.

Long before the vamp emerged, writers considered certain types of criminals to be vampires. In 1819, a poem called *The Pirate* described its title character as a vampire.[22] Prentiss Ingraham's dime novel *The Ocean Vampire; or, The Heiress of Castle Curse* (1882) featured a pirate.[23] T. C. Harbaugh's *Captain Cutlass, the Ocean Spider; or, The Buccaneer's Girl Foe* (1884) chronicled a seafaring fiend who commands a vessel named the *Vampire*.[24] The title of *The Vampire*, an 1899 British musical composition by Michael Watson, also referred to a pirate ship.[25] And *The Captain of the Vampire or, The Smugglers of the Deep Sea*, published in the *New Nick Carter Weekly* in 1904, made reference to a Chinese word that sounds "exactly like" the term vampire:

> In a word, Dan, it means smuggler; but like all Chinese character words, it comprehends a whole lot of other things with it. For example, your mere opium smuggler would not be a vampire, but if he happened to smuggle opium and other things for the purpose of concealing the fact that he also smuggled Chinese girls into the country to sell them to Chinamen here, for wives, then he would be a vampire. Do you understand?[26]

Nick Carter adds that the Chinese word for vampire can appropriately label a criminal or a ship engaged in smuggling.

Criminal vampires seemed to be everywhere, on land and sea. As Nina Auerbach has observed, "Vampires go where power is," and sometimes that meant financial power.[27] In 1818, a newspaper published these comments regarding American bankers:

> The wealthy Vampyres, through their Agents, those Vultures on Society called Brokers, will pursue the same legalized robbery, under the plausible and specious terms of *premium* and *discount* which they do at present, though not to so great an extent.[28]

Eight decades later, lyrics to an 1896 song swore to "drive the money-changers out," to "drive these vampires from our land" and to "break up their Wall Street nest."[29]

Less powerful crooks could also be vampires. In 1851, a journalist disparaged, "The gamblers, and those who are generally known as sporting characters who, producing nothing themselves, live by preying upon the community, and fatten by sucking the blood of others."[30]

In 1860, the *Chicago Tribune* condemned gangs of thieves who "live vampyre-like, by preying upon their more honest and law-abiding fellows."[31] A newspaper article in 1878 mentioned "the 'vampire,' the 'extortioner,' the 'thief'" as if they were synonymous.[32] And a definition of the word "bandit" published in 1883 advised readers to "see also Brigand, Riff-Raff, Scoundrel, Assassin, Thief, Leper, Highwayman, Horse-thief, Ruffian, Traitor, Spy, Perjurer, Scalawag, Pickpocket, Vulture, Wild-Beast, Ghoul, Vampire &c."[33]

Describing the denizens of a particularly violent district of Chicago in 1906, a writer denounced the:

> "Bad men," who want nothing better than an excuse to commit a murder; common "stickup" men, who will only shoot when they have to in order to escape arrest; "kick-in" men, who make a specialty of robbing tailor shops; tough boys, waiting for a chance to assault somebody; and "dope fiend" and degenerates of the worst type respond to the darkness in the Maxwell Street district like so many vampires.[34]

Murderous vampires plied their trade outside of the Windy City.[35] One newspaper referred to Jack the Ripper as a vampire, for example.[36] Even those who sympathized or cheered for murderers – like the anarchists who celebrated President McKinley's assassination in 1902 – could be called vampires.[37]

Popular American literature drew upon the vampire–criminal connection repeatedly, including in *Dandy Dutch, the Decorator from Dead-Lift; or, Saul Sunday's Search for Glory* (1889), *Dauntless Dan, the Freelance; or Old Kit Bandy in Arcadia* (1890), *The Trail of the Vampire; or, The Mysterious Crimes of Prospect Park* (1904), and *The Vampire's Prey; or, Nick Carter's Blow* (1910).[38] The title of *The City Vampires; or, Red Rolfe's Pigeon* (1888) construed a gang of robbers and kidnappers as the "Bowery Vampires," their schemes "petty," but their purpose "diabolical."[39] And the title character of *"Vampire," the Bravo: or, Man of Many Disguises* (1891) was a "noted thief and assassin."[40]

Figure 3.1 The cover of the dime novel *"Vampire," the Bravo: or, The Man of Many Disguises* (1891).

Given the ongoing currency of the vampire-as-criminal metaphor, including in dime novels, it is not surprising that American filmmakers saw potential for story material. Publicity indicated that the villain of Kalem's *The Usurer* (1910) was a "human vampire," bleeding his victims into bankruptcy. Two years later, *The Forest Vampires* (Domino, 1914), a two-reeler written by Thomas H. Ince and William Clifford and starring J. Barney Sherry, chronicled a gang of crooks in medieval France.[41] *Motion Picture News* believed it achieved a number of "pretty scenes."[42] The same issue of *MPN* also described the one-reeler *Vasco the Vampire* (Universal, 1914, aka *Vasco, the Vampire*), which featured a cast of children under the age of nine years old. In it, a detective agency finally brings the title character – "a notorious villain, who is a mesmerist" – to justice.[43] Rather than prison, he is "sent back to a foreign land, where he is disgraced."[44]

Figure 3.2 Movie poster for *Vasco the Vampire* (Universal, 1914). (Courtesy of Heritage Auctions.)

Titled *The Vampire*, episode six of the serial *The Exploits of Elaine* (Pathé, 1915) was in some respects more fascinating than its predecessors. In it, Elaine (Pearl White) shoots the lackey of a criminal mastermind known as "The Clutching Hand" (Sheldon Lewis). The only way to save the lackey's life is a "blood transfusion."[45] And so the Clutching Hand:

> sees an opportunity of killing two birds with one stone, that is, to save his tool's life and destroy that of Elaine. He sends two accomplices to Elaine's home, chloroforms her, and confines her within a suit of armor which stands in the reception room of her own home. The next morning an expressman is sent for this suit of armor, which has been damaged and orders repairing which [has] been given, and thus the helpless Elaine is boldly kidnapped in broad daylight, and taken to the Clutching Hand's abode. There her arm is bared, strapped to that of the wounded man, and the great doctor prepares to perform the critical operation.[46]

The police rescue Elaine, halting the operation and saving her life. The lackey "breathes his last almost immediately afterwards."[47] The Clutching Hand makes his escape through a sliding panel in the wall.

Moving Picture World believed that the episode would make viewers' "nerves creep at the uncanny ability of the terrible band and the blood boil at the audacity of the leader of it." The trade publication added, "This is an unusual situation, and we suspect that no one has ever used it before – be it remembered that no one sees all pictures."[48] What exactly was the unusual situation? *Moving Picture World* presumably meant a story in which a criminal tried to force the heroine into giving her own blood to save another criminal.

America was not alone in bringing vampire criminals to the screen. In Roberto Roberti's *La vampira indiana/The Vampire of Indiana* (Aquila, 1913), a woman murders a man to help her brothers and then

Figure 3.3 *Vampires of the Night* (Aquila, 1913), originally titled *La belva della mezzanotte*.

has an innocent man convicted of the crime.[49] *Maggese Cinematografico* applauded its cinematography.[50] *L'Araldo della Cinematografia* praised its "artistic element" and "glorious staging."[51] The following year, Vittorio Rossi Pianelli's *Il vampiro* (Gloria, 1914) featured a crime which "leads the innocent to jail," though eventually there was the "punishment of the guilty and the triumph of justice." While praising the cinematography, *La Vita Cinematografico* believed the film to be "not very original." The critic also claimed the audience made "murmurs of wonder and denial and a few ['unflattering'] laughs."[52]

Aquila produced *La belva della mezzanotte* in Italy in 1913; it became a vampire film due to a new title bestowed on it, *Vampires of the Night*, first in England in 1913 and then in the United States in 1914.[53] The story tells of Judith, daughter of a criminal, whose grandmother switches her into the cradle of an heiress, leaving the heiress to be raised as a "singing girl at a rough inn." Nevertheless, the heiress comports herself as a lady, while Judith behaves horribly, even luring the heiress "into a trap door, down which she falls into the city sewers."[54] Vampires could not be denatured, it would seem. *Moving Picture World* told readers:

> The story is, of course, just a mystery tale; there is nothing great about it. But as an offering to the public eager for entertainment, it should rank high. In staging and acting it is above the ordinary, and, as we have said, the story is written so as to leave its impression on us as a whole and not merely as a collection of sensational episodes. It is a safe offering.[55]

Variety and *Motion Picture News* were less kind, praising the mise-en-scène while arguing that the film's running time should have been shortened.[56]

Figure 3.4 Theo Ortner's poster for *Der Vampyr* (Sport-Film, 1920), which starred Fred Stranz.

German filmmakers created several of their own vampire criminals. As early as 1914, Luna-Film-Gesellschaft's "detective" drama *Vampyre der Großstadt/Vampires of the Big City* featured a band of miscreants known as "The Vampires" who kidnap a wealthy man's daughter.[57] And the title villain of *Der Vampyr* (Sport-Film, 1920), portrayed by Hugo Schneider, was a "Parisian impresario, who takes talented children from the scenic but decadent Apache section of the city, trains them and then bleeds them to death [metaphorically]."[58] He owns a pub that caters to criminals, one where he makes the youngsters work in "pure hell." Amid a background of circus performances, a circus fire, and an escaped lion, the daredevil Texas Fred (Fred Stranz) bests the wicked Vampyr.[59] One review praised its "nerve-wracking sensations that ... make your blood run cold."[60] Along with the title, an original movie poster painted by Theo Ortner attempted to further the connection to vampirism by depicting a monstrous, bat-like villain beginning sink his teeth into a nude female victim.

More elaborate, at least in narrative scope, was a trio of German features produced by Dua-Film in which the heroic detective John Hopkins battled a vampire named George Corvin. The first, *Apachenrache* (*Apache Revenge*, aka *Apachen-Rache*), bore the subtitle *In den Krallen des Vampirs* (*In the Vampire's Clutches*).[61] The second instalment featured the subtitle

In den Krallen von Gg. Corvin, dem Ausbrecher-König (*In the Clutches of Geo. Corvin, King of Escapes*, 1920). The third film, *Der Sklavenhalter von Kansas-City* (*The Slaveholder of Kansas City*, 1920), was also known as *John Hopkins III*.[62] Bela Lugosi played Corvin in *Der Sklavenhalter*, and possibly in the first and/or second films as well, marking his initial onscreen appearance as a vampire, even if one of the felonious rather than supernatural variety.

France provided the most notable home to criminal vampires on the screen.[63] The use of the vampire metaphor in this context was not unknown in French literature, ranging from some aspects of Paul Féval's novels *La Vampire/The Vampire* (1865, earlier serialized in 1855) and *La Ville-Vampire/ Vampire City* (1875) to Michel Morphy's *Le Vampire: les mystères du crime* (1886).[64] The first film of this type was probably Pathé Frères' one-reeler *Les Vampires de la côte/Vampires of the Coast* (1908). *The Nickelodeon* referred to its villains as "pirates."[65] A company plot synopsis stated:

> A band of outlaws on the sea coast make their miserable and dishonest living by luring ships from their course to be dashed to pieces on the rockbound coast. They tie a lantern on the horns of a cow and lead her along the beach, and the ship, seeing its gleam, heads for the light, and as a consequence is soon on the rocks, where it is dashed to pieces. The pirates gather up the rich merchandise as it floats to shore, and make the surviving crew and passengers prisoners, taking them to a cave, where the casks and boxes are broken open and the spoils distributed among the gang.[66]

The tale – which was not dissimilar to Daphne du Maurier's later novel *Jamaica Inn* (1936) and its 1939 film adaptation directed by Alfred Hitchcock – ends happily thanks to a male robber who redeems himself by rescuing a female prisoner. The two escape and marry.[67]

Figure 3.5 Léonce Perret's *Le Mystère des roches de Kador*, released in the United States under the title *In the Grip of the Vampire* (Gaumont, 1912).

In 1912, Gaumont retitled Léonce Perret's three-reeler *Le Mystère des roches de Kador* as *In the Grip of the Vampire* for the American release. Its story tells of an evil guardian who drugs his young female ward and leaves her for dead, hoping to claim her inheritance. Though she temporarily goes "insane," the ward recovers. *Moving Picture World* published one of the film's explanatory intertitles, which explained how an "up-to-date scientist" uses a projected image to restore her sanity: "The vibrations of cinematographic images transmitted by means of an optic nerve from the retina of the eye to the cells of the brain cause a state of hypnotism which lends itself admirably to suggestion."[68] The pseudo-scientific trick works, with the police catching the vampiric guardian at a masquerade ball. The ward enjoys a happy ending. *Motion Picture News* praised the film's "scenic effect," adding that it featured "more than the ordinary number of thrills."[69]

Fascinating too was Éclair's *L'Oiseau de Mort/ The Bird of Death* (1914), retitled *The Vampire* for its UK release.[70] In this approximately 2,000-foot film, a scholar named René Farjas marries his second wife, Geneviève. Though he is happy with her, he also "seeks to divine the secrets of mysterious India." That gives him an opportunity to wed someone else, "a lovely creature dressed in Indian style, arms adorned with bracelets, adorned like a sumptuous idol . . . It is Djeliah, the daughter of the great Master of the Mysou, the living goddess of the Masters of fire." To free himself and inherit Geneviève's money, René decides to murder her. The two travel thus to the Château de Plemeur. According to the *Eclair Bulletin Hebdomaire des Nouveautés*:

> They arrive at night; the landscape wears a mournful aspect. Geneviève fears isolation and the shadows surrounding her. Farjas reassures her. Finally, in her bedroom, alone and anxious as a child, she falls asleep.
>
> Farjas crosses the sinister countryside; he skirts thick little woods, fantastic in the moonlight. Here he is near the raging sea, climbing dark rocks; the waves lash the rugged coast. Farjas finds an iron door, hidden in the rock. With a violent push he opens it. Wondrous spectacle, in the center of the crypt of Plemeur, illuminated with a thousand lights, Djeliah appears.[71]

Djeliah gives René a sandalwood box containing a vampire bat. That night, he releases it into Geneviève's bedroom. It "flutters into the room, scraping its wings against the walls, descends onto the sleeper's neck. Ferociously the bat sucks the blood of its victim." But René's dead first wife saves Geneviève from the bat, night after night, for a full week, and then reveals her ghostly presence to René, who is dumbfounded. Djeliah flees and throws herself off a cliff. Geneviève survives. The thrilling film anticipated Jean Yarbrough's *The Devil Bat* (1940), at least insofar as the repeated use of a bat as an instrument of murder.

Louis Feuillade's *Les Vampires* (Gaumont, 1915–16) brimmed with far more thrills than any of its predecessors. His ten-chapter serial was an enormous hit in France, as well as in England and America, where it was released as *The Vampires*. *Les Vampires* became a monumental release, an "immense success," as ads in *Ciné-journal* rightly touted in 1916.[72] And *Les Vampires*' fame continues to the present day for many reasons, from its influence on filmmakers like Fritz Lang and Alfred Hitchcock to Olivier Assayas' film *Irma Vep* (Dacia Films, 1996), in which a character attempts to remake Feuillade's serial. As Chapter 1 indicated, *Les Vampires* is notable in terms of the vampire dance depicted in Episode 2, *La Bague qui tue/ The Deadly Ring* (aka, *The Ring That Kills*). The serial is crucial given the emphasis on the term "vampires," not only in its title, but also for the name of an organized criminal gang in Paris, The Vampires, its leader being known as Le Grand Vampire/ The Grand Vampire.

Figure 3.6 *La Tête coupée/ The Severed Head*, Episode 1 of Louis Feuillade's *Les Vampires* (Gaumont, 1915–16).

Unlike prior vampire-as-criminal films, *Les Vampires* was unique given its twentieth-century setting and narrative reliance on modern technologies, including the telephone, automobile, phonograph, and motion picture. Particularly important is Feuillade's ability to make The Vampires seem strange and mysterious and uncanny, from secret panels and hidden passageways to their murderous methods, which include decapitation and poison. Episode titles speak to the serial's weird and horrifying potential: *La Tête coupée/ The Severed Head* (Episode 1, aka *The Detective's Head*), *L'Évasion du mort/ The Corpse's Escape* (Episode 5, aka *Dead Man's Escape*), and *Les Yeux qui fascinent/ Hypnotic Eyes* (Episode 6, aka *Eyes That Hypnotize* and *The Eyes That Hold*).[73] Vénénos (Maurice Boyer), the gang's "chemist and criminal genius," is something of a mad scientist, while Madame d'Alba is a masterful hypnotist. She is also a fake spiritualist, one of the many ways that Feuillade invokes the supernatural, even though it is never actually at play. Other examples include the name Satanus/Satanas, one of the gang's leaders, as well as the title of Episode 4, *Le Spectre/The Spectre* (aka *The Ghost*).

Allusions to supernatural vampires are numerous, ranging from artistic bats on publicity materials to imagery inside the serial's chapters.[74] While conducting nefarious and covert activity, gang members dress in black, creating "strange occurrences" in the night. At night, they scale buildings with ease, not unlike Dracula crawling on the side of his castle in Stoker's novel. The Grand Inquisitor of the Vampires, a member of its elite Black Council, keeps a red codebook, as noted in the title of Episode 3, *Le Cryptogramme rouge*. And then there is the title of Episode 10, *Les Noces sanglantes/The Bloody Wedding* (aka *The Terrible Wedding*).

Figure 3.7 *Le Cryptogramme rouge/The Red Codebook*, Episode 3 of Louis Feuillade's *Les Vampires* (Gaumont, 1915-16).

Irma Vep (Musidora) is the most notable member of the gang, her bizarre name being an anagram for "vampire," a fact addressed visually in Episode 3, when newspaper reporter Philippe Guérande (Édouard Mathé) examines a poster promoting her performance at a seedy nightclub. Thanks to film animation, the letters of her name rearrange, instructively and ominously. Irma Vep at times wears dark eye makeup and clothing, being reminiscent of Hollywood vamps. Her dark, hooded cloak in Episode 8, *Le Maître de la foudre / The Master of Thunder* (aka *The Thunder Master* and *Lord of Thunder*), is particularly vampiric. Collectively, these are likely the reasons why *Motion Picture News* believed *Les Vampires* was "hair-raising."[75]

After *Les Vampires*, the most notable vampire-as-criminal film was Roland West's American feature *The Bat* (United Artists, 1926). Together with collaborator Avery Hopwood, Mary Roberts Rinehart adapted her novel *The Circular Staircase* (1908) for the stage in 1920, renaming it *The*

Bat and adding the new title character, a sophisticated criminal who relies on modern means to steal valuables. As the *New York Times* explained:

> The scheme is to coop up a handful of miscellaneous people, as on a boat or in a quarantined house, and there let loose theft and arson and murder, to the accompaniment of crashing lights, mysterious knocks and sliding panels. The general impression created is of a madhouse just before the end of the world . . . while the finger of suspicion moves steadily along the list of characters, reading from right to left.[76]

According to the *New York Sun*, *The Bat* marked nothing less than the "apotheosis of the detective drama."[77]

The *Chicago Tribune* believed The Bat was an "enjoyable bandit," a "spectacular outlaw" whose "portentous insignia" was a "strange device," a "neatly florid touch, symbolic of the restless age and the passion for publicity."[78] The character was not a bandit or highwayman living in the forest, but a modern criminal mastermind, his exploits gripping Broadway audiences. *The Bat* became a massive success, its character likely inspired by *Les Vampires*.[79] Not surprisingly, as early as 1920, one magazine declared the play would make for an "admirable movie."[80]

And so it did. Roland West himself was no stranger to the theater, having worked in vaudeville prior to directing a 1925 film adaptation of Crane Wilbur's play *The Monster* (1922). His film version of *The Bat* (United Artists, 1926) features eerie sets designed by William Cameron Menzies, who served as art director on Raoul Walsh's *The Thief of Bagdad* (United Artists, 1924), Clarence Brown's *The Eagle* (United Artists, 1925), and West's *Alibi* (United Artists, 1929), before becoming a director himself.[81] Arthur Edeson provided expert cinematography for *The Bat*; he later shot James Whale's *Frankenstein* (Universal, 1931), *The Old Dark House* (Universal, 1932), and *The Invisible Man* (Universal, 1933), as well as John Huston's *The Maltese Falcon* (Warner Bros., 1941) and Michael Curtiz's *Casablanca* (Warner Bros., 1942).

Onscreen, *The Bat* remained largely faithful to its theatrical source (including a direct request that audience members not reveal the villain's secret identity to their friends), but the film proved far more visually striking. It begins with a closeup of a bat before showing another of the species flying ominously around a modern American city. The title character (played by Charles Herzinger) wears a bat costume, a mask with large ears and fangs. He easily climbs a tall building and leaves a taunting, bat-shaped note for the city police: he will give them a break by heading "to the country for a short vacation." Then, in the dark of night, a bat flies around a small-town bank, which The Bat robs successfully. His first two crimes not only link him to bats, but also imply that he might be supernatural, even

Figure 3.8 Trade advertisement from 1926.

transforming from winged bat to bat-like human. A newspaper headline underscores this possibility, reporting that The Bat "flies away" with some famous jewels. And yet the same account suggests he might be a "Merchant, Lawyer or Doctor by Day," requiring us to ask exactly who or what is this mysterious burglar?

The bulk of the story takes place at a country estate, one that the maid Lizzie (Louise Fazenda) believes to be haunted. A bat silhouette projected on the wall initially seems supernatural, but it turns out to be nothing more than a moth stuck on a car's shining headlight. Eventually, The Bat is unmasked as a human criminal, thus shifting any fantastical possibilities into the supernatural explained. As one theater manager disclosed in 1926, "you can hear one big loud 'Oh' from all over your theater when the mask is pulled off 'The Bat.'"[82]

Figure 3.9 Roland West's *The Bat* (United Artists, 1926).

Moving Picture World praised *The Bat*'s "soul-stirring thrills and chills, weirdness, mystery, [and] uncanny happenings."[83] A review in *Motion Picture News* declared:

> There probably isn't a human creature, young or old, hard-boiled enough to sit through a session of *The Bat* without having spine chills develop as a result of its eerie, creepy, blood-curdling atmosphere or experiencing a sense of welcome relief when a thrust of slapstick comedy momentarily changes horror to hilarity.[84]

Such critical reaction was not uncommon in the trade press or New York newspapers.[85] *The Bat* proved successful onscreen, so much so that Roland West remade it as *The Bat Whispers*, a talkie released in 1930.

Surprisingly or not, the word "vampire" is never used in the text of Rinehart and Hopwood's play, nor does it appear in the intertitles of West's silent version. Critics did not rely on the term either, even though the vampiric associations seem so very evident, so very stark. Here then is a criminal vampire without the term to identify him, something of the reverse of *La belva della mezzanotte*, which had to be retitled in English as *Vampires of the Night* to benefit from the metaphor. Like Feuillade, West created a particularly modern criminal vampire, one very much suited for its era. After all, The Bat does not really fly. Rather, he drives an automobile, and American newspapers of the twenties repeatedly ran headlines about "Vampire Car" crimes, referring to those hit-and-run drivers who left death and destruction in their smokey, oil-fueled paths.[86]

While such crimes continue to the present day, the vampire terminology used to describe them faded out during the Great Depression. The vampire-as-criminal covered in this chapter largely died as well, apart from a small number of possible considerations like Frank Strayer's *The Vampire Bat* (Majestic, 1933), Phil Rosen's *Spooks Run Wild* (Monogram, 1941), Wallace Fox's *The Corpse Vanishes* (Monogram, 1942), Riccardo Freda's *I Vampiri/Lust of the Vampire* (Titanus, 1957, aka *The Devil's Commandment*), John Gilling's *Mother Riley Meets the Vampire* (Renown, 1952), Crane Wilbur's *The Bat* (Allied Artists, 1959), Robert Hossein's *The Vampire of Düsseldorf* (Panta Cinematografica, 1965), George Romero's *Martin* (Libra, 1977), and Robert Bierman's *The Vampire's Kiss* (Hemdale, 1988).

Perhaps the last, great vampire heist was one in which a character detailed herein became victim instead of predator. Comic book writer and artist Bob Kane purloined the title villain from *The Bat* (more specifically West's *The Bat Whispers*), transforming him from thief to vigilante, from bad guy to good.[87] The lasting legacy of the criminals lurking in this chapter is not the original metaphor, meaning the "salt-water pirate" or "red-handed highwayman," but instead a different kind of imposter, meaning Batman, heroic star of comics, television shows, and blockbuster films. Under the lunar influence, but no lunatic, Batman makes safe the night for law-abiding citizens by combatting evildoers wherever he finds them. In Michael Goguen's animated feature *The Batman vs. Dracula* (2005), the superhero even defeated Stoker's vampire count.

Notes

1. *The Mystery of Ravenswald: A Tale of the First Crusade* appeared in *The London Reader of Literature, Science, Art, and General Information* over twelve issues during 1878. The vampire quotation appears in chapter IV, as published on July 20, 1878, 274.

2. "Our Weekly Gossip," *New York Dispatch*, December 17, 1878, 7.
3. C. A. Kinkaid, "*The Vampire's Treasure*," in *The Anchorite and Other Stories* (London: Humphrey Milford, Oxford University Press, 1922), 188.
4. *The Three Vampires; or, Maids Beware of Moonshine*, Playbill, Coburg Theater, London September 4, 1823.
5. *Invisible Prince! Or, the Island of Tranquil Delights*, Playbill, National Theatre, Boston, MA, October 6, 1854.
6. John Jones, *Lines to a Mosquito Upon My Wife's Bosom*, *The People's Advocate*, April 10, 1844, 1.
7. Untitled, *Newport Mercury*, February 29, 1763, 1.
8. Joel Barlow, "*The Conspiracy of Kings*," *The New York Magazine, or Literary Repository*, June 1792, 375.
9. "Manly Eloquence," *Herald of Liberty*, December 10, 1798, 10. In this case, the journalist meant that England wished to suck the blood out of a particular Irishman.
10. "The Confederate Flag," *Commercial Advertiser* (Buffalo, NY), October 29, 1863, 4.
11. Count Ernst zu Reventlow, *The Vampire of the Continent* (New York: Jackson Press, 1916).
12. Advertisement, *Worcester Daily Spy*, November 20, 1885, 20; advertisement, *Anaconda Standard*, September 12, 1900, 5.
13. "Vampyre of the Ocean," *National Gazette* (Philadelphia, PA), September 21, 1824, 3; "For Circus People," *Billboard*, January 12, 1901, 8.
14. "Rapid Experimenting," *Rock Island Weekly Advertiser*, April 23, 1856, 3; Albert F. Porta, "Sun's Osculation of 'Vamp' Planet Causes Volcano," *Atlanta Journal*, March 10, 1918, 50.
15. Anthony Comstock, "Vampire Literature," *North American Review* 153, no. 417 (August 1891): 160–71.
16. The Wife of a Medical Man, *The Vampyre* (London: A. W. Bennett, 1858).
17. "We Are a Nation of Vampires Feasting on Human Blood," *New York Sun*, February 16, 1906, 2.
18. Advertisement, *Show World*, September 4, 1909, 32.
19. "*Beatrice Fairfax*," *Moving Picture World*, October 21, 1916, 451.
20. "A Drama of the Underworld," *Motography*, June 28, 1913, 462.
21. "Feature Previews," *Exhibitors Trade Review*, September 1, 1923, 611.
22. "The Pirate," *New-England Galaxy and Masonic Magazine*, February 5, 1819, 68.
23. Prentiss Ingraham, *The Ocean Vampire; or, The Heiress of Castle Curse* (New York: Beadle & Adams, 1882).
24. T. C. Harbaugh, *Captain Cutlass, the Ocean Spider, or, The Buccaneer's Girl Foe: A Tale of the Tropic Seas and Shores* (New York: Beadle and Adams, 1884).
25. Michael Watson, *The Vampire (A Pirate Song)* (London: E. Ascherberg & Co., 1899).

26. "The Captain of the Vampire or, The Smugglers of the Deep Sea," *New Nick Carter Weekly*, October 8, 1904, 10.
27. Nina Auerbach, *Our Vampires, Ourselves* (Chicago: University of Chicago Press, 1995), 6.
28. "On the National Bank," *Lancaster Intelligencer and Journal*, September 19, 1818, 2.
29. Untitled, "An Infamous Thief," *Utahnian*, July 4, 1896, 10.
30. "Letter from California," *Zion's Herald and Wesleyan Journal*, April 23, 1851, 1.
31. "Wholesale Rascality," *Chicago Tribune*, July 31, 1860, 2.
32. "The Quintessence of Socialism," *St. Louis Evening Post*, May 15, 1878, 2.
33. Untitled, *Stark County Democrat*, April 14, 1883, 3.
34. "The Wickedest District in the World Where Scores of Men and Women Are Murdered Every Year," *Chicago Tribune*, February 11, 1906, F2.
35. "A Human Vampire," *Fisherman and Farmer*, August 26, 1892, 8.
36. "Whitechapel's Admonitions," *Ashland Times*, December 13, 1888, 3.
37. "Human Vampires Jubilate," *Los Angeles Times*, September 9, 1902, A1.
38. Oll Coomes, *Dauntless Dan the Freelance; or, Old Kit Bandy in Arcadia* (New York: Beadle and Adams, 1890); "*The Trail of the Vampire; or, The Mysterious Crimes of Prospect Park*," *New Nick Carter Weekly*, September 24, 1904; "*The Vampire's Prey; or, Nick Carter's Blow at Policy*," *New Nick Carter Weekly*, January 8, 1910.
39. T. C. Harbaugh, *The City Vampires; or, Red Rolfe's Pigeon* (New York: Beadle and Adams, 1888), 2, 3.
40. F. Lusk Broughton, *"Vampire," The Bravo: or, The Man of Many Disguises* (New York: Munro's Publishing House, 1891), 3, 4.
41. "Stories of the New Photoplays," *Reel Life*, May 9, 1914, 18.
42. "Mutual Program," *Motion Picture News*, May 16, 1914, 56.
43. "Universal Program," *Motion Picture News*, May 16, 1914, 56.
44. "Imp," *Moving Picture World*, May 16, 1914, 1012.
45. "*The Vampire*," *Motography*, February 13, 1915, 266.
46. Neil G. Caward, "Dog Actor Displays Wonderful Skill," *Motography*, February 13, 1915, 243.
47. Ibid., 243.
48. Hanford C. Judson, "The Vampire," *Moving Picture World*, February 13, 1915, 987.
49. Aldo Bernardini and Vittorio Martinelli, "*La vampira indiana*," *Bianco e Nero*, no. 3–4 (1993): 328.
50. A. Berton, *Maggese Cinematografico*, January 10, 1914, quoted in Aldo Bernardini and Vittorio Martinelli, "*La vampira indiana*," 329.
51. *L'Araldo della Cinematografia*, December 31, 1913, quoted in Bernardini and Martinelli, 329.
52. Pier da Castello, *La Vita Cinematografica*, February 22, 1915, quoted in Aldo Bernardini and Vittorio Martinelli, "*Il vampiro*," *Bianco e Nero*, no. 3–4 (1992): 280.

53. Advertisement, *The Bioscope*, October 9, 1913, xlvi; advertisement, *Moving Picture World*, April 11, 1914, 273. Ads for *Vampires of the Night* in the United States listed its running time as five reels, whereas ads for the film in Great Britain listed it as four reels.
54. "*Vampires of the Night*," *Moving Picture World*, April 4, 1914, 122.
55. Hanford C. Judson, "*Vampires of the Night*," *Moving Picture World*, March 21, 1914, 1513.
56. "*Vampires of the Night*," *Variety*, March 13, 1914, 23; "Special Film Reviews," *Motion Picture News*, January 24, 1914, 37. Not dissimilar was the review in *The Billboard*, which privileged *Vampire of the Night*'s cinematography and "beautiful scenes" over its narrative. See "*Vampires of the Night*," *The Billboard*, March 14, 1914, 58.
57. "Film-markte," *Kinematographische Rundschau*, September 13, 1914, 21.
58. "*Der Vampyr*," *Der Film*, no. 27, 1920, 49.
59. "München," *Der Kinematograph*, August 20, 1919, 19.
60. Ibid., 19.
61. The first *Apachenrache* film, *In den Krallen des Vampirs* (*In the Vampire's Clutches*, 1920), is a distinctly different film than Heinz Sarnow's film *In den Krallen des Vampyrs* (*In the Vampyre's Clutches*, 1919). Given the near-identical title, the two have been conflated in some prior filmographies.
62. Filmographies that list *Der Sklavenhalter von Kansas-City* and *John Hopkins III* as different films are mistaken. They are different titles for the same film.
63. "*The Usurer*," *Kalem Kalendar*, December 16, 1912, 9.
64. Michel Morphy, *Le Vampire: les mystères du crime* (Paris: Coustillier, 1886).
65. "Pathe Freres [*sic*]," *The Nickelodeon*, April 1909, 116.
66. "*Vampires of the Coast*," *The Film Index*, March 20, 1909, 7.
67. "*Vampires of the Coast*," *The Billboard*, March 27, 1909, 17.
68. "*In the Grip of the Vampire* (Gaumont)," *Moving Picture World*, 1308.
69. "*In the Grip of the Vampire*," *Motion Picture News*, December 21, 1912, 13.
70. "*The Vampire*," *The Bioscope*, March 26, 1914, 5.
71. "*L'Oiseau de Mort*," *Eclair Bulletin Hebdomaire des Nouveautés*, no. 14, April 3, 1914, 3–6.
72. Advertisement, *Ciné-journal*, March 4, 1916, unpaginated.
73. For this chapter, I am using the English translations of the serial chapter titles and onscreen intertitles as they appear in the 2012 restoration released on Blu-ray by Kino International.
74. For an example of an ad featuring a bat, see *Moving Picture World*, November 16, 1917, 1112.
75. F. G. Spencer, "*The Vampires*," *Motion Picture News*, December 23, 1916, 4040.
76. Alexander Woollcott, "The Play," *New York Times*, August 24, 1920, 15.
77. "*The Bat* Intensely Interesting Play of Mystery Here," *New York Sun and Herald*, August 24, 1920, 7.
78. Percy Hammond, "An Enjoyable Bandit, *The Bat*," *Chicago Tribune*, December 27, 1920, 17.

79. "*The Bat* Breaks Records," *The Billboard*, September 25, 1920, 19.
80. "The Appeal of *The Bat*," *Outlook*, October 13, 1920, 272.
81. For more information, see James Curtis, *The Shape of Films To Come: William Cameron Menzies* (New York: Pantheon Books, 2015).
82. "United Artists," *Exhibitors Herald*, July 3, 1926, 68.
83. C. S. Sewell, "Through the Box-Office Window," *Moving Picture World*, March 27, 1926, 283.
84. George T. Pardy, "*The Bat*," *Motion Picture News*, March 27, 1926, 1418.
85. "Newspaper Opinions on New Pictures," *Motion Picture News*, April 3, 1926, 1528.
86. See, for example, "Vampire Car Seen After Crash, Driver Drunk, Witness Says," *Duluth News-Tribune* (Duluth, Minnesota), December 1, 1920, 6; "Arrest 'Vampire Car' Suspect," *Rockford Daily Register-Gazette* (Rockford, IL), October 2, 1923, 1; "Vampire Auto Kills as Fight on Speed Grows," *Chicago Tribune*, September 21, 1924, 4.
87. Bob Kane, *Batman and Me* (Forestville, CA: Eclipse Books, 1989), 38–40.

CHAPTER 4

Supernatural Vampires

"[T]o fail here is not mere life or death.
It is that we become as him."

– Bram Stoker
Dracula, 1897

"[I]f you're so lonely, why don't you make more vampires?"
– E. Elias Merhige
Shadow of the Vampire, 2000

Are vampires good at mathematics? Perhaps those who were once accountants and bankers. Perhaps those who failed algebra courses not so much. In fairness, even for vampires who own calculators, it might be hard to keep track of how many victims they have bled over the decades, over the centuries.

In some folkloric traditions, vampires who encounter spilled grain or seeds must count them, apparently due to a type of supernatural arithmomania.[1] Woe to the less-educated vampire who could not count as high as the number of seeds on the ground. Or to the vampire who kept losing count and had to start anew repeatedly until it dawned on him or her that it was dawn. Perhaps there are times when it's preferable to be the Count von Count of *Sesame Street*.

Such mathematics may or may not be important, but to the vampire hunter, the vampire enthusiast, and the vampire scholar, one number is as dramatic as it is baffling: the global vampire population. According to much folklore and literature, vampires give rise to more vampires. Biting one creates another, the process repeats, and then repeats, and so it goes. In Bram Stoker's *Dracula*, Van Helsing refers to the title character as the "King Vampire." At the end of the nineteenth century, there were fewer than two billion people in the world. But how many supernatural vampires were there, if not in the real world, then in the world of fiction? Over how many undead did Dracula reign?

Put another way, the problem is that, by a given point in time, every person would either die or transform into a vampire. As more vampires are spawned, more blood is necessary, and so the scarcer it gets. Eventually there would probably be, as the title of Ubaldo Ragona and Sidney Salkow's 1964 film warned us, *The Last Man on Earth*. Then he too would become either dead or undead. Thus, earth could accurately be called, to borrow the title of Mario Bava's 1965 film, *Planet of the Vampires*. But in most vampire fiction, that mathematical probability does not come to pass. The problem of population growth is ignored, to the detriment of numbers, but to the benefit of narratives.

Both of the aforementioned films came long after the silent era ended. The same was true of Richard Matheson's novel *I Am Legend* (1954), on which *The Last Man on Earth* was based. In it, Robert Neville, the title character, tries to reduce the "unholy numbers" of the unholy undead, but Matheson explains that Neville is not as exacting mathematically as he could be: "If he had been more analytical, he might have calculated the approximate time of [the vampires'] arrival."[2]

Whether or not we excelled in basic arithmetic, we must attempt to be analytical in our discussion about the arrival of supernatural vampires onscreen. To be sure, silent cinema seems overpopulated with metaphorical vampires, to the extent that calculating the exact number of screen vamps – as well as the number of times the words "vamp" and, in that context, "vampire" appeared in intertitles – proves challenging. Vamps beget vamps beget vamps. And yet, that did not occur with supernatural vampires, not during the early twentieth century. The title characters in *Loïe Fuller* (Pathé Frères, 1905) and *Vampyrdanserinden/The Vampire Dancer* (Nordisk, 1912, aka *Vampyr-danserinden*) did not bite many victims, it would seem (See Chapter 1). Vampires did not go viral, despite how infectious they can sometimes be.

Instead of living in cinematic world in which there are an ever-increasing number of vampires – as occurred from the 1950s (if not the 1930s) to the present – the silent era represents the opposite, the mirror reverse of Robert Neville's nightmarish world, much to the puzzlement of some film scholars. Matheson's novel states, "[B]efore science caught up with the legend, the legend had swallowed science and everything."[3] Here is perhaps another explanation for why viewers have mistaken the title character of Georges Méliès' *Le Manoir du diable/The Devil's Castle* (1896) for featuring a vampire: we want more of them.[4] The lure of the vampire in silent cinema is strong. Their legend can easily swallow our science, our reason. If the vampire population is too low, let us locate more of them; if we cannot locate them, let us create them.

In 2022, internet posts on Facebook heralded a rediscovered silent vampire, one that allegedly appeared in Theodore and Leopold Wharton's *The Mysteries of Myra* (Pathé Exchange, 1916), a fifteen-chapter American serial.[5] In *Silent Serial Sensations: The Wharton Brothers and the Magic of Early Cinema* (2020), Barbara Tepa Lupack writes:

> Structurally, *The Mysteries of Myra* (which survives only in a few random reels and fragments) employed a familiar serial framework: a young, attractive heroine, supported by a devoted admirer with considerable sleuthing skills, who protects her from a powerful antagonist who wants to do her harm and steal her money . . . Yet, while its basic storyline was consistent with the pattern of *The Exploits of Elaine* [Pathé Exchange, 1914] and other early serials, *The Mysteries of Myra* departed radically from its predecessors in other ways. Nowhere was that departure more evident than in the use of occult elements, evoked by a series of special effects that the Whartons, working in concert with skilled set designer Arch Chadwick and electrician Leroy Baker, created through unusual angles, lighting, and superior technical work.[6]

While most of the serial's episodes are lost, historian Eric Stedman completed an amazing restoration of four of them by relying on various archival materials.[7] Detailed plot synopses for every episode exist, as do numerous photographs and a 1915 novelization (though the novelization includes plot elements, dialogue and other details that did not necessarily appear in the actual serial). In 2010, Stedman republished that novelization with other contemporaneous text. Together with his episode restorations, Stedman's book has allowed us to unravel at least most of Myra's mysteries.

Without doubt, *The Mysteries of Myra* is one of the most important horror-themed serials or films produced in America between 1915 and 1931, a key link between those of the early cinema period and the release of Tod Browning's *Dracula* (Universal, 1931) and James Whale's *Frankenstein* (Universal, 1931). *The Mysteries of Myra* brims with the supernatural unleashed, rather than explained, its terrors so plentiful that the serial form was probably necessary. A single feature film would hardly have had the running time to contain all of them. Here are occult forces, spirit materializations, and astral projections. Here is a demonic Fire Elemental, a Frankensteinian "Thought Monster," and a secret cult known as the Black Order. Episode titles provide further insight into the serial's thrills and chills: *The Mystic Mirrors* (Episode 3); *The Wheel of Spirit* (Episode 4); *The Hypnotic Clue* (Episode 6); *The Nether World* (Episode 8); *Invisible Destroyer* (Episode 9); *Levitation* (Episode 10); *Elixir of Youth* (Episode 12); *Witchcraft* (Episode 13); and *Suspended Animation* (Episode 14).

Does a vampire appear in *The Mysteries of Myra*? Metaphorically speaking, the answer is yes. When the Master of the Black Order dies, his heir is

"The Vampire Woman," his ex-paramour, one he has kept imprisoned in his hideout.[8] She drinks no blood. She is not undead, but very much alive. She is yet another human vamp of the Philip Burne-Jones and Rudyard Kipling variety, one made more intriguing because she is adjacent to the supernatural goings-on. The Vampire Woman of *The Mysteries of Myra* is perhaps spookier than some of her kith and kin, but she is not at all supernatural.

With all the horrors that *The Mysteries of Myra* does explore, it hardly seems necessary that it needed to include a supernatural vampire. That said, it is possible to perceive a few elements akin to later vampire films.[9] In one scene, a bat flies around outside of Myra's bedroom, then the astral body of the Master and another character appear at her bedside. But neither are vampires. They are would-be murderers. Elsewhere in the serial, a demon declares he would like to obtain some of Myra's blood, but his goal is to deliver it to the Fire Elemental. A period synopsis of the serial clearly states that the Fire Elemental requires a "blood sacrifice."[10] And while it may or may not have been factored in the serial's running time, the novelization claims that it is the Master of the Black Order who suggests the idea of a blood sacrifice to the Fire Elemental, rather than the other way around.[11]

To be sure, the synopses of the film episodes themselves are what are important for us, not what appears in a novelization that could have altered and/or expanded from the serial's storyline. And none of the episode synopses suggest these characters are blood-drinkers, let alone supernatural vampires. To argue for the appearance of a supernatural vampire in *The Mysteries of Myra* is probably an error, one driven by the understandable but ultimately problematical goal of population growth. As early as 1969, Ron Borst published an article that clearly indicated there was no vampire in *The Mysteries of Myra*, despite earlier claims to the contrary made by Walt Lee, Jr., claims made decades prior to modern internet rumors.[12]

And so, the error has continued, and it is not alone. For example, in a 1958 article, Peter John Dyer claimed Arthur Robison's film *Nächte des Grauens/Night of Horror* (Lu Synd-Wartan-Film GmbH, aka *Nächte des Schreckens/Night of Terror*, completed in 1916 but not publicly screened until February 9, 1917) to be a forerunner of Browning's *Dracula*.[13] Arguably the statement was true, but some readers wrongly took Dyer to mean Robison's film featured one or more vampires.[14] Period synopses make clear that it certainly did not.[15] Later, J. Gordon Melton described Kai Hansen's Russian Pathé production *The Secret of House No. 5* (1912) as "possibly the first vampire film."[16] However, the surviving print and Denise J. Youngblood's careful analysis of it indicate that no supernatural vampire appears in the film.[17]

Other writers have cited Gino Zaccaria's Italian film *La torre dei vampiri/The Vampire's Tower* (Ambrosio, 1913), though contemporary plot synopses make clear that it featured nothing more than the admittedly deserted and spooky title architecture, around which some bats fly.[18] The word "vampire" is enough to generate excitement in some historians who may not be all that exacting. David J. Skal has gone so far as to catalogue *Vamping Babies* (F.B.O., 1926) in a vampire filmography, even though it doesn't feature a supernatural vampire or even a vamp, just a young couple in love who elope after an "irate father" won't give his permission for them to marry.[19]

And if a film title does not feature the word "vampire," then change the title, as has happened in at least one case. While the title character of Robert Wiene's German film *Genuine* (Decla-Bioscop, 1920) might appropriately be called a vamp, she is not a supernatural vampire. In Germany, the film's subtitle was originally *Die Tragödie eines seltsamen Hauses*, meaning *The Tragedy of a Strange House*. However, modern writers have claimed its subtitle was *The Tragedy of a Vampire* (and it might have been in some other country where it was screened, though no evidence of that possibility has surfaced after a thorough search).

Some vampire filmographers have been so starved for fresh cinematic blood that they have even catalogued two Italian silent films, Roberto Danesi's *Vampe di gelosia/Blaze of Jealousy* (Savoia-Film, 1913) and Ugo Falena's *Cenere e vampe/Ashes and Flames* (Tespi-Film, 1918).[20] Neither film features vampires; in fact, *Cenere e vampe* was meant to build support for Italian war bonds.[21] Here the errors stem from the inaccurate translations, with English speakers wrongly believing "Vampa" means "Vamp" or even "Vampire." The Italian word "Vampa" actually means blaze, as in a large flame, with "Vampe" being its plural form.

By way of confession, I am not immune from this persistent pestilence, as I am tempted to write at length on a trio of nonfiction moving pictures that depicted vampire bats, particularly Frank Newman's *The Vampire Bat and Armadillo* (Special, 1911), which depicted the title animals as well as a "giant tarantula."[22] Such images seem prescient of the nocturnal Transylvanian sequence in Browning's *Dracula*. Our impulse to grow the species and to feed our own desires is very strong, but none of these films feature supernatural vampires. Let us curb our appetites by recalling what Keats wrote in *Lamia* (1820), "Over the solitary hills he fared, Thoughtless at first, but ere eve's star appeared/His phantasy was lost, where reason fades, In the calm'd twilight of Platonic shades."

Other cases of mistaken identity are more complicated and arguably more fascinating, cases in which reason does not fade or sleep, but produces monsters nonetheless. In June 1963, Forrest J Ackerman included the following brief item in an issue of *Famous Monsters of Filmland*: "Eric Jason, specialist in stage monsters, once told me he was sure there'd been a Russian version of *Dracula*."[23] Over time, this rumor morphed into a legend about a silent Russian film adaptation of Stoker's novel, allegedly directed in 1920 by Viacheslav Turzhanskii (later known as Viktor Tourjansky).[24] In *The Dracula Book* (Scarecrow Press, 1975), Donald F. Glut wrote about the early twenties, noting, "Other film versions are reported to have been made about this time – one being Russian – but there is no real verification to substantiate these claims."[25] Later, in *The Vampire Book: The Encyclopedia of the Undead* (Visible Ink, 1994), J. Gordon Melton told readers, "The first movie that attempted to bring the novel *Dracula* to the screen may have been a silent film made in Russia (1920), but no copy has survived."[26] Later writers have ignored Glut and Melton's tempered language, disregarding such qualifications as "may have been."

In Stoker's *Dracula*, Mina informs Lucy Westenra, "I hear rumours, and especially of a tall, handsome curly-haired man???" We hear rumors of another man, this Russian vampire, and they are certainly difficult to believe. To explain this version of *Dracula*'s missing status, one internet story suggests prints might have been destroyed during the Russian Civil War, but the film's fate is not our major concern.[27] By contrast, we must ask if this *Dracula* could really have been produced. Given the importance of the film business to Lenin and the Soviet government, it seems extremely unlikely that they would have adapted a novel written by a British, capitalist author. At that time, Soviet filmmakers concentrated on educational propaganda.[28] To have spent scarce money and resources on a vampire movie seems, to rework an earlier phrase, hard to swallow.

No period announcements, production information, or reviews of any kind have ever been found to prove that this version of *Dracula* was planned, let alone filmed. All that we have are modern rumors, which have continued into the twenty-first century. The following tale appeared on a Russian website in 2012:

> [T]he very first film about Dracula, the Russian-Ukrainian film of 1920, which most likely took place, disappeared without a trace. For many years, historians have tried to get access to the most ancient archives of the Gosfilmofond . . . First, in 1921 at one of the studios filmed the film *Meetings on Khreshchatyka*. The film was shot on schedule – from 7 am to 8 pm. The studio was then released. For what? As it turned out, at night they shot a picture of horrors. No one knew if it was true or not. It was believed that the studio was closed for the night, and the operator and the director remained there to inspect the materials. However, in the case of this film, a short note was preserved: "Ekaterina Alexandrovna, we are waiting for you in our studio. Come up at 9:00. The movie is interesting. Not horror, but horror."

The note was written with many errors. Most likely, the note was written by the operator or director of one of the actresses who agreed to take part in the film. They also found documents about the dismissal from the work of the operator Alexander Mallo, for constant delays at work, non-punctual delivery of the camera for storage and even suspicion of using the equipment for personal purposes. He was also credited with the disappearance of several roll-ons of film. Most likely, the film was shot on a professional camera, but with the lack of a few details. The camera was alone, the installation was carried out manually, the projection of the film is extremely unprofessional.

That is, we can say that it was the first amateur film in the history of cinema. Unfortunately, the quality left much to be desired. Almost the entire film was lost, many of the shots are illuminated or too murky. The director of the film, most likely, was Yuri Ivarono, who shot *Meetings on Khreshchatyka*. The actress in the main role is Ekaterina Ivanko. Dracula was played by Ivarono himself. There are only three frames left of the entire film . . . The first image shows a woman's face in blood. On the second – a man in a cape and a hat, with sharp teeth. It was probably Dracula. The third frame shows a house and a bat. I couldn't find out more about the film. It is only known that both Mallo and Ivarono hurriedly left the country.[29]

Such information is as fascinating as it is difficult to believe. To be sure, adding the Ukrainian location and describing this *Dracula* as an "amateur film" makes the story more plausible, situating the production outside of Soviet control.[30] And the mention of Kreshchatkyka seems credible, as it is the name of a boulevard in Kyiv. Nevertheless, none of the archival materials mentioned have been made public, if they exist. And should they exist, the cited note about a "not horror, but horror" story would not automatically indicate an adaptation of Stoker's novel. The trio of film frames might, though they might also suggest a vampire story other than *Dracula*. But these issues are less important, as the overall story becomes particularly unbelievable when we confront that which we finally must: none of the people named in the aforementioned quotation seem to have existed, let alone worked in the cinema.[31] As Denise J. Youngblood and

Figure 4.1 A frame from *Drakula (1920)*, a modern fake.

other historians have determined, the entire story and the evidence it mentions are almost certainly a hoax.[32]

As of 2022, the only three "period" documents we have for the 1920 Russian *Dracula* are without doubt fakes produced in the modern era. Two are fragments from the film, the first allegedly discovered in Serbia prior to being posted on YouTube in 2013 under the title *Drakula (1920)*. With a running time of approximately 3:17, the fragment depicts Dracula welcoming Harker to his dinner table and serving him wine. Later we see Harker at a desk, writing in his diary, or perhaps authoring a letter to Mina. The footage is clearly bogus, showing no registration error. It was filmed digitally, which accounts for its stability, and then manipulated in post-production to look old. The film damage overlays repeat, yet another obvious sign of its modern origin.[33] The acting style is incorrect, and Harker's haircut is too modern. That said, the footage illustrates talented and dedicated work. As Academy Award-winning editor Bob Murawski has observed, "whoever made it did a good job."[34] While it cannot fool trained filmmakers and scholars, *Drakula (1920)* has fooled at least a few viewers.

In 2021, a different fragment appeared online under the title *Apakyna/Dracula*. It runs approximately 2:17. The accompanying description claims that Viacheslav Turzhanskii shot the film in Yalta in 1919, which seems potentially credible, given that Turzhanskii resided in that region until February 1920. The description notes that an unnamed person discovered the partially burned fragment near Kyiv. There is also a vague and unattributed claim that *Apakyna*'s "creepy atmosphere" shocked its original viewers. If anyone saw this footage in circa 1920, they would have had very good reason to be shocked, as it is really a prank film edited nearly one century later. *Apakyna* largely consists of footage appropriated from *Мазепа/Mazepa*, directed by Vasili Goncharov in Russia in 1909; that was a film about two lovers who elope after a parent disallows their marriage. We also

Figure 4.2 Film poster for *Apakyna*, another modern fake.

see approximately ten seconds of footage from W. K. L. Dickson's *The Newark Athlete* (1891), heavily blurred in an effort to obscure its origins as well as to appear "creepy." The fragment also features title credits designed in the twenty-first century, mimicking the style of Russian films from circa 1910 and digitally manipulated to appear old.[35]

Along with these two counterfeits, a phony movie poster for *Apakyna* has circulated online. Generating supernatural vampires is difficult to do unless one is a supernatural vampire: hence, the ersatz films and ephemera. Let us turn now not to Van Helsing, but instead to Stoker's character Swales, who so readily condemns the falsehoods he sees all around him, even in a cemetery:

> It makes me ireful to think o' them. Why, it's them that, not content with printin' lies on paper an' preachin' them out of pulpits, does want to be cuttin' them on the tombstones ... Lies all of them, nothin' but lies of one kind or another!

In *The Vampire Almanac: The Complete History* (Visible Ink, 2022), J. Gordon Melton writes "no copy [of the Russian Dracula film] has emerged to confirm the rumor."[36] In all likelihood, no authentic copy ever will emerge, because it is almost certain that no such film ever existed, the tale representing a mistake from the 1960s that spawned hoaxes in the twenty-first century.

Aside from the *Loïe Fuller* and *Vampyrdanserinden*, what supernatural vampires *do* lurk in the silent cinema? There are at least two, the first having languished virtually unknown, particularly to English-speaking readers. In 1915, Viacheslav Turzhanskii directed *Zagrobnaia skitalitsa/The Afterlife Wanderer* (aka *Skazka nebes bez kontsa i nachala/The Sky Fairy Tale of Heaven with No Ending or Beginning* and *Zhenshchina vampir'/The Vampire Woman*) for T/d "A. Taldykin, N. Kozlovskii, S. Iuriev and K." It starred Olga Baclanova, who would later immigrate to America and play a leading role in Tod Browning's *Freaks* (1932).[37] It is likely that Turzhanskii's film – which was definitely produced and released, and which unquestionably features a supernatural vampire – provided the modern Russian Dracula fraudsters with a tenable director name.

An advertisement in *Kine-zhurnal* promoted *Zagrobnaia skitalitsa* as being the "first Russian occult drama," one provocative enough that the mayor of Petrograd banned it.[38] A synopsis published in *Proektor* told readers:

> Mad love for the artist Amosov has captured Vera, an innocent young girl. When her mother found out about their relationship, she cursed Vera. However, Vera's love for Amosov was stronger than this misery. Soon a terrible misfortune befell Vera. She saw that Amosov took her as a toy, a temporary pastime of a Don Juan spoiled by success with women. Under the pressure of grief and disappointment, Vera commits

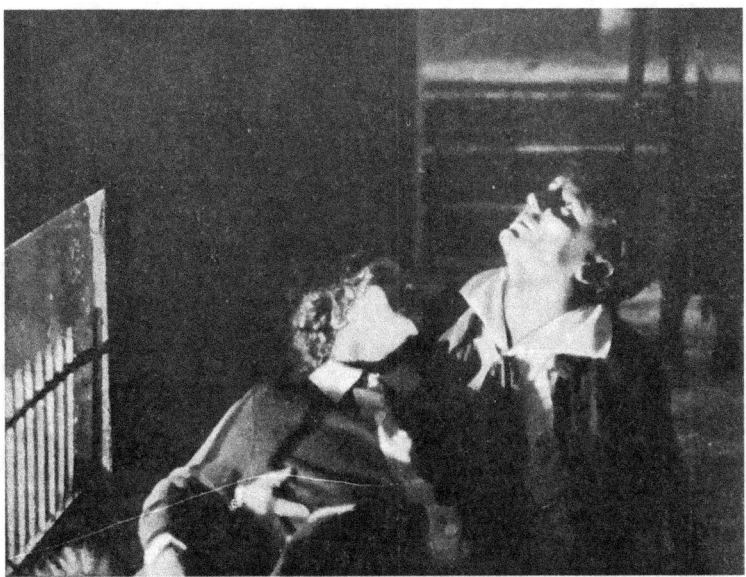

Figure 4.3 Viacheslav Turzhanskii's *Zagrobnaia skitalitsa/ The Afterlife Wanderer* (1915). (Courtesy of *Daydreams Database: Cinema of the Russian Empire and Beyond*, edited by Anna Kovalova and developed by Alexander Grebenkov.)

suicide. But death did not give her peace, because she loved life too much. Even death could not end her unsatisfied desire for love. In order to return to life, Vera's soul merges with the soul of a girl who looked like Vera. Twenty years have passed since Vera's reincarnation, and now she is married. Her husband loves her and surrounds her with wealth and happiness, and life could be a bright holiday for her. However, incomprehensible sweet and cruel anticipation of something, some unearthly joys, excite Vera's soul and blood and undermine her health, remaining a mystery to doctors who do not know how to treat this disease. She can only restore her strength by sucking the blood of people who surround her . . . Thanks to Amosov and the spiritualist Intyre, the secret of the vampire woman is revealed, and the nightmare that hung over the family and life of Vera's husband comes to its end.[39]

A review printed in a subsequent issue of *Proektor* mentions a "vampire who sucks the blood of the living people at night."[40] Similarly, a review published in *Teatral'naia gazeta* described a "vampire woman sucking blood from loved ones."[41]

The appearance of a supernatural vampire hardly impressed *Teatral'naia gazeta*, its critic observing, "The audience does not understand much, shrugs their shoulders in bewilderment and does not experience the slightest horror."[42] *Pegas* went further in condemning the film, declaring "Whoever wrote a screenplay like *The Afterlife Wanderer* should burn with

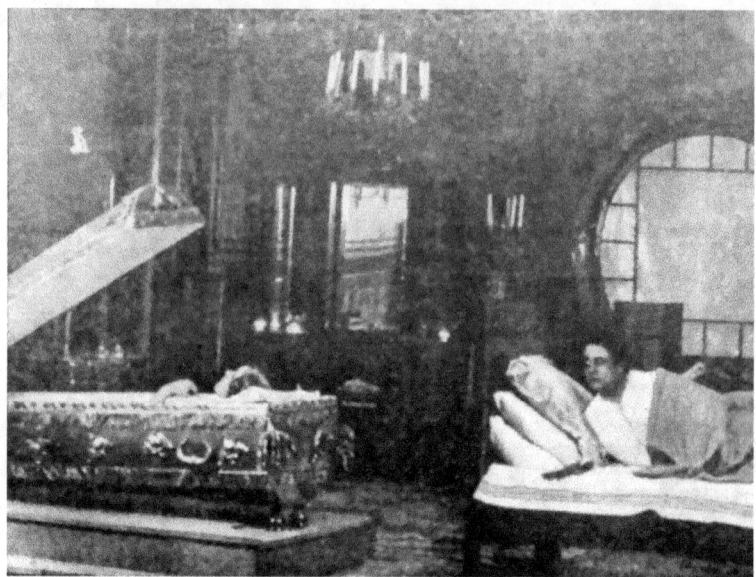

Figure 4.4 Olga Baclanova in *Zagrobnaia skitalitsa/ The Afterlife Wanderer* (1915). (Courtesy of *Daydreams Database: Cinema of the Russian Empire and Beyond*, edited by Anna Kovalova and developed by Alexander Grebenkov.)

shame all his life." The publication – which made repeated mention of the film's supernatural vampire – praised Baclanova's performance as Vera, though its text was probably intended to be ironic: "We must do justice to the actress who played the vampire woman. She undoubtedly studied her bloodthirsty expressions and voluptuous gestures at the zoo, watching tigers and leopards while they were eating raw meat."[43]

Zagrobnaia skitalitsa became the first supernatural vampire feature film in the history of cinema, and perhaps the first supernatural vampire film of any length, mitigated by how we view *Loïe Fuller* and *Vampyrdanserinden*. "A vampire who drank human blood must die," *Pegas* explained, and so that came to pass, for Vera and for *Zagrobnaia skitalitsa*, which became largely forgotten, save for being catalogued in a 1945 book on Russian cinema.[44] The film deserves much renewed attention, assuming its appropriately paramount place in vampire cinema history.

The other major supernatural vampire of the era came in the form of Lilith, Adam's first wife in Hebrew and Mesopotamian mythology. In some iterations, she sucked the blood of children, and so she at times been considered a vampire.[45] As *Photoplay* magazine argued in 1921, Lilith was not a "Vamp in name only, but a real, full-grown night-flying Vampire of the kind that stand no nonsense."[46] Metaphorical Lilith characters appeared onscreen in Komet Films' *Lilith, das Mädchen vom See/Lilith, the Girl from the Lake* (1912, aka *Lilit, das Mädchen vom See*) and in William C. DeMille's *The Tree of Knowledge* (Paramount, 1920), but it was yet another motion picture that depicted Lilith's penchant for drinking blood: the Austrian film *Lilith und Ly/Lilith and Ly* (1919), directed by Erich Kober for FIAT-Film-Gesellschaft. Fritz Lang wrote the script. According to Lang's biographer Patrick McGilligan:

> Perhaps it was [Lang's] very first script. Although Fritz placed the film in 1919, it seems possible, nevertheless, that *Lilith und Ly* was one of Lang's earliest hospital scenarios (the one he vaguely recalled as a "werewolf story"), and that it was filmed in Austria without his knowledge or participation shortly before he left Vienna in late 1918.
>
> The film's director was the founder of the Fiat Film company in Vienna, Erich Kober ("a director apparently unknown outside Austria," in Lotte Eisner's words), whose short-lived company made several silent pictures. The leads of the film were Elga Beck and Hans Marschall, the latter quite well-known, both as an actor and director, in Austria.
>
> Contemporary newspaper notices claimed the *Lilith und Ly* script was inspired by an original Sanskrit manuscript ("parchment strips"), which Lang acquired during his "extensive" travels in Asia. But the film's main idea, of an artificial creature brought to life with a slip of parchment, is clearly pinched from the Jewish legend of golem, a monster of clay which can only be brought to life by placing a sacred text in its mouth.[47]

By the time that Lang wrote his script, Paul Wegener had twice appeared as the Golem onscreen, first in Paul Wegener and Henrik Galeen's *Der Golem/The Golem* (Deutsche Bioscop, 1915) and then in Paul Wegener and Rochus Gliese's *Der Golem und die Tänzerin/The Golem and the Dancer* (Deutsche Bioscop, 1917).

Figure 4.5 Elga Beck as Lilith in Erich Kober's
Lilith und Ly/Lilith and Ly (1919).

In *Lilith und Ly*, a scientist named Landov (Marschall) brings a statue of a woman to life using a Sanskrit parchment that he discovered inside a mummy's tomb.[48] The mystical process requires an inscribed ruby to work. Landov and the statue-turned-woman (Beck) live together in bliss until a shattered test tube cuts him. According to one synopsis, the woman "pounces greedily at the drop of blood, which she quickly kisses away." Her behavior changes, with Landov coming into possession of another parchment, one that explains:

> [I]f an accident should happen that the creature learns of its origin, it will become a vampire. It will have secret powers; it will be able to make itself invisible, and the vampire will drink blood wherever it finds it, because it needs it to exist.

While Lilith's vampirism is unleashed, Landov falls in love with a real woman named Ly (also played by Beck). Landov dispatches Lilith by destroying the statue of her with a Tibetan sword. He also throws away the inscribed ruby, "the heart of the vampire." But a happy ending is not possible: Ly's father requires that Landov never again see his true love.

Neue Kino-Rundschau gave *Lilith and Ly* a brief but glowing review, praising its "exciting plot" and "artistic direction."[49] The publication also printed a lengthy plot synopsis with numerous photos.[50] However, FIAT-Film-Gesellschaft soon went bankrupt and sold the movie to another German company. *Lilith und Ly* then appeared under two subsequent titles in Austria and Germany, the first being *Das Kind des Teufels/The Devil's Child* (1919). Two years later, Lilith returned from the cinematic grave under the title *Der Vampyr im Spiegel/The Vampire in the Mirror* (1921).[51] While there is no surviving print, a fragment of *Das Kind des Teufels* exists in the Österreichisches Filmmuseum. Lilith's reputation as a vampire, the use of the term in the film, and her blood-drinking qualify *Lilith und Ly* as a supernatural vampire film, one of the very few of the 1910s.

Where might other vampires be found? In a 1984 article, Lajos Matos wrote that Sándor "Alexander" Korda's Hungarian film *Mágia/Magic* (Corvin, 1917) "included elements of the Dracula theme."[52] A period plot synopsis explains:

> Count Merlinus, the proud lord of the castle, is identical to Sinesius, the famous medieval alchemist who in 1590 invented the Philosopher's Stone, to which he owes his eternal youth. But the miracle stone has magical powers only if its owner sacrifices a young man every thousandth full moon, i.e., every human lifetime. Count Merlinus hires Paul, a poor philosopher from Pest, to organize his library, and he has chosen him as his next victim. Paul finds the book on the Philosopher's Stone and suspects Merlinus' plan. The Count's young and unhappy wife is attracted to Paul and enjoys spending time in his company. One day, they find the Count's magic mirror from Arabia, which reveals to them the story of Sinesius' life. They see how, in the fifteenth century, Sinesius killed his own assistant to prolong his own life by a man's lifetime. The stunned Paul recognizes his own features in the victim.[53]

Figure 4.6 The scene in which Lilith (Elga Beck) drinks Landov's (Hans Marschall's) blood in *Lilith und Ly/Lilith and Ly* (1919).

Matos was correct when he wrote the film echoed *Dracula* in some respects, but are these similarities enough to characterize it as a vampire film? Merlinus is a count and lives in a castle. He sheds blood, but period articles make clear that he does not drink it. Instead, the archaic Hungarian phrase "take one's blood" means nothing more than murder.[54] And while Merlinus possesses eternal life, he is not undead.

Though it has been mistakenly included in some vampire filmographies, *Mágia* did not feature a supernatural vampire.[55] Nor do there seem to have been vampires in *Il Trovatore* (Lubin, 1909), *Il Trovatore* (Pathé Frères, 1911), or *Il Trovatore* (Centaur, 1914), though film adaptations of Verdi's 1853 opera might take us closer to the undead than, say, *The Mysteries of Myra* or *Mágia*. Its shapeshifting witch – her soul condemned to live in this world – appears on the rooftops ("Sull'orlo dei tetti"), transforming into an owl or raven before "flying through the dawn like lightning" ("sull'alba fuggente al par di saetta!"). The possible vampirism here would rest not only on the character's description, but also in how she was described in

Figure 4.7 *The Poet of the Peaks* (American Film Manufacturing, 1915).

the early cinema period. During the years from 1908 to 1910, for example, Victor Records repeatedly referred to its release of *Sull'orlo dei tetti* with the following English phrase: *As a Vampire You May See Her*.[56] We might see her as a vampire; we might not, and with good reason, as she would be best understood using the language heard in the opera. She is a "fattucchiera," a "strega," meaning a witch.

We could also search for vampires in film adaptations of specific literature. *The Poet of the Peaks* (American Film Manufacturing, 1915) featured Vivian Rich in a story based on Keats's *La Belle Dame sans Merci*.[57] *Motion Picture News* called Rich an "irresistible vampire," the reference presumably meaning a vamp, though *Reel Life* referred to her character as a "phantom" who causes a "crazed" character to fall from a cliff to his death.[58] We could similarly consider Germaine Dulac's *La Belle dame sans Merci* (1921), which *Cinéa* praised for its "taste and style" and its "beautiful rhythm."[59] Certainly James B. Twitchell has made the case to consider the title character of Keats's poem to be a supernatural vampire.[60]

Twitchell makes an even more compelling argument for Samuel Taylor Coleridge's *The Rime of the Ancient Mariner* (1798), interpreting its "Life-in-Death" character as undead.[61] Coleridge's poem tells us:

> Her lips were red, her looks were free,
> Her locks were yellow as gold:
> Her skin was as white as leprosy,
> The Nightmare Life-in-Death was she,
> Who thicks man's blood with cold.

She thickens blood, but she does not drink it. Instead, Coleridge's blood drinker is fear – not embodied, but rather the emotion – which seems to sip the main character's "life-blood" as if from a cup.

Figure 4.8 Pictured on the right, Life-in-Death (Gladys Brockwell) rolls dice with Death (Robert Klein) in a scene from *The Ancient Mariner* (Fox, 1925).

In 1925, Henry Otto and Chester Bennett directed an adaption of the poem for Fox starring Leslie Fenton and Clara Bow. *The Ancient Mariner* featured a modern story bookending Coleridge's tale, which included the famous scene of Life-in-Death (played by Gladys Brockwell) rolling dice with Death. Some period sources like *Motion Picture News* referred to the character as Life-in-Death; others, including the studio pressbook, simply call her "Life."[62] *The Ancient Mariner* does not survive, alas, and so how the onscreen intertitles referred to her is difficult to know. Likely, the pressbook mirrors the film's word choice, but then again, pressbooks occasionally made errors.

Nevertheless, *The Ancient Mariner* might take us closer to the undead than most of the films in this chapter. If there is any other worth considering, it would probably be Aleksandr Panteleev's Russian film *Derevo Smerti, ili Krovozhadnaia Susanna/The Death Tree, or Bloodthirsty Susanna* (T-vo "Khudozhestvennaia lenta," 1915), in which a botanist uses a fantastical tree as an instrument of torture. According to a synopsis published in *Sine-Fono*, "The bloodthirsty Susanna is a vampire tree that feeds on the blood of people and animals: having huge tentacles, it squeezes its victim with them and sucks the blood out of it."[63] But of course if a fantastical blood-drinking tree suffices as a supernatural vampire film, so too should the aforementioned nonfiction films about

Figure 4.9 Aleksandr Panteleev's *Derevo Smerti, ili Krovozhadnaia Susanna/ The Death Tree, or Bloodthirsty Susanna* (1915).

vampire bats. Or even a nonfiction film like *Odd Fresh Water Creatures* (Pathé, 1917), which depicted *Piscicola geometra*, a species of leech that punctures the skin of fish and sucks their blood.[64]

Most importantly, aside from *Zagrobnaia skitalitsa* and *Lilith und Ly*, we must consider that the silent cinema examined in this chapter requires us to expand our definition of what a supernatural vampire *is*, a process that would quickly make all demons, devils, ghosts, and revenants into vampires. Therein lies, if not madness, an approach so broad as to achieve little more than to satisfy our urge for population growth. As Van Helsing asks, "Does not the belief in vampires rest for others . . . on them?" Ernest Jones explained in his book *On the Nightmare* (1931) that vampires possess two "essential characteristics," being undead and imbibing blood.[65] Consider also Nick Groom's commentary:

> There are plenty of trans-historical, transnational surveys that cherry-pick demons, witches, werewolves, and ghosts from world culture to propose that the vampire has been an eternal (indeed, undying) threat to humankind . . . Instead, I argue that the vampire is a recognizable thing that dates from a precise period in a certain place, and which consequently has recognizable manifestations and qualities – especially concerning blood, science, society and culture.[66]

The reality is that the supernatural vampire was an endangered species in silent cinema. After all, there is a definable supernatural, undead, bloodsucking vampire, one identifiable to everyone from Dom Antoine Augustin Calmet and Montague Summers to Bela Lugosi and Stephen King, one identifiable to most of us, within certain parameters at least, rather than parameters be damned.

And yet, perhaps we should also guard against being too restrictive with our definitions, to avoid becoming those Summers disparaged with the phrase, "Inconsulti abuent sedemque odere Sibyllae."[67] In *I Am Legend*, Matheson reworks dialogue from Hamilton Deane and John L. Balderston's *Dracula –The Vampire Play* (1927) and Browning's *Dracula*: "The strength of the vampire is that no one will believe in him."[68] Following a YouTube post that decried the *Apakyna* fragment for being fake, another viewer responded, "Сам ты фейк этот фильм настоящий," meaning, "You yourself are fake; this movie is real."[69] And so it is; the film is very real, although it was edited from found footage in the twenty-first century. But we might still be missing the larger point, even if not the larger pointed teeth.

At the end of *I Am Legend*, right after Neville commits suicide, Matheson describes the fledgling vampire planet, one "entering the unassailable fortress of forever."[70] Perhaps *Le Manoir du diable*, *La Légende du fantôme/ Legend of a Ghost* (Pathé Frères, 1908), and the motion pictures discounted in this chapter *are* vampire films, even if they are not films featuring supernatural vampires.[71] Rather than being an endangered species, perhaps vampire films are everywhere we look in silent and sound cinema. Let us rethink Lord Godalming's dialogue in Stoker's *Dracula* when he says, "I thought I saw a face, but it was only the shadows."

Perhaps the shadows onscreen are always the face of vampires, in silent films and in talkies. In Stoker's novel, Van Helsing told us, the "vampire is known everywhere that men have been." The unassailable film fortress of forever might be overpopulated with vampires, if we think of them metaphorically rather than supernaturally, if we think of them as adjectives in a descriptive, behavioral capacity, rather than nouns in a literal, "real" sense. Other chapters in this book examine vamps and thieves because filmmakers described them as vampires during the silent era. And so perhaps we should label every film character as being vampiric, at least those who feed off others emotionally, romantically, spiritually, or financially? They are become vampires, each and every one.

Nearly 150 years before Matheson's *I Am Legend*, John Herman Merivale (under the pseudonym "Arminius") authored *The Dead Men of Pest*,

A Hungarian Legend, which was published in 1807. The two stories have much in common. Merivale wrote:

> It was the Cor[p]ses that our Churchyardes filled,
> That did at Midnight lumberr up our Stayres;
> They suck'd our Bloud, the gorie Banquet swilled,
> And harrowed everie Soule with hydeous Feares.

By the end of the tale, vampires populate the entire city, save for two humans, one a storyteller, the other a listener, their conversation unfolding not unlike an author and a reader. Perhaps *The Dead Men of Pest* serves as a warning against too many vampires. Or perhaps it serves as an invitation for more of them, ever more of them.

Notes

1. Montague Summers, *The Vampire, His Kith and Kin* (London: K. Paul Trench, Trubner, 1928), 170.
2. Richard Matheson, *I Am Legend* (New York: Tor, 1995), 1.
3. Ibid., 17.
4. For a lengthy discussion of *Le Manoir du diable*, please see Chapter 1.
5. Eric Stedman kindly referred me to the internet discussion about *The Mysteries of Myra*, which appeared as posts at the *Silent and Pre-Code Horror Group* on Facebook in 2022. One version of the story apparently dates to at least the late 1960s, given that Ron Borst mentioned the serial's alleged vampire in "The Vampire in the Cinema," *Photon*, Number 18, 1969, 19. An announcement and discussion of the serial's alleged vampire can notably be found David Annwn Jones' paper "Cinema's First Vampires: Theodore and Leo Wharton's *The Mysteries of Myra* and Alexander Korda's *Mágia*," presented at the World Vampire Conference in 2016.
6. Barbara Tepa Lupack, *Silent Serial Sensations: The Wharton Brothers and the Magic of Early Cinema* (Ithaca, NY: Cornell University Press, 2020), 140, 142.
7. *The Mysteries of Myra*, DVD (South Hampton, Pennsylvania: Serial Squadron, 2018). The four restored chapters are Episode 1 (*The Dagger of Dreams*), Episode 5 (*The Fumes of Fear*), Episode 12 (*The Elixir of Youth*), and Episode 15 (*The Thought Monster*).
8. "Mysteries of Myra," *Moving Picture World*, August 19, 1916, 1299.
9. I am grateful to Eric Stedman for sharing these observations.
10. "The Mysteries of Myra," *Moving Picture World*, July 15, 1916, 534.
11. Stedman, *The Mysteries of Myra*, 252. The novelization finds one character saying, "elementals are vampires and are blood hungry" (267), but two points must be made. The first is that contextually this dialogue seems to be a comparison of the two different creatures, presumably due to the blood sacrifice. The second is that there is absolutely no evidence whatsoever that

this dialogue or anything similar to it appeared in the film serial, and it is the film serial that is under review. After all, the history of films and their novelizations show repeated examples of variations and contradictions between the two. Indeed, the book's dialogue about vampires seems somewhat contradictory with the earlier account that it is actually the Master of the Black Order who suggests the blood sacrifice.
12. Borst, 19. In his article "Vampire Film Checklist" (*Photon*, no. 19, 1970, 27), Borst repeated his belief about the lack of vampires in *The Mysteries of Myra*.
13. Peter John Dyer, "All Manner of Fantasies," *Films and Filming*, June 1958, 1315. Dyer's article was reprinted in *Journal of Frankenstein*, no. 1 (1959): 10–13.
14. Mention of *Nächte des Grauens* as a possible vampire film appears at least as early as Borst's "The Vampire in the Cinema" article in 1969. Borst notes, "Whether [Dyer's] statement refers to the vampiric element or the atmospheric element is unknown to me" (19). Future writers, including many on the internet, have avoided Borst's caution and have stated without merit that *Nächte des Grauens* features one or more supernatural vampires. For example, Raymond T. McNally and Radu Florescu catalogue the film in their book *In Search of Dracula: The History of Dracula and Vampires* (Greenwich, CT: New York Graphic Society, 1972), 216. David J. Skal also includes the film in his vampire filmography in the book *V is for Vampire: An A–Z Guide to Everything Undead* (New York: Plume, 1996), 234.
15. I am very grateful to Lisa Roth and the Deutsche Kinemathek for providing an extensive original plot synopsis for *Nächte des Grauens/Nächte des Schreckens*.
16. J. Gordon Melton, *The Vampire Almanac: The Complete History* (Detroit, MI: Visible Ink Press, 2022), 166.
17. Denise J. Youngblood, *The Magic Mirror: Moviemaking in Russia, 1908–1918* (Madison, WI: University of Wisconsin Press, 1999), 94–5.
18. Giorgio Bertellini, email to Gary D. Rhodes, November 2, 2022.
19. "*Vamping Babies*," *Moving Picture World*, August 7, 1926, 366. Skal lists *Vamping Babies* in the filmography published in *V is for Vampire*, 233.
20. For example, Raymond T. McNally and Radu Florescu list *Vampe di gelosia* in their book *In Search of Dracula: The History of Dracula and Vampires* and mistranslate the title as *The Vamp's Jealousy* (216). They also include *Cenere e vampe*, misspelling it as *Ceneri e vampe* and misdating it as 1916 (216). While they do not attempt to translate the title, they do include it in their vampire filmography. In *V is for Vampire*, Skal lists *Cenere e vampe*, with the same misspelling and incorrect date (233).
21. Giorgio Bertellini, email to Gary D. Rhodes, December 5, 2022.
22. "*The Vampire Bat and Armadillo*," *The Bioscope*, March 26, 1914, ix. The other two nonfiction films depicting vampire bats are *Curious Indian Animals* (1913) and an entry in a series of "Scenic Travel Pictures" that C. L. Chester filmed in conjunction with *Outing* (aka *The Outing Magazine*) in 1918. See "*Curious Indian Animals*," *The Bioscope*, December 18, 1913, v; "*Outing*-Chester," *The Billboard*, April 6, 1918, 30.

23. Forrest J Ackerman, *Famous Monsters of Filmland*, June 1963, 43.
24. "*Dracula* (Lost Russian Film; Existence Unconfirmed; 1920)," accessed August 11, 2022, https://lostmediawiki.com/Dracula_(lost_Russian_film;_existence_unconfirmed;_1920).
25. Donald F. Glut, *The Dracula Book* (Metuchen, NJ: Scarecrow Press, 1975), 101.
26. J. Gordon Melton, *The Vampire Book: The Encyclopedia of the Undead* (Detroit, MI: Visible Ink Press, 1994), 175.
27. "*Dracula* (Lost Russian Film; Existence Unconfirmed; 1920)."
28. For more information on this period of Russian film, see Denise J. Youngblood, *Soviet Cinema in the Silent Era, 1918–1935* (Austin, TX: University of Texas Press, 1991).
29. Our Homeland–USSR, Historical Group, November 10, 2012, accessed August 14, 2022, https://vk.com/wall-9771_20766?lang=en.
30. I would note that no film produced in 1920 would qualify as the "first amateur film in the history of cinema," given that amateur filmmaking predates that year.
31. The full account, in text not reproduced in this chapter, does mention one person who did exist, Gosfilmofond cofounder Georgy Avenarius.
32. Denise J. Youngblood, email to Gary D. Rhodes, September 27, 2022.
33. *Drakula (1920)*, accessed August 19, 2022, https://www.youtube.com/watch?v=Qk8imiYs_OQ.
34. Bob Murawski, email to Gary D. Rhodes, August 22, 2022.
35. *Аракуna (1920)*. Т/Д А. Ханжоков, реж. Виктор Туржанский, accessed August 12, 2022, https://www.youtube.com/watch?v=mON9xgeYbKQ.
36. J. Gordon Melton, *The Vampire Almanac*, 166.
37. *Zhenshchina vampir'* – as rendered with the apostrophe – is the correct transliteration. However, it is commonly transliterated as *Zhensh'ina-vampir*.
38. Advertisement, *Kine-zhurnal*, no. 9–10 (1915), 33; "Khronika," *Proektor*, no 1 (1915): 31. I am deeply grateful to Anna Kovalova for all primary sources on *Zagrobnaia skitalitsa* and the translations of them.
39. "Opisaniia kartin," *Proektor*, no. 2 (1915): 41.
40. "Kriticheskoe onozrenie," *Proekto*r, no. 9 (1916): 14.
41. "Stranitsy ekrana," *Teatral'naia gazeta*, no. 17 (1916): 15–16.
42. Ibid., 16.
43. "*Zagrobnaia skitalitsa*," *Pegas*, no. 5 (1916): 80–1.
44. V. E. Vishnevskii, *Khudozhestvennyie fil'my dorevoliutsionnoi Rossii* (Moscow: Goskinoizdat, 1945), 61.
45. See, for example, Augustine [*sic*] Calmet, *The Phantom World: or, The Philosophy of Spirits, Apparitions, &c., Volume I* (London: Richard Bentley, 1850), 76; Summers, 227.
46. Svetozar Tonjoroff, "Vamps of All Times," *Photoplay*, May 1921, 40.
47. Patrick McGilligan, *Fritz Lang: The Nature of the Beast* (Minneapolis, MN: University of Minnesota Press, 1997), 47.
48. More plot summary appears in Walter Fritz, "Der Vampyr im Fernsehstudio: *Lilith und Ly* ein vergessener Film von Fritz Lang," *Aktion*, April 1969, 26–8.
49. "*Lilith und Ly*," *Neue Kino-Rundschau*, July 12, 1919, 14.

50. "*Lilith und Ly*," *Neue Kino-Rundschau*, July 12, 1919, 17–32.
51. "Neuestes aus Deutschland," *Neue Kino-Rundschau*, June 11, 1921, 7.
52. Lajos Matos, "A Valószínűtlen Lehetséges," *Filmvilág*, January 1984, 13–21, https://filmvilag.hu/xista_frame.php?cikk_id=6536.
53. I am grateful to Gyöngyi Balogh for this plot synopsis, which appears in her encyclopedia manuscript *Magyar Filmográfia Játékfilmek (1901–1929)*.
54. Here I am deeply grateful to my colleague Tamás Gyurkovics, who kindly translated period text regarding *Mágia* and provided insight into the particulars of word choice and contemporary meanings of relevant phrases therein. I would also thank my colleague Mirjam Dénes, who also provided important context on the phrase "take one's blood."
55. For an example, see Skal, 233.
56. See "*Il Trovatore* Series," *New Victor Record Catalogue*, May 1908, 120; "*Il Trovatore* Series," *New Victor Record Catalogue*, July 1909, 104; "*Il Trovatore* Series," *New Victor Record Catalogue*, January 1910, 50; "*Il Trovatore* Series," *New Victor Record Catalogue*, July 1910, 53.
57. Neil G. Caward, "*The Poet of the Peaks*," *Motography*, April 17, 1915, 605.
58. T. S. Mead, "*The Poet of the Peaks*," *Motion Picture News*, April 17, 1915, 89; "Stories of the New Photoplays," *Reel Life*, April 10, 1915, 10.
59. "*La Belle Dame sans Merci*," *Cinéa*, May 13, 1921, 8.
60. James B. Twitchell, *The Living Dead: A Study of the Vampire in Romantic Literature* (Durham, NC: Duke University Press, 1981), 54–8.
61. Twitchell, 145–60.
62. "Pictures and People," *Motion Picture News*, October 3, 1925, 1572. A copy of the studio pressbook for *The Ancient Mariner* is archived in the Billy Rose Theatre Division at the New York Public Library.
63. "Novye lenty," *Sine-Fono*, no. 5–6 (1916): 134–5. I am grateful to Anna Kovalova for this primary source and the translation of it.
64. "*Odd Fresh Water Creatures* (Pathe)," *Moving Picture World*, April 14, 1917, 268.
65. Ernest Jones, *On the Nightmare* (London: Hogarth Press, 1931), 99.
66. Nick Groom, *The Vampire: A New History* (New Haven, CT: Yale University, 2018), xv.
67. Montague Summers, *The Vampire in Europe* (New York: Random House, 1996), xi.
68. Matheson, 17. In the Deane-Balderston play, the dialogue is as follows: "The strength of the vampire is that people will not believe in him."
69. "Знакомьтесь робот" posted this comment in July 2022, accessed September 10, 2022, https://www.youtube.com/watch?v=mON9xgeYbKQ.
70. Matheson, 159.
71. *Le Manoir du diable* and *La Légende du fantôme* are discussed at length in Chapter 1.

CHAPTER 5

Drakula halála

"Those standing nearby fell under the spell of Drakula's powerful words. An awkward silence followed."

– *Drakula halála* novella, 1924

Dracula was not Hungarian. Bela Lugosi, who famously portrayed the title role in Tod Browning's *Dracula* (Universal, 1931), was born in Hungary, but Dracula was not.

Vlad III, also known as Vlad Drăculea (Vlad Dracula) and Vlad Țepeș (Vlad the Impaler), remains a hero in Romania. As Voivode of Wallachia for three separate reigns during the fifteenth century, he was at times at war with Hungarians, at times allied with them. But no one mistook Vlad III's heritage, not even the Germans, his greatest detractors in the years after his death.[1]

Bram Stoker's Dracula recounts his own complicated history with Hungarians in the 1897 novel:

> Is it a wonder that we were a conquering race; that we were proud; that when the Magyar, the Lombard, the Avar, the Bulgar, or the Turk poured his thousands on our frontiers, we drove them back? Is it strange that when Arpad and his legions swept through the Hungarian fatherland he found us here when he reached the frontier; that the Honfoglalas was completed there? And when the Hungarian flood swept eastward, the Szekelys were claimed as kindred by the victorious Magyars, and to us for centuries was trusted the guarding of the frontier of Turkey-land . . . When was redeemed that great shame of my nation, the shame of Cassova, when the flags of the Wallach and the Magyar went down beneath the Crescent? . . . Again, when, after the battle of Mohács, we threw off the Hungarian yoke, we of the Dracula blood were amongst their leaders, for our spirit would not brook that we were not free.

Histories fiction and histories nonfiction reside in a similarly complex place: Dracula was not Magyar; he was not Hungarian. And yet he was never far from the country and its people, including in the cinema.

In the late twentieth century, a few historians discovered that F. W. Murnau's *Nosferatu* (Prana-Film, 1922) was not, as long believed, the first time that a filmmaker adapted Stoker's *Dracula* for the screen.[2] Even though it was hardly faithful to the novel, Hungarian director Károly Lajthay's *Drakula halála/The Death of Dracula* (1921, aka *Dracula's Death*) marked the character's earliest screen appearance, incorporating Stoker's vampire character into a tale that also drew heavily on Robert Wiene's *Das Cabinet des Dr. Caligari/The Cabinet of Dr. Caligari* (Decla-Film, 1920).

Initial mention of *Drakula halála* in the English language probably came in a 1971 fan magazine, its title listed in a vampire filmography.[3] Then, in 1981, Forrest J Ackerman's book *Mr. Monster's Movie Gold* published a publicity still allegedly from a Hungarian silent version of *Dracula*, though it didn't name *Drakula halála* by title.[4] Ackerman's image actually depicted Pál Fejös' film *Lidércnyomás/Nightmare* (Mobil, 1920, aka *Jóslat/Prophecy*), based on Oscar Wilde's mystery *Lord Arthur Savile's Crime* (1887).[5] And so little was known of *Drakula halála*'s production or its storyline in English-language texts until an earlier version of the present chapter was published in *Horror Studies* in 2010.[6]

Figure 5.1 *Lidércnyomás/Nightmare* (1920, aka *Jóslat/Prophecy*).

Announcing *Drakula halála*'s production in January 1921, the Hungarian trade publication *Képes Mozivilág* wrote:

About twenty years ago, H. G. Wells' novel *Drakula*, one of his most interesting and exciting stories, was published as a serial in the *Budapesti Hírlap*, and then later published here as a book. The novel was highly acclaimed at the time, because the reader was fully absorbed into its exciting plot that featured so many unexpected turns.[7]

Although *Képes Mozivilág* mistakenly named Wells as the author rather than Stoker, the publication was correct that *Budapesti Hírlap* had serialized *Dracula* from January to March 1898.[8] In May of that same year, a publisher

Figure 5.2 Károly Lajthay in *Vorrei morir* (Rex, 1919).

released a Hungarian-language version of *Dracula*, with two more editions being published before 1910.[9] To some degree, Stoker's vampire became known, even popular, in Hungary.

Képes Mozivilág also claimed that Lajthay intended to translate the "basic ideas" of Stoker's *Dracula* onto the screen. Whether due to copyright concerns or the influence of *Caligari* or yet some other reason, Lathjay would shoot a script that featured the novel's character but not its narrative. Bram Stoker's Dracula became Károly Lajthay's Drakula, a madman in a mental institute who believes himself to be an immortal, supernatural vampire.

Born in Marosvásárhely, Lajthay was an important figure in the Hungarian film industry during the 1910s. At times he was a writer, as for *Átok vára/The Cursed Castle* (Cosmos, 1918, aka *Lobogó vér/Burning Passon*) and *Júlia kisasszony/Miss Julia* (Triumph, 1919). And on at least one occasion before *Drakula halála* he was a producer, for *Tláni, az elvarázsolt hercegasszony/Tláni, the Enchanted Princess* (Triumph, 1920). But the bulk of Lajthay's credits were as director and actor. He used the screen name Charles Lederle for approximately thirteen Hungarian feature films, including *Nászdal/Wedding Song* (Star, 1918), which co-starred Bela Lugosi.

Lajthay greatly admired Emil Jannings, believing his performance in Ernst Lubitsch's *Anna Boleyn/Deception* (PAGU, 1920) was "unforgettable." As for his own work, Lathjay told *Képes Mozivilág*, "I think the only actors who can become exceptional in the cinema are those who excel on stage as well." He added, "A good stage actor cannot become a terrible movie actor; this is also impossible the other way around."[10]

According to censorship records, the Lapa Film Studio produced Lajthay's *Drakula halála*.[11] In late 1920, Lajthay visited Budapest and rented space at the Corvin Film Studio for a project then known as

Drakula. By that time, the theatre magazine *Színházi Élet* had named Lajthay as one of several leading Hungarians who had left for Vienna. In an interview with the publication, Lajthay explained:

> Film production in Vienna is virtually under Hungarian control, because Hungarian directors dominate the industry there. [Sándor] Korda and [Mihály] Kertész are extremely successful there . . . Now I am directing my film entitled *Drakula* [for a Vienna-based company].[12]

In January 1921, *Képes Mozivilág* added that Lajthay would direct a "Viennese troupe" of actors for his "grandiose" new film.[13]

Lajthay coauthored the *Drakula* script with Mihály Kertész, who had already been a prominent film director in Budapest, having worked at Phönix with Bela Lugosi on such films as *99-es számú bérkocsi/Rental Car Number 99* (1918). By the time of *Drakula halála* (as the film became known at some point during its production), Kertész was making films in Austria. Years later, using the name Michael Curtiz, he directed such Hollywood movies as *Doctor X* (Warner Bros., 1932), *Mystery of the Wax Museum* (Warner Bros., 1933), and *Casablanca* (Warner Bros., 1942). It is likely that Lajthay and Kertész saw *Das Cabinet des Dr. Caligari* in 1920, whether in Vienna, where it opened in September of that year, or elsewhere, presumably before Béla Colussi finally distributed the film in Hungary during the spring of 1921.[14]

The story Lathjay and Kertész crafted features characters not in Stoker's novel, with "Drakula" becoming a mad composer locked in an asylum, a "picturesque panopticon" in which "humans [are] reduced to shadows."[15] Here is a framing story reminiscent of *Caligari*, with the inmates suffering from various delusions, one of them believing himself to be Stoker's vampire, another believing himself to be the minister of finance.

That said, the bulk of the story unfolds as a nightmare in which the composer actually is Drakula, at least until the dreamer awakens. Drakula appeared similar to Beelzebub, descriptions of him being satanic, "like a ghost from Hell," with "his deep fiery black eyes glow[ing] with dark flames." Most descriptions drew upon Stoker, though another seems to refer to Vlad III. In the film, Drakula is the "devil's son," an apt translation of the name Drăculea/Dracula.

During the dreamscape, Drakula is similar to Stoker's character in other respects, from wearing a black cloak and being powerless against the cross to having undead brides in his castle. Drakula pursues a character named Mary much as Dracula pursues Mina. Nevertheless Lathjay and Kertész largely jettisoned Stoker's story in favor of their new creation, one featuring a beautifully ghoulish wedding scene and nighttime chases through the snowbound countryside. Here was not a faithful adaptation of Stoker nor a mere recapitulation of *Caligari*. Dracula's first screen appearance instead inaugurated an approach dozens of future films would repeat, meaning the use of Stoker's vampire in a story not based on Stoker's novel.

To shoot the film, Lajthay employed Eduard Hoesch, believing him to be the "best cameraman in Vienna."[16] Hoesch would shoot *Drakula*'s interiors, though later credits suggest he was only one of two cinematographers who worked on the film. The other was Lajos Gasser, who had previously shot *Júlia kisasszony*.[17] Unfortunately, no known records indicate the names of the other crewmembers.

For the role of Drakula, Lajthay cast Paul Askonas, a member of the Deutsches Volkstheatre in Vienna. Askonas had previously appeared as Svengali in Jacob and Luise Fleck's film version of *Trilby* (Österreichisch-ungarische Kino-Industrie, 1912). In the years after his work as Drakula, Askonas would portray Dr. Mirakel in Max Neufeld's *Hoffmanns Erzählungen/Tales of Hoffmann* (Filmindustrie AG Wien, 1923) and Diener in Robert Wiene's *Orlacs Hände/The Hands of Orlac* (Pan-Film, 1924).

Figure 5.3 Paul Askonas as Mephistopheles in 1927.
(Courtesy of George Chastain.)

As for the other two key roles in *Drakula halála*, Lajthay cast Deszö Kertész (Mihály's brother) as the young male lead George and Margit Lux as the heroine Mary Land. Lux had previously appeared in such films as Fejös' *Lidércnyomás* and Kertész's *Alraune* (1918, co-directed with Edmund Fritz). Of the latter, *Képes Mozivilág* wrote she "stood out due to her beauty and refined acting."[18] Lux informed the same publication that her main goal was to learn English and star in Gaumont films produced in London.

Margit Lux's appearance in *Drakula halála* has been the matter of a minor controversy, as a January 1921 issue of *Képes Mozivilág* claimed that Lene Myl (who was in fact a Serbian named Miléne Pavlovic) would play "the role of the heroine"; they remarked on her "impressive appearance," and went so far as to say that she would "ensure the success" of *Drakula halála*.[19] Though she was essentially unknown, Myl had appeared in small film roles at studios in Rome and Berlin. Lajthay probably spotted her in the Austrian film *Königin Draga/Queen Draga* (Allianz-Film, 1920), in which she had a supporting role alongside Askonas. However, every other source from 1921 to 1923 claimed that Lux portrayed Mary Land, not Myl.[20] Moreover, it is definitely Lux who appears with Askonas in a *Drakula halála* publicity photograph published in *Szinház és Mozi* in 1921; its caption specifically credits Lux as playing Mary.

It is evident that *Képes Mozivilág* – the same publication that had incorrectly claimed that H. G. Wells wrote *Dracula* – simply made an error. Lux definitely portrayed Mary Land, whereas Myl played some other, lesser role. For example, 1921, Lajthay said, "The major parts are played by Margit Lux, Lene Myl, and Askonas."[21] A cast list published in 1924 also listed Lux as Mary Land, with Lene Myl in a different, unnamed role. Given *Drakula halála*'s storyline, Myl appeared either as a nurse or – more likely, if an extant publicity photograph of her for the film accurately reflects her onscreen costume – as one of Drakula's brides.[22] As for Lux, she would claim in late 1921 that working on *Drakula* was one of her fondest memories.[23]

With Askonas, Kertész, and Lux in the lead roles, Lajthay cast such actors as Lajos Réthey – who had costarred with Bela Lugosi in the Phönix release

Figure 5.4 Autographed photo of Margit Lux.

99-es számú bérkocsi – as the "Fake surgeon," and Karl Götz – aka Carl Goetz, who would later portray Schigolch in *Die Büsche der Pandora/Pandora's Box* (Nero-Film AG, 1929) – as the "Funny Man." Others included Elemér Thury, who had acted in Hungarian films since at least 1912, and Aladár Ihász, who appeared in a small number of films between 1913 and 1944.

Figure 5.5 Paul Askonas (left) in *Drakula halála*. This scene likely depicts the wedding ceremony between Drakula and Mary Land.

In December 1920, Lajthay directed some of *Drakula halála*'s exteriors in and around Vienna, including in the village of Melk.[24] The following month, beginning on January 2, 1921, he shot interior scenes at the Corvin Film Studio in Budapest, which he believed to be "better equipped than any studio in Vienna."[25] Afterwards, he returned to Vienna to film additional exteriors in the nearby Wachau Valley.[26]

During the Corvin shoot, a journalist from the publication *Színház és Mozi* visited the set and wrote a story about the film's production, the most in-depth to be published:

> It was not one of our famous prima donnas' weddings, nor one of our celebrated actors, or for that matter one of successful writers, poets, sculptors, or painters; however, I nonetheless must insist that I attended a wedding. Firstly, because I de facto did; secondly, because it was the most unusual and extraordinary wedding ever witnessed by anyone.
>
> I attended a wedding – at the Corvin Film Studio. The bridegroom – an actor – was none other than Asconas [*sic*], the most celebrated actor in Vienna, and the bride – an actress, of course – is Margit Lux, the nice, talented film actress who has been so highly acclaimed for crying so realistically on the screen.
>
> Asconas [*sic*], Drakula *in persona* –a phantastic creature, some kind of modern bluebeard – brings a new woman into his amazing castle, this new woman being played by Margit Lux. He stops at nothing in order to possess the woman: he summons demons and spirits and strange creatures to gain control over her, but then a cross

around her neck comes into view . . . and Drakula, this wonderful, and at the same time mysterious creature, is dispelled by it.

That's how Drakula's wedding took place – in the Corvin studio, namely. Since I might not be able to give away anything by admitting now that *Drakula* is a film, I will say that it is a film destined to become sensational, the plot of which must not be told due to the extraordinary excitement it conveys and the fact it will depend upon suspense when it appears on the screen.

Drakula's wedding gives a taste of the film's energies. There is an immense hall, dressed in marble, with a very, very long and dark corridor in the middle. That is where Drakula lives his mysterious life. It is night. The flutter and shrieks of a multitude of beasts can be heard, and the door in the middle of the hall opens. Beautiful women parade through it, all dressed in dreamlike costumes, all of them being Drakula's wives. But now Drakula awaits his new woman, the most beautiful and desirable of all. She will be welcomed with a rain of flowers.

How beautiful it will appear on the screen, I thought to myself while watching *Drakula* being shot at Corvin. Károly Lajthay, the great film director, worked all day without interruption to have Drakula welcome his new bride; when the film is finished, this scene will constitute just a small section of a four-act film. On the screen, this scene will not last more than five minutes, whereas it takes a full day's work to produce. The viewer, sitting in the theatre, will have no idea what extraordinary talent was required from the director to rehearse, shoot, and edit the sequences one by one.[27]

Színház és Mozi then quoted Lajthay as claiming the film would be a "super production," which were coincidentally the same words that Universal Pictures used a decade later to describe Browning's *Dracula*.[28]

Figure 5.6 Paul Askonas and Margit Lux in *Drakula halála*.

Színház és Mozi later reported in the past tense that a successful press screening of *Drakula halála* occurred in Vienna in 1921. No corroborating data has yet surfaced in Austrian trade publications, though the exhibition and its publicity could have been relatively meager. If nothing else, it is difficult to believe that Lathjay would not have shown the film to at least a few persons in 1921, including its financial backers, its cast, and possible film distributors. At any rate, the 1921 screening – presuming it actually occurred – remains shadowy.

Why the film did not premiere in Budapest in 1921 or go into general release anywhere that year is unknown. Perhaps there were problems with censors or even legal troubles. After all, there is no indication that Lajthay had obtained any rights from Bram Stoker's estate. Whatever the case, *Drakula halála* seems to go missing until November of 1922, when *Képes Mozivilág* reported:

> The well-known Lapa Studio of Vienna moved to Budapest in recent weeks. The studio is led by Károly Lajthay, the excellent director, whose name is familiar even to foreign audiences, and who is currently preparing his elaborate and (for the Hungarian movie industry) very important program. Lajthay's name and previous projects are guarantees that the Lapa Studio will enrich the Hungarian movie industry with excellent, meaningful productions.
>
> First and foremost, the studio will release two of Lajthay's recent works, one of them being the Dalmatian *Olavi* with an engaging story situated entirely in a Dalmatian environment. The other is the *Marriage of the Vampire*, which paints an unprecedently interesting and suspenseful portray of a strange creature. The excellent lead of *Olavi* is played by Paul Kronegg, while the titular character in *Marriage of the Vampire* is brought to life with a very strong performance by Paul Askonas.[29]

It is clear that *A vámpír násza/Marriage of the Vampire* was *Drakula halála* under a different title. Was the purpose to make the unreleased film seem new, or to distance it from Murnau's *Nosferatu* and/or Stoker's copyrighted novel? The answers are unknown, but here is the distinct possibility that the film might have screened under an alternate title in 1921 or 1922, one that did not draw attention to Stoker's character.

According to the April 1923 issue of *Mozi és Film*, it is certain that distributor Jenő Tüchten presented *Drakula halála* under that title to Hungarian audiences at the Tivoli Theater on April 14, 1923.[30] Running 1,448 meters in length, the film headlined a bill that also included an American movie, Fred J. Balshofer's *The Haunted Pajamas* (1917), as well as a series of seven dances performed by Sebastian Droste and the infamous actress and provocateur Anita Berber. These examples of "modern ballet" included *Whipdance*, *Morphium*, *Night of the Borgias*, *Martyrs*, *Vision*, *Cocaine*, and *Astarte*.[31]

Figure 5.7 Paul Askonas in a publicity still for *Drakula halála*.

Though some articles implied that Berber and Droste would appear in person, the Tivoli actually screened *Tänze des Grauens, des Lasters und der Extsase/Dances of Horror, Vices and Ecstasy* (Filmwerke, 1923), a Viennese film of their dances produced between November 1922 and January 1923.

Advance publicity for the Tivoli event published in *Színházi Élet* sheds further light on *Drakula halála*:

> Drakula is the hero of horrible nights, nameless terrors and mysterious glooms. The legendary vampire, whose life was watched by thousands of moviegoers, will return to the cinemas. Károly Lajthay, the German-born excellent director with many amazing productions to his name, adapted the atmospheric and grateful story under the title *Drakula halála* with a new and original style. In his adaptation, Drakula is no mere nightmare, but a living person, who is kept in an insane asylum as an inmate. On Christmas evening, a young girl arrives with her fiancé to the institution, to visit her dying father. It is this place where Drakula meets the girl, his later deadly nemesis. He kidnaps her into his terrifying, decaying castle, and tries to end her in this torturous, horrible place. The groom only gets to the dreadful castle after a series of chilling adventures, where he saves his beloved in the last minute from the deadly kiss. Drakula, whose demonic souls manifested in a human body, repents with the death by a revolver shot for his sins.
>
> The grandiose film with scenes shot among the snowy mountains of Transylvania, will be brought to Budapest by the distributor company of Jenő Tüchten, and the premier will be held at the Tivoli. Beyond the fortunate and interesting plot, the main strength of the movie lies in Margit Lux, the wonderful, young actress, who we haven't seen in an acting role for two years. Drakula is played by Paul Askonas, who is said by German critics to be the greatest actor to play scheming characters. His mask was designed in a competition with a prize worth of half a million forints, on which almost every theatric figurine designer participated. Those who had the fortune to see this mask only spoke of it with infatuation, stating that nothing as mysterious and terrifying could be imagined.[32]

Here is the only known mention of location shooting in Transylvania, as well as of the Drakula "mask." Neither detail comports with other sources and should thus be treated skeptically.

Figure 5.8 Advertisement published in *Mozi és film* on March 23, 1923.

In April 1923, *Budapesti Hírlap* published an article about the film's "grand premiere," explaining that:

> "Variety is the spice of life" – that is the principle of the Tivoli's managers, upheld by creating the most diversified program possible for this Saturday evening. It contains suspenseful sensations to stretch the nerves till the breaking point, light humor to summon laughter and spicy dances to bring dreamlike rapture.
>
> *Drakula halála* is a drama in five acts, adapted to film by Károly Lajthay from the world-famous English novel, with a thrilling, exciting plot . . . Excellent foreign and domestic actors bring this wonderful tale to life. . . .[33]

In yet another example of the contradictions surrounding *Drakula halála*, *Belügyi Közlöny* claimed in 1923 that the film unfolded in four acts, not five.[34] Shortly after the "grand premiere," the *Pesti Hírlap* published a review of the film:

> Premiere fever in real theatres is typical of actors before the first performance. But in cinema, it's typical of the audience. Such feverish interest precedes Saturday's big premiere at the Tivoli, which will satisfy the needs of three different audiences in one evening. The three big attractions will entertain in three different styles. *Drakula halála* makes an impact with its intriguing, exciting plot. This fantastic tale takes the viewer to a demon's castle after the secrets of a madhouse. The seduced girl is saved from the demon by the cross. The demon is afraid of incense smoke. The cross triumphs against the intrigue/insidious. We don't usually give away the tricks of the movies, but in order to keep the nerve-wrecking scenes from hurting the audience, we'll let you in on the secret that half of these scenes are – a dream. But an interesting dream.[35]

Drakula halála next played the Royal-Apollo on April 18 and 19, 1923, and then the Olympia on May 12.[36]

The Olympia booking likely occurred to compete with Murnau's *Nosferatu*, which opened at approximately the same time at Budapest's Royal-Apollo. An advertisement in the April 1, 1923 issue of *Mozi és Film* promoted a "reprise" screening of *Nosferatu*, which in Hungary was titled *Drakula*. The industry publication announced, "Drakula is coming. THE REAL DRAKULA IS NOT DEAD! But he continues his triumph in full health, and appears again . . . at the Royal-Apollo!"[37] *Magyaroszág*'s review of *Nosferatu* told readers:

> At the beginning of this season, a strange film kept the audience in Pest in suspense for weeks: the *Drakula*.
>
> The eccentric realisation of its eerie theme and the novelty of the direction were far from the usual template, *it was different in every sense of the word*.
>
> 'A symphony of horror,' people said, and packed the cinemas to enjoy, shiver and be convinced that the nerve-wracking and the artistically beautiful (aesthetic) had come together in this film.
>
> For those who love *grand guignol* themes: *Drakula* is a real treat, because it is a collection of nerve-wracking scenes. For those who have read the novel before, the strange and peculiar characters are brought to life with startling realism, to capture and hold the viewer's heightened imagination with their mystical fate.[38]

Had a ticket-buyer in Budapest desired, he or she could have viewed both *Nosferatu* and *Drakula halála* on the very same day: May 12, 1923.

Drakula halála made its next appearance at the Uránia Theater on June 20 and 21, 1923.[39] A notice in one newspaper touted the film as a "demon circus."[40] Four years later, in 1927, *Drakula halála* reappeared briefly, playing the Petőfi cinema in Kiskunfélegyháza.[41] Then, in late 1931, *Újság* published an article about Lathjay, calling him an "excellent Hungarian film director from the post-war years," one who produced the "first film version" of Stoker's *Dracula*.[42] It was the only Lathjay movie mentioned by name, probably because of the currency of Browning's *Dracula*.

From there, *Drakula halála* vanishes. No evidence has yet surfaced that it was ever re-released in Hungary, or that it was screened in any other country. Perhaps it was shown under another title, or perhaps not. Regrettably, there are no surviving prints of *Drakula halála*. However, four publicity photographs have surfaced in Hungary. Two of them are portraits: one of Lene Myl, and the other of Askonas as Drakula, clad in black, his eyes glaring, his eyebrows accentuated by makeup, and his dark hair forming a widow's peak on his forehead. What is fascinating is that Lajthay apparently deviated from Stoker's description of Dracula, including his "long white moustache." The clean-shaven Askonas appears none-too-different than Lugosi would in Browning's *Dracula*.

Though it is difficult to glean much information from the two surviving scene stills – and it is certainly dangerous to generalize too much based upon them – they tantalizingly suggest the film bore the influence of German Expressionism, which may not be surprising given the apparent influence that *Caligari* had on the film's script. One of them shows Drakula and Mary Land with his brides; the other shows Drakula peering through a window (or open door, perhaps) at Mary.[43] Both feature some evocative shadows, and the latter depicts an artistically painted flat of a building and dreary sky in the distance. Though certainly not as stylized or exaggerated as *Caligari*, the image creates an eerie and unreal landscape.

Only one other artifact survives that can help us understand the screen's first Dracula: a short novella that acted as something of a "book-of-the-film," one that does not feature a byline. Possibly written by Lajos Pánczél (the editor of *Mozi és Film*, who had been a friend of Bela Lugosi's before Lugosi left Budapest in 1918), the novella *Drakula halála* was copyrighted and published in Temesvár in early 1924.[44] How closely it adapted the film's storyline is unknown, but it was evidently intended to be faithful, as the book opens by discussing the film and offering a list of its cast members. Moreover, it was promoted as "Number 6 in a Series of Film Books." (Pánczél wrote a similar book in Hungarian on Lubitsch's 1919 film *Madame Dubarry/Passion*, and was likely the author of yet another on Chaplin's 1921 film *The Kid*).

Figure 5.9 The cover of the *Drakula halála* novella.

Along with having seen *Drakula halála*, Pánczél had likely read Stoker's novel. Consider the novella's line, "The dim light of the lamp cast strange images around the room, and Mary believed she could see shadows flickering on a white wall." The imagery is not unlike Harker's first view of Dracula in Stoker's novel: "He held in his hand an antique silver lamp, in

Figure 5.10 The title page for the *Drakula halála* novella.

which the flame burned without chimney or globe of any kind, throwing long quivering shadows as it flickered in the draught of the open door."

The full text of the novella *Drakula halála* is reprinted herein, a translation I undertook with Péter Litván. It was originally published in "*Drakula halála* (1921): The Cinema's First Dracula," in *Horror Studies* 1, no. 1 (2010): 25–47.

The Death of Drakula:
A Novella of the Phantasy Film
Likely Written by Lajos Pánczél
Translated by Péter Litván and Gary D. Rhodes

Preface

This mystical story ushers us into the bizarre realm of unrestrained human fantasy. Entering into this stormy night of dreams and magic, we are faced with an ominous tale frightening black shadows, of the dying, and of the living dead . . .

In the midst of this piteous ensemble, there grows a budding, young girl; she is like an oasis in a barren desert wasteland, but unbridled madness savagely threatens her fragile existence. The weak little soul is a helpless captive of fate, which unmercifully forces her into life's raging waters, down its cascades towards impending doom, until – after much suffering – the golden gate opens, and the heroine reaches the shores of a bright and happy future.

This is brief summary of *Drakula*'s enthralling plot, the film version of which is a product of the great Hungarian cinema industry. Written and directed by Károly Lajthay, the film is enacted by the following cast:

Drakula	Paul Askonas
Märy	Margit Lux
George	Dezsö Kertész
The Chief Surgeon	Elemér Thury
The Fake Surgeon	Lajos Réthey
His Assistant	Aladár Ihász
Funny Man	Karl Götz

Also featuring Lajos Szalkay, Károly Hatvani, Oszkár Perczel, Béla Timár, Paula Kende and Lene Myl.

I. The Tragedy of Old Mr. Land

In the midst of some giant mountains covered with everlasting snow could be found a little Alpine village. Here, in majestic silence, far from the bustle of the world, lived little Mary Land, a poor seamstress. Each day in the life of this little lady passed sadly. Mary tried to overcome her loneliness and her heart's endless sorrow by devoting herself to work. She toiled unceasingly, night and day, in order to earn a meager salary, which she used to support her sick father who was kept in the mental asylum in the nearby capital city.

In the poor little house where Mary lived, the sewing machine was forever buzzing; her soft, fragile little fingers were always moving.

Outside of Mary's home, the wintry landscape seemed to gleam with power. Surrounded by snowy mountains, the little village lived its own dreamlike life as if it was a tiny island surrounded by the sea's endless waters. A deep calm enshrouded the village, its peaceful citizens taking a rest from the year's hardships.

Mary's tiny house, where she had been born sixteen years earlier, had once been a home to great happiness. Her parents were wealthy; their home was free of sorrow, filled instead with laughter and joy. However, during a recent spring, Mary's mother fell ill, and not too long afterwards, Death delivered the poor woman from her misery.

Mary's heart bled for her deceased mother, and old Mr. Land's grief was indescribable. The tragedy had such a terrible impact on him that he eventually lost his mind, causing Mary to follow the doctors' advice and have him committed to a mental asylum.

From that time onward, Mary lived a lonely existence in her home at the end of the village. She worked without rest in order to earn a living and pay for her father's care. After two sad years, though she was worn down by hard work, Mary's will power did not weaken. She would have sacrificed her own life to help her father. But regrettably, two years of care in the asylum did not improve old Mr. Land's condition. He lingered inside the asylum like a living corpse. The doctors eventually came to the conclusion that his mental state was beyond repair, that he had mere days to live, and that a quick death would be an act of mercy for such a broken, suffering old man.

Mary visited her father every week, causing Mr. Land's confused eyes to light up, beaming with renewed energy. When he would see his daughter, the old man nearly broke into euphoria: he hugged, kissed, and caressed his only child, because in secret he knew that the end was near and that he would soon have to bid his treasured daughter farewell. For her part, Mary tried to comfort her father, and, even when she was reduced to tears, she tried to remain silent. She bravely endured the painful goodbyes, and neither of them openly admitted that their world would never be the same . . . They beguiled one another . . . Their tearful glances were lies, promising a happy future and the hope of a new life, but deep inside they both heard the sorrowful sound of "Fare-thee-well."

Both of them spent their time yearning for their next encounter, but when they parted, they did so with the terrible feeling in their hearts of those who know, who *feel*, that death is at hand, and that they might see each other never more . . .

II. Mary and George

During those sad, wearisome days, Mary's only comfort was George Marlup, who eventually became her fiancé. He loved her, and his heart brimmed with affection for the blossoming young girl. Though George worked as a woodcutter in the neighboring village, he still called to see Mary every day. Those became her few happy hours . . . It was only then that Mary's heart was freed from sorrow. It was only then that she could forget about her pain and imagine a happy future, one that would make up for all the agony she had suffered.

George devoted himself to Mary with tender love and attention. He also tried to spare his little bride-to-be from exhaustion, warning her that she was too obsessed with work and that it was too much a burden for her sensitive nature. But Mary would not yield; she would not stop working. When George visited her on the holy day of Christmas, he could not believe that she was still working, working as hard as ever.

"Again you have been awake, working all night, my little Mary! Why don't you take better care of yourself? After all, today is a holiday, the holy day of Christmas, and I brought you this little tree. When I come back this evening, we will decorate it together."

"My destiny is labor and self-denial," Mary answered in a solemn voice. "But I am not complaining . . . I have had to deal with my situation in my own way . . . I must keep carrying life's heavy burden."

Then a tear welled in Mary's sad eyes . . . The young man put the little fir-tree on the table, bestowed a kiss on her lips, and departed.

"God be with you, my sweetheart!" George said, turning back to look at her before leaving. "Goodbye!"

* * *

That same night, George returned to his bride-to-be, and together they decorated the fir-tree, a beautiful symbol of peace and love . . . Then they prayed to the Lord in Heaven with their hearts full of gratitude, and as they prayed, they heard the chapel bells in the little village begin to chime, summoning the pious to midnight Mass.

They had already decorated the little fir-tree with many glittering ornaments and candles, which cast a silvery light onto the two lovers. It seemed to create a halo around Mary's golden hair . . .

At that minute, they heard someone mysteriously knocking on the door. George answered it to greet the unexpected visitor, who turned out to be the town's postman, delivering a registered letter for Mary. The maiden hastily opened the envelope:

To Miss Mary Land

We regret to inform you that your father's condition has worsened. You should attempt to visit him as soon as possible.

Yours sincerely,

Municipal Mental Asylum
Dr. Faigner, Head Surgeon,
and Director

Mary's eyes, which had been gleaming with joy, ran wet with tears . . . Although she was well aware and prepared for the fact that her father had limited time, she was still taken aback by the news and tearfully placed her head on George's shoulder.

Then she quickly raised her head and said: "We must not miss the midnight Mass. Let's hurry, George!"

Without saying a word, the young man took his fiancée by the arm. The little chapel's bell was still ringing throughout the village, and its devout citizens were busily making their way to the worship service . . .

Neither Mary nor George would have missed the midnight Mass. The maiden and her fiancé looked to Almighty God, praying from the depth of their hearts that He might prolong old Mr. Land's days . . .

When the service was over, Mary nervously said to her fiancé: "My dear, wonderful father! Who knows whether he will still be alive when I reach the asylum? The next train leaves in the morning . . . I'm scared that I might be too late."

George understood Mary's fears and tried to comfort her: "Not a minute must be lost, Mary! Let me harness the horses, and then we will set out! Dawn will see us arrive at the asylum!"

Quick as it was thought, it was done. George readied the horses and a sleigh, and within a few minutes he was outside Mary's house, ready for departure. With great care, the young man seated the sad maiden in the sled, her own thoughts consumed by worry and fear.

The horses raced along with the lovers in full gallop. The little sleigh boldly glided down the frozen, snowy path, and the fairylike chime of its silver bells echoed throughout the darkness of the night . . .

For hours, heavy, thick snowflakes floated down from the skies . . . It was long after midnight. Worn out by grief, Mary lay down in the sleigh in order to sleep.

* * *

The rising sun was already casting its golden rays when the lovers approached the city. With a few minutes, they reached the gates of the mental asylum. It was morning . . . a crisp, fresh, winter morning. But soon the light of the sun struggled to beam through an increasingly dismal, cloudy sky . . .

Frowning gloomily down at the young couple was an immense, sad, desolate building: the madhouse.

Mary shuddered, "Oh!"

George embraced her tightly and sheltered the fainting maiden in his arms: "What happened, my dear? What is wrong?"

"Every time I arrive at this place, I am nearly overcome. I am reminded that my poor father must live here, his life empty and his mind hardly conscious. Oh, George, what a terrible fate! This house is the realm of the living dead; the most unhappy of men dwell here, and among them is my father! I could never forget the way he was. His wonderful face, his tender look, and the great devotion he had towards me. He raised me with so much love, and yet he's ended up here! Is this the end of his journey?"

George tried to comfort his fiancée, softly explaining: "Be calm, dear. We cannot know the ways of providence, and we must live with God's will, however painful it is. Now be brave. I am confident that your father is still alive."

George's words calmed Mary, and soon the couple reached the door of the madhouse.

Before entering, Mary said: "Thank you, George, for bringing me here. I will return home on the evening train. Goodbye, my sweetheart!"

The lovers parted with a gentle kiss.

"Please do not be late, Mary," George said at last. "God be with you. Goodbye!"

Then the girl entered the house of sorrow. As she nervously walked through its archway, her heart filled with grief and her spirits sank. She was shaking with fear over her father's fate.

Mary anxiously asked the first man that crossed her path: "Could I speak to Doctor Tillner, please?"

As soon as she asked for him, Doctor Tillner appeared. One of the most important doctors at the asylum, Tillner was wearing a white coat, preparing for his morning rounds. By that time, Mary knew Tillner quite well, because her father was a member of his ward.

With her eyes wide open, Mary questioned the doctor: "How is my father? Is he alive? Please doctor, tell me everything!"

Tillner remained silent for a moment, and then he tried to calm down his desperate visitor by saying: "Take comfort, Miss! Death will be salvation for your poor father. Come along and have a look at my patients. What a pitiful life these poor wretches must live!"

III. Humans Reduced to Shadows

With an air of curiosity, Mary followed him. Doctor Tillner ushered her into the garden of the hospital, where so many of the inmates were gathered. They instinctively wanted to be outside on such a bright winter morning, which had a calming effect on their dead nerves and paralyzed spirits.

With scared and troubled eyes, a host of inmates stared at Mary, the unknown and unexpected interloper, as if they were all part of some picturesque panopticon. She kept close to the doctor, because – even though she did recognize a few of the patients from her previous visits – she was scared by the bizarre appearance of them gathered together. Her fear heightened when some of them moved towards her. Their eyes radiated with madness, and their slow steps dragged frail, wrecked bodies towards her as if she was their enemy.

Growing aware of the danger, Doctor Tillner motioned for the patients to withdraw. They moved away, but their gaze revealed a hateful, murderous light.

"Do not be afraid, my dear child," Tillner said, trying to reassure Mary. "They are all innocent people who wouldn't hurt a fly. It is only their appearance that is threatening. They are cowards, who would shrink back at the mere rustle of a leaf."

Mary remained fearful of the poor, death-bound pariahs, and so the doctor continued to speak to her as he approached one of the inmates: "This man here," he said, "was a famous scientist, who now has the belief that his foot is made of glass and prone to break if he steps on it."

Doctor Tillner then pointed out the fact that his feet were wrapped in thick scarves: "Now he believes that he is the Minister of Finance. He constantly doles out checks worth billions to his friends."

Mary observed the thin, haggard man dressed in bizarre clothes; he manically wrote in his notebook and then tore out pages from it, giving them to other inmates who passed his way. Each time he did, his pale face lit up with joy and happiness.

Then she became aware of a tall, gaunt man with bushy hair and a face that resembled Beelzebub. Turning to the doctor, she asked, "Who is this formidable man? He is staring at me as if I am his prey. He virtually swallows me with his eyes, which are ablaze with all the terrible colors of Hell."

"He used to be an excellent composer," Tillner replied. "Now he believes himself to be a ruler. He wouldn't part from his royal cloak even to go to sleep."

"He resembles the organ player who some years ago taught me how to sing," Mary said.

"If you are not afraid, you are certainly welcome to speak to him," the doctor said. "I ask him questions in vain. He will not reply."

IV. Drakula

Encouraged by the doctor, Mary slowly approached the man dressed in the cloak, who gazed upon her with a terrifying smile. Growing more confident among the patients, she asked him: "How are you, master? . . . Don't you remember me? My name is Mary Land . . . Five years ago in the school . . ."

"I don't remember," the horrible man replied. "I do not remember anything. I am Drakula . . . the immortal!"

A wild fire then flared inside the man's heart. In a commanding voice, he exclaimed once again: "Yes! I am Drakula . . . the immortal!"

Mary Land shuddered at the sight of the awful man. She quickly regretted having spoken to him, but continued the conversation: "Try to remember, master . . . I was in the second row . . . I sang soprano, and you often stroked my hair as a token of affection . . . a long time has passed, but I can still remember everything."

The madman shuddered: "I have been alive for a thousand years and I will live forever . . . Mine is immortality . . . Immortality! I possess eternal life . . . People will die, the world will be destroyed, but I will keep living!"

Deeply shaken, Mary shrunk away from Drakula, who continued speaking: "My life is a life eternal! Death will never come for me! Oh, do not believe that I, too, am mad! I stay here only because I love the living dead. I deeply pity them, and I want to gift all of them with life!"

Mary listened nervously to Drakula, the human monster, whose voice sounded like a roar from Hell, and whose deep fiery black eyes glowed with dark flames. Then he towered over fragile little Mary as if he was going to squeeze her to death with one single movement.

Doctor Tillner, who had been watching the scene from a distance, rescued Mary and escorted her back into the hospital. The doctor ushered the girl into an operation room and said to her: "Please, take a seat here while I have a word with the director about giving your father a room of his own."

Mary replied in a trembling voice, "I am so very disturbed by that terrible man dressed in black . . . Drakula."

"Please relax," the doctor told her. "Drakula only looks terrifying. You mustn't be scared of him. Calm down."

Mary nervously sat down in the sterile, white operation room. She was still shuddering. Faced with an irrepressible and unceasing image, her thoughts struggled with Drakula. And while she was waiting, consumed by her thoughts, one of the doors opened and a man who appeared to be a doctor entered quietly.

Mary grabbed at her chair. She was terrified by the stranger's weird looks. Though he wore a doctor's white coat, the man was one of the inmates. He was tall and had a bony face. The madman believed he was a doctor, always wore a doctor's coat, and always arrogantly tried to examine and operate on the other patients.

"I am Professor Wells," he told Mary. "A doctor of universal medicine. If you don't mind, Miss, I will examine you." He then sat down next to her, staring at her with his eyes wide open.

V. The Two Doctors

Mary had no idea that "Professor Wells" was a madman disguised as a doctor, but she instinctively felt that danger was near. She feared, abhorred, and then shrank from this man who gazed her with great intensity.

"Tell me, please, do your eyes not hurt?" the madman said, breaking the silence, and all of a sudden he started to examine her. "My diagnosis is very clear! You are suffering from severe eye disease, Miss," the fake doctor pronounced. "If we do not operate at once, you will go blind!"

Mary was taken aback. Her doubts about the man vanished. She believed him and was convinced that he was indeed a doctor.

At that very moment, the door opened and another man wearing a doctor's coat entered. Professor Wells's face lit up and he said to Mary: "If you don't believe me, ask my colleague," and he pointed to the man who had just entered.

The other pseudo-doctor scrutinized Mary's eyes and produced his diagnosis: "Vulpis doloris! To be operated on without delay!"

Utterly terrified, Mary changed her opinion once more and tried to get away from the two men. But they grabbed the young maiden and threw her onto the operating table. They strapped down her hands and feet. Professor Wells then appeared over her brandishing a surgical knife that he had removed from one of the cupboards. All of this occurred within a few moments.

A terrible shriek then escaped from Mary's throat: "For God's sake . . . Let me go! Help!"

"Be quiet!" one of the fake doctors shouted at her.

"You should be glad that we have chosen to operate on you!" the other madman exclaimed. "You will owe us your life, your eyesight . . . It will take only a minute or two, and then it will be over!"

Mary cried: "No! I won't let you do it! Let me go! Please, let me go!"

But the two madmen, their eyes wildly ablaze, swooped down on the maiden, who was now fighting with all her might. She desperately wanted to escape from the operating table, and while she was struggling, she kept crying: "Help! Help!"

Her words echoed throughout the white operating room, but fate seemed determined to keep her where she was. Like a bird caught in a net, she was helplessly trapped in the claws of the two madmen. As an ominous, cruel silence fell across the room, Mary suddenly quit crying. The two madmen were just about to pierce open her eyes, when Doctor Tillner and his assistants rushed into the operation room, grabbed hold of the madmen, and freed the maiden from her straps.

Mary was lying there, swooning. She didn't recover consciousness for more than an hour. Doctor Tillner watched over her, checking her heavy breath and the convulsions of her body, which was still heavily affected by the terrifying adventure she had experienced. Eventually, she opened her eyes.

"What happened to me?" she asked with a frightened voice, her eyes full of terror. "Have I dreamt an evil dream, or did those awful things actually happen to me?"

The doctor tried to comfort her as best he could. "There is nothing that can hurt you now, little Mary!" he said. "Forget what happened; consider it nothing more than an ugly dream."

"It's so awful to think about!"

"You shouldn't have been in here alone, Mary, but nobody could have guessed that you might attract such strange visitors."

Hoping to banish the terrible memories from her mind, Mary wiped her forehead, and then she left the operation room with Doctor Tillner's help.

Finally Mary went to see her father, who was near death. Though weak, he embraced his daughter. Mary's tears washed down her face . . . then she heard a loud groan . . . the father's outstretched arms lost their strength . . . his bony fingers stiffened . . . his head dropped to one side . . . his confused eyes were forever shut . . .

In tears, Mary held onto her father's corpse. Doctor Tillner raised her and took the sad, shaken young maiden out of the ward. Had his death, and her strange adventure with the two doctors, really happened, or were they simply a dream?

The doctor helped the poor, fainting creature into a little room adjacent to the director's office and laid her on a couch so she could rest. But Mary longed to get away. To run from this house of Hell, where she had suffered so utterly, where the most horrendous memories of her life had been born.

"Away . . . I want to go away . . . to escape . . . My life is threatened here! Let me go!" the frightened little maiden kept crying.

Doctor Tillner was hardly able to keep Mary from fleeing: "In such a terrible state of mind, you cannot leave," the doctor said. "Stay here for the night and have a rest. In the morning you will be fine, and then you can leave for home."

The maiden felt inclined to follow the doctor's kind advice. She lay down on the couch, but said in a frightened voice, "I beg you . . . don't hurt me . . . I haven't done anything." Her eyelids then closed, and she fell asleep.

VI. Drakula's Assault

Mary had been asleep for several hours . . . When the tower clock struck midnight, Drakula appeared in the room like a ghost from Hell. He quietly approached the sleeping girl and then touched her shoulder with his long, bony fingers, which caused Mary to awaken. Taken aback, she looked up at Drakula, whose eyes burned with all the horrendous colors of Hell. A satanic smile formed on his lips before he grabbed the girl and began to drag her across the room.

"Follow me!" he commanded. "We are going to my castle, the home of lust and delight! I want to save you! All of these men here are evil. They want to destroy you just like they destroyed your father!"

Mary listened in terror while Drakula continued: "Flee this Hell! Follow me and trust me. I am immortal, and I possess supernatural powers! Come!"

"No! . . . For God's sake, leave me alone," Mary protested. Then she nervously asked him a flurry of questions: "Who are you? What do you want of me? By what right do you command me to follow you? Where do you want to take me?"

Without responding, Drakula grabbed her and set off for his castle like a whirlwind so that they would reach it before dawn.

Outside, the mysterious veil of night enshrouded the town. Large, soft snowflakes fell to the earth, and this black-and-white panorama created a weird, haunting effect.

The human monster dragged Mary into the night as if she was a helpless puppet . . . Their desperate journey lasted for hours, until they finally reached a strange, enormous building: Drakula's Castle.

Mary shuddered. Shaking in the icy wind, she was completely bewildered by her weird companion. She wanted to escape from Drakula's arms, but the monster was holding her firmly.

"Hah, my dear," he laughed in his satanic voice. "Joy and ecstasy are awaiting you! Why would you try to flee?"

"Let me go! Let me go!"

"You, too, will enter the realm of immortality, the palace of wonders: Drakula's Castle! Do not be afraid; do not shudder! Be happy instead, for bliss is awaiting you! Come!"

And so the young maiden's protests were all in vain. Drakula's power overcame her. Then an immense stone gate creaked open before them. Drakula had reached home with his prey.

Though scared, Mary was curious, and so she looked around in the interior of the palace. Its weird architecture, its phantastic illumination reminded her of the strange realms that appear in fairy tales.

And then she smelled a weird and rank odor in Drakula's castle, the smell of death and decay. And this heavy, suffocating smell nearly intoxicated the mentally broken young maiden.

"But why have you brought me here?" Mary finally asked. "What do you want from me?"

Drakula replied triumphantly: "You will never be able to flee! Tomorrow we will celebrate our engagement! You will be my bride! I will marry you with an immortal kiss, and you will stay here with my other wives, all of whom possess eternal life!"

Then, with a wave of Drakula's hand, the marble floor in the middle of the palace opened. A blue-violet light appeared from below . . . the lush sounds of supernatural music could be heard . . . and twelve beautiful women could be seen, who, with their attractive bodies covered in veils, danced to the rhythm of the soft music . . .

Drakula told Mary: "Before the sun rises twice, you will be among my subterranean residents!"

"No . . . I don't want to be here, not for all the treasures in the world," Mary screamed. Filled with despair, she grabbed the cross hanging around her neck and beseeched God to save her from such horrors.

"Damnation! . . . Hell! . . . The only means by which my power is paralyzed! . . . Away with it!" Drakula shouted after seeing the crucifix.

VII. The Wedding

Soon the palace was lit up by the first light of dawn. As he began to flee, Drakula scowled, "I hate the sunlight! It forces me away. But I shall see you again, tonight!"

Drakula disappeared, and all the gates of the palace closed behind him. Mary was left alone in the mysterious castle, and yet in every corner she could still see Drakula's satanic image grinning at her . . . She wanted to flee from the terrible phantom, but her actions were all in vain . . . Drakula's power prevented her from escaping.

Hours of agony passed . . . Mary helplessly moved around in her prison . . . She dragged her trembling limbs from one room to the next, in search of some relief, but to no avail . . . The horrendous image of Drakula's cruel, grinning face seemed to be everywhere.

Evening was soon at hand . . . Mary ran down into the park of the palace . . . Just as she did, the great gate opened with majesty and Drakula entered . . .

"How kind of you to receive me!" he said to the terrified maiden.

Drakula took Mary by her arm and led her through the palace. He told her: "Go now, and dress for our marriage ceremony."

Drakula then waved to his slave women, who surrounded Mary and led her into a beautiful, flowery room. Inside it was a wedding dress adorned with gold, silver and priceless jewels. The slave women dressed Mary, and when they had finished, Drakula's newest bride was led into the great hall of the palace, where the devil's son was eagerly expecting her.

Drakula approached her, offering her a lustful smile. Deprived of her own will, as if trapped in a dream, Mary yielded to the power of the satanic man.

"You are welcome, my beautiful bride," Drakula flattered Mary. "We are now celebrating a feast of joy, the eve of our nuptials!"

Shrill music was then heard . . . It was the loud, weird music of some devilish wedding march, to which some strangely costumed ballerinas offered a wanton dance. The whole palace was covered in a mystical light . . . Shocking colors interchanged. A flash of colorful light appeared and then faded, only to be followed by the next one. Drakula's engagement feast was luxurious, but strange.

"After the rain of flowers, my kiss will unite us for ever!" the bridegroom said to the bride.

In the wake of these words, thousands and thousands of flowers fell from the ceiling of the palace, like summer rain, covering the floor. Horrible, death-like odors filled the enormous hall. Then, Drakula bent his head towards Mary in order to bestow a kiss onto her lips. His mouth trembled from wild desire, and he opened his arms to embrace her.

But at that very moment Mary pushed Drakula away, reached for the cross hanging around her neck, and bravely revealed it to him, her eyes flashing as she did.

"The cross! . . . The cross!" Drakula roared, shrinking back from the girl in terror.

At the sight of the crucifix, the entire hall was seized with panic . . . Drakula and all of the other evil spirits fled. Mary seized her opportunity. She rushed through the castle gate and into the snowy night.

VIII. Down the Path of Death

Mary fled from Drakula and the palace of Hell, but her tired legs could not take her very far. Fainting, she fell on some snowy ground beside a tree trunk; the rays of dawn were just starting to shine upon her. Later that same morning, a nice family discovered her and took her back to their house so she could rest. But they were unable to revive her.

Mary Land was unconscious, though a fever had taken control of her mind. She was tormented by cruel, gruesome images. Drakula's hellish face never ceased grinning at her. His eerie eyes, his satanic features, and his terrible hands seemed always ready to possess her. Those images danced in front of her unconscious eyes.

"No . . . no . . . Don't hurt me!" Sometimes a word or two escaped from between her parched lips, causing Mary's rescuers to watch her with great sympathy.

"We must call a doctor," the head of the household decided. "We won't learn anything from her until she regains consciousness. There might be information we need to know before then." His younger brother then journeyed into the town to call a doctor.

All the while, Mary's agony persisted. She was tormented by nightmares that seemed as if they might destroy her. The family covered her burning forehead and face with snow in an effort to help ease her fever.

Hours later, the room was almost silent. Only poor Mary's panting could be heard. But the quiet was broken when the door opened unexpectedly. Mary's rescuers saw a visitor clad in black standing at the threshold. It was Drakula. The devilish creature made the family shudder in fear.

Outside the wind was howling and thrashing snow into the room. Without saying a word, Drakula closed the door behind him and quietly approached Mary. He paid no attention to the family members staring with wonder at his appearance.

"I am here because she requires medical help. Nothing else is more important," Drakula informed the onlookers.

"But who sent you?" the head of the household asked. "How did you know to come here? My brother has left to get a doctor from the town."

Drakula chose not to answer. Instead, he approached the still-unconscious Mary, looked at her briefly, and then said: "This young maiden is insane and must have escaped from a mental asylum. She must be removed from here as soon as possible, since she is a threat to herself and those around her."

Those standing nearby fell under the spell of Drakula's powerful words. An awkward silence followed. Drakula's blazing eyes hypnotized the family, who helplessly suffered as a result. Then it seemed as if he would never remove his violet, flashing eyes from Mary's poor body, which had become more and more disturbed since Drakula's arrival.

"Don't surrender me! Rescue me! Help . . . ! He is killing me!" she screamed, trapped in a state of extreme terror. Then Drakula displayed once again his cruel, hellish smile.

With his arms crossed, he stood beside Mary, while the horrified family watched.

Meanwhile the head of the household's brother arrived with a real doctor from the town.

"This doctor considers the young woman to be a dangerous maniac," the head of the household said to the new doctor.

After examining Mary, the real doctor turned to Drakula and said: "You seem to be wrong, dear colleague. All I can perceive are wounds . . . and a fever." Then he proceeded to say: "This seems to be quite an extraordinary case! Whatever it is, I will remain here, in order to watch over her."

Disgusted by the real doctor's words, Drakula immediately disappeared from the house.

* * *

Days passed . . . Mary struggled to regain her health, and after a week had gone by, she was in much better form. She was cheerful again, as if nothing had happened. In fact, she could hardly recall the horrible events that had transpired. She just felt as if she had awoken from a terrible nightmare, but one that she could hardly really remember. The family continued to watch over Mary as if she was one of their own relatives.

One day, after examining the little patient, the doctor happily announced: "Mary is definitely getting better. Soon she will be fully recovered!"

IX. A Cruel Night

One night, when everyone in the household was sitting together, a man arrived at their door. "You have been requested," he said to the surgeon. "Somebody has had an accident at the sports field! They are waiting for you!"

"Who are you?" the doctor inquired.

"I am a coachman," man replied. "It is me who takes the hotel guests to the train and back."

"But it is pitch dark outside," the doctor said with a concerned voice.

"You needn't be afraid, doctor! I know the road by heart, and my horse is very reliable," the coachman said reassuringly.

The doctor understood his duty and left with the coachman. He promised Mary and the others that he would return as soon as he had finished his work.

Outside the sky was pitch black and a heavy fog blanketed the landscape. The snow crunched under the two men's steps. The doctor took a seat inside the little carriage, the coachman sat on the box, lashed the horses, and the wooden frame was set into motion.

The doctor turned back to look behind them. The bright window of the nice little house became an increasingly distant image as the carriage moved forward through the white snow.

The coachman drove faster and faster; the carriage seemed to fly on wings, as the road it travelled over could not be seen. The blackness of night and the thick fog seemed to hide everything. As he smoked his cigar during the long journey, the doctor thought about Mary, and he rejoiced in the fact that he helped the blossoming young woman regain her life.

The carriage continued its journey, faster and faster, and the sound of the horses suggested a hint of life in the otherwise desolate and mysterious night. After a quarter of an hour had passed, the doctor asked the coachman, "What are you actually headed for?"

Perhaps the question escaped the coachman's attention, or perhaps he chose not to hear it, as he kept silent and continued to drive the horses.

The doctor was puzzled and so he asked even more loudly: "Where are you heading for? Where are you taking me? Stop!" But this call, too, was lost in the night. The doctor then felt his pockets; he had no weapon. He was aware now that his guide was part of some cruel plan.

However, the doctor did not lose faith. Encouraged by a sense of urgency and danger, the doctor once again raised his voice: "Tell me, will you, where you are taking me? What is our destination?"

At that very moment, the little carriage reached a hazardous stretch of road that ran alongside a deep abyss . . . Even a slight landslide would cause the carriage to fall to its doom.

Realizing the risk they faced, the coachman admitted: "A strange man clad in black gave me a gold coin and ordered me to bring you here, doctor."

"You miserable man! Turn back at once!" the doctor said. "Our lives are in danger!"

The graveness of the situation and the doctor's warning did not fail to have an effect on the coachman who had been bribed by Drakula. He cautiously turned the carriage around and took his passenger back to the home where Mary now resided.

On the return journey, the doctor questioned the coachman further, but he was unable to give anything more than a vague description of his employer. Nonetheless, his information was enough for the doctor to realize that the man who bribed the coachman was the same "doctor" that he had met at Mary's sick bed. That man had suggested that Mary should go to a mental institute as a ruse to kidnap her. But all of this information was of limited help, since the doctor did not know where the mysterious stranger lived.

Meanwhile, the family's house was enshrouded by the deep silence of the night. The whole family was asleep; only little Mary was restless . . . At about midnight, Mary awoke to an odd, frightening sound . . . It was as if she heard the ghostlike wail of an owl . . . Her entire body shuddered . . . She looked around in the half-lit gloom of the house . . . Her eyes turned towards a dim lamp . . . She looked for the source of the mysterious sounds, but she saw nothing. Mary then sank back to her bed and tried to sleep.

The wind outside howled viciously, and so Mary was unable to close her eyes. The dim light of the lamp cast strange images around the room, and Mary believed she could see shadows flickering on a white wall.

Drakula invaded her thoughts . . .

The kind family and the good doctor had helped her forget about the horrors of the past: its terrible memory had grown distant, but this horrible night brought it back to the forefront of her mind.

"To-whoo . . . To-whoo . . . To-whoo . . . " Mary heard the hoots of an owl, but she did not know whether she really heard it or if it was just another delusion . . . And the dark shadows kept creeping around the room. Sweat beaded her forehead; her body was burning with fever. Overcome with distress and terror, she tossed around in her bed.

Mary desperately tried to forget everything, keeping her eyes closed in stubborn determination and pushing her head into the pillows. She wanted sleep, nothing but sleep. Her lips murmured prayers, beseeching God to grant her a deep and restful sleep.

But try as she might, her eyes did not close. On the contrary, no matter how hard she tried, her eyelids remained open. "My God . . . don't leave me!" she whispered, feeling that her fate was about to reach a terrible turning point.

Outside the wind howled more horribly than ever. It caused the windows to shake with a vengeance. Mary felt she could hear countless cries echoed in the roaring wind.

The minutes passed slowly, which weighed on the poor maiden as if they were hours.

When Mary looked once again into the vanishing lamplight, it crashed down onto the floor, flames erupting in its wake, setting the carpet on fire and spreading across the little room. Jumping out of her bed, Mary fled from the sea of fire into the cold winter night . . .

As if pursued by something, she ran and ran through night . . . She didn't feel the cold of the snow or the lashes of the icy wind. She just ran and ran and ran . . .

X. The Devil Has Flown Away

At last the terrible nightmare ended.

Mary woke up and, with her frightened eyes, she looked around the operating room, where the snow-white furnishings and the operating table were reminiscent of death. They had a ghastly effect on the poor creature, who had just been freed from her terrible dream . . .

The red rays of the rising sun appeared. Nature was waking up, and the hospital, too, with its wretched patients, was also coming to life. Looking worried, Mary ran across the room. She raised her frail hand to stroke her forehead.

Shuddering, she remembered her awful experiences, but her soul cheered up at the thought that they had only been a dream.

But then a terrible fear gripped her, and Mary began to worry once more. Since she had entered the madhouse, so many bizarre things had happened:

the incident in the operating room and the cruel nightmare that seemed so real. Her nerves began jumping, and her heart was beating heavily. Then she heard a horrible sound that seemed to come from the asylum's garden.

Remembering her poor father, who had lost his mind, Mary grew worried. The icy hand of suspicion crept across her body. "What if . . . what if . . . if I too . . . ?" she shuddered.

At that moment, the door of the room began to creak open, but Mary wasn't strong enough to look at who entered.

* * *

Doctor Tillner's morning rounds brought him to the operation room. Mary was still lying on the couch. Her eyes were open, but she was too weak to get up. The nurse standing beside her approached the doctor.

"She must have had very horrible dreams. She was crying out all night," the nurse explained.

Doctor Tillner tenderly held the maiden, who was still shaking with fear and distress and looking about the room, still in tremor from the satanic Drakula . . .

"What is it . . . what happened to me?" Mary nervously asked the doctor. "Am I awake . . . or I am still trapped in that awful nightmare?"

"Calm down, my dear," Tillner said to her. "It was just a dream; please try to forget about it."

XI. Drakula's Death

The mental patients had already gathered in the garden of the asylum. They continued with their strange habits. The scientist feared for his "glass leg," the "Minister of Finance" doled out checks, and Drakula, the one-time composer, gave a speech about his immortality to a group of patients who quickly grew bored with him.

Among these living dead stood a heavyset little man who wore a tall, pointed top hat. A pair of enormous spectacles weighed down his thick nose. His old, parchment-colored face displayed a permanent smile, as if he was forever caught in a distorted laugh. He never ceased making strange jokes and was always kidding his companions. He liked to fool the others, though they were long used to his ways.

This morning, the "Funny Man," as he was nicknamed, had somehow discovered a loaded revolver, which he began pointing at his panicked companions. The armed madman then appeared before Drakula, pointed his gun at him, and laughed with that distorted grin.

Drakula nearly erupted with joy, telling the Funny Man: "At last I can prove that I am immortal! Shoot!"

Drakula's voice boomed throughout the garden, causing the other patients to gather around them.

Drakula then thundered: "What are you waiting for, you cowardly mongrel! All of you have always stared at me like fools, not believing in my immortality. Now, come here all of you, gather around and witness the truth! Drakula is safe from your bullets; they will not penetrate my body. Drakula is immortal! Hahaha! Come . . . here . . . all of you! And you . . ., raise your revolver!"

The Funny Man nervously began to back away from Drakula.

"No . . . I dare not do it . . . I dare not do it!" – he said, slowly lowering the revolver.

"So you are afraid? You coward! Shoot, as I command you to do! Here – aim at my chest!" Drakula shouted.

The terrified group that surrounded the two madmen surveyed the scene with heightened interest. Then, obeying his stern command, the Funny Man cocked the trigger of his pistol and fired . . .

The bullet hit Drakula in the heart and killed him at once. His blood poured forth, staining the fresh snow with the color red.

After the gun was fired, the terror-stricken patients scattered throughout the garden. Within moments, Doctor Tillner and his assistants stood beside Drakula's body.

"Drakula is dead," one of the assistants told the doctor after examining him. "The Funny Man has killed him with a stolen gun."

At the sight of his gruesome deed, the mad murderer was at first seized with panic, but soon he began giggling once again. While the assistants tied him up and took him back to his cell, the Funny Man's face grew even more disfigured by his insane laughter.

XII. Down the Road of Love

A sleigh stopped in front of the madhouse. It was George, Mary's fiancé, who climbed out of it. After having waited in vain for his bride-to-be the previous night, he had rushed to the city, in order to find her and take her back home.

Overjoyed at the sight of George, Mary ran up to him, fell into his arms, and then the two lovers shared a long kiss . . .

"Thanks God," the young man said with the sound of relief and happiness in his voice. "At last we are reunited . . . I was so worried . . . so anxious that something might have happened to you! . . . But please tell me, why didn't you come back last night? What kept you?"

A flood of questions poured out of George's lips, but Mary did not have the time or desire to answer them: Doctor Tillner was approaching. He bid the young couple farewell, and they set out across the garden to leave the hospital. As they were walking arm in arm, they came across two assistants who were carrying Drakula's corpse on a stretcher. When the procession passed in front of her, Mary caught sight of Drakula's formidable face, which caused her even more fright than when he was alive. Nearly fainting, she drew close to George. Not knowing about her horrible dream, George was puzzled by her reaction.

The assistants carried Drakula away. As they did, a notebook dropped out of his pocket. George picked it up and examined the cover:

A DIARY OF MY IMMORTAL LIFE
AND OF MY ADVENTURES
– DRAKULA

Glimpsing the title and growing even more frightened, Mary demanded: "Throw it away at once! I don't want to look at it! This man was the cause of my terrible dream!"

George followed her wishes. He threw the diary away, took Mary by the arm, and then helped her into his sleigh. Its little wooden frame then carried the lovers back home, back to happiness and to bliss.

During the journey, George repeatedly tried to get Mary to talk, but her lips remained sealed. She did not tell him a single word about the agony she had suffered because of the terrible dream. George would not learn what had happened. Realizing she wished to remain quiet, he never spoke about it again.

The End

Translation copyright © Gary D. Rhodes, 2009

Notes

1. For more information, see Kurt W. Treptow, *Vlad III Dracula: The Life and Times of the Historical Dracula* (Las Vegas: Center for Romanian Studies, 2020).
2. See, for example, Jenő Farkas, "Nosferatu Előtt: A Magyar Drakula," *Filmvilág*, December 1997, accessed September 15, 2018, http://www.filmvilag.hu/xista_frame.php?cikk_id=1714. I would note that all modern scholarship has been greatly assisted by the hard work and research of Gyöngyi Balogh at the Hungarian Film Institute in Budapest.
3. Ron Borst, "The Vampire Film in the Cinema: Additions and Corrections," *Photon*, no. 21 (1971): 25.

4. Forrest J Ackerman, *Mr. Monster's Movie Gold* (Virginia Beach, VA: Donning, 1981).
5. It is worth noting that Margit Lux appeared in both *Lidércnyomás* (1920) and *Drakula halála* (1921).
6. Gary D. Rhodes, "*Drakula halála* (1921): The Cinema's First Dracula," *Horror Studies* 1, no. 1 (2010): 25–47. My original article also appeared as a chapter in Olaf Brill and Gary D. Rhodes, *Expressionism in the Cinema* (Edinburgh: Edinburgh University Press, 2016).
7. "*Drakula*–Károly Lajthay's Latest Film," *Képes Mozivilág*, January 16, 1921, 21.
8. The *Budapesti Hírlap* serialized Stoker's *Dracula* from January 1, 1898 to March 29, 1898.
9. Gary D. Rhodes and Bill Kaffenberger, *Becoming Dracula: The Early Years of Bela Lugosi, volume I* (Orlando, FL: BearManor Media, 2020), 68–9.
10. "Lajthay, Károly," *Képes Mozivilág*, February 6, 1921, 10.
11. I am very grateful to Gyöngyi Balogh for this information.
12. "Hungarian Film Directors in Vienna," *Színházi Élet*, no. 52, 1920.
13. "Lajthay, Károly," *Képes Mozivilág*, January 9, 1921, 21.
14. Advertisement, *Arbeiter - Zeitung* (Vienna, Austria), September 3, 1920, 8; advertisement, *Pesti Hírlap* (Budapest, Hungary), March 12, 1921.
15. This quotation stems from the *Drakula halála* novella reproduced in this chapter.
16. "Lajthay, Károly," 21.
17. Ibid., 21.
18. "Margit Lux Has Returned from the Netherlands," *Képes Mozivilág*, March 23, 1920, 9.
19. "*Drakula* – Károly Lajthay's Latest Film," 21.
20. It should be noted that *Képes Mozivilág* never actually said that Myl would portray Mary Land. Rather, the publication claimed that she would play the "heroine."
21. "I Attended a Wedding," *Színház és Mozi*, January 1921, 26–7.
22. Anna Marie Hegener and Magda Sonya might well have portrayed Drakula's other brides; both are named in the article "Hungarian Film Directors in Vienna."
23. "Lux, Margit," *Képes Mozivilág*, December 25, 1921, 22.
24. Ibid., 26–7. (In this publication, Lajthay notes that he "completed external shots last month," meaning December 1920, "near Vienna." The article "Hungarian Film Directors in Vienna" was more specific, quoting Lajthay about shooting in Melk. However, in "*Drakula* – Károly Lajthay's Latest Film," *Képes Mozivilág* reported that – following the interiors at the Corvin Film Studio – Lajthay would "resume the external shots in the Wachau near Vienna" (21).)
25. "I Attended a Wedding," 27.
26. "Hungarian Film Directors in Vienna."
27. "I Attended a Wedding," 26–7.
28. Gary D. Rhodes, *Tod Browning's Dracula* (Sheffield: Tomahawk Press, 2014), 227, 231, 233, 235.

29. "The Elaborate Plans of Károly Lajthay," *Képes Mozivilág*, November 5, 1922.
30. "Calendar of Events," *Mozie és Film*, April 1923, 23.
31. "Nagy premier a Tivoliban," *Budapesti Hirlap*, April 28, 1923, 5.
32. "Akinek halálára mindenki kiváncsi . . . ," *Színházi Élet*, March 25, 1923.
33. "Nagy premier a Tivoliban," 5. This same article appeared in the newspapers *8 Orai Újság* (April 28, 1923) and *Világ* (April 28, 1923).
34. Untitled, *Belügyi Közlöny*, March 25, 1923, 396.
35. "A Tivoli mai nagy premierje," *Pesti Hírlap*, April 28, 1923, 7.
36. "Színház," *Egyetérés*, April 18, 1923, 2.
37. Advertisement, *Mozi és Film* April 1, 1923, 4.
38. "Mozi," *Magyaroszág*, May 13, 1923, 11.
39. "Színház," *Magyar Jovő*, June 19, 1923, 3.
40. Untitled, *Reggeli Hírlap*, June 12, 1923, 6.
41. "Fényes ünnepi előadások a Petőfi moziban," *Csonka Magyarság*, August 14, 1927, 3.
42. "Lathjay Károly Budapesten," *Újság*, October 15, 1931, 9.
43. Neither image of Askonas as Drakula suggests that he is wearing a mask, as *Színházi Élet* implied.
44. Untitled, *Friss Hírek*, January 5, 1923, 3. Pánczél edited the "Series of Film Books," but it is possible that someone else wrote *Drakula halála*.

CHAPTER 6

Nosferatu, eine Symphonie des Grauens

"And as softly thou art sleeping
To thee shall I come creeping
And thy life's blood drain away."[1]
— Heinrich August Ossenfelder
Der Vampir, 1748

"You witches and ghosts,
Close cheerfully the circle,
Soon our master will be here with us!"[2]
— Heinrich Marschner
Der Vampyr, 1828

Given the many fascinating qualities that Dracula possesses, we may well forget his memory, meaning his ability to remember, and he does have such a very long history, he and his forebears, as he explains to Harker in Bram Stoker's 1897 novel:

> We Szekelys have a right to be proud, for in our veins flows the blood of many brave races who fought as the lion fights, for lordship . . . What devil or what witch was ever so great as Attila, whose blood is in these veins? . . . Ah, young sir, the Szekelys – and the Dracula as their heart's blood, their brains, and their swords – can boast a record that mushroom growths like the Hapsburgs and the Romanoffs can never reach.

Dracula has other memories as well, including memories of love, as he reminds his trio of brides after interrupting their lustful attack on Harker: "[Y]ou yourselves can tell it from the past. Is it not so?"

By contrast, in E. Elias Merhige's *Shadow of the Vampire* (Lions Gate, 2000), Max Schreck (Willem Dafoe), who plays Graf Orlok, has an extremely poor memory. He cannot recall when he became a vampire or where he was born. One character chides him, complaining, "Count Dracula wouldn't say he couldn't remember." But Schreck/Orlok must

Figure 6.1 Albin Grau's publicity artwork for F. W. Murnau's *Nosferatu, eine Symphonie des Grauens/Nosferatu, a Symphony of Horror* (Prana-Film, 1922).

say it. He is ancient, so very ancient, that his memory has faded. Is it possible to conceive of a time before he existed? Such is difficult for him as well as for us. Might we recall the date of his birth, even if he is unable? Let us reconstruct that night, for it was indeed at night, when Orlok's symphony of horror was first heard in Germany, when he first cast his shadow on a Berlin theater screen, when not a single scratch appeared on a pristine print that advanced through a film projector, its teeth sinking into *Nosferatu*'s sprocket holes with each turn of the take-up reel.

The most accurate and detailed of memories would necessarily recall that F. W. Murnau's *Nosferatu* made its screen debut in The Netherlands in February 1922. But its formal premiere came in Berlin on March 4, 1922, as part of an elaborate "Fest des Nosferatu/Festival of Nosferatu," named not for the film title, but for the vampire himself, as if he was the master of ceremonies. Ads excitedly and wrongly claimed that night would mark *Nosferatu*'s first public exhibition. And so that night represents our *memento vampiri*, an unforgettably forgotten event, one that separates history before and after Orlok's arrival, a momentous occasion, even for a German cinema that had broached the supernatural time and again, from Stellan Rye's *Student von Prag/The Student of Prague* (Deutsche Bioscop, 1913) and Paul Wegener and Henrik Galeen's *Der Golem* (Deutsche Bioscop, 1915) to Richard Oswald's *Unheimliche Geschichten/Eerie Tales* (Richard Oswald-Film AG, 1919) and Robert Wiene's *Das Cabinet des Dr. Caligari/The Cabinet of Dr. Caligari* (Decla-Film, 1920).

To consider how new *Nosferatu* was, let us begin with the following text from a writer in 1922 who pondered the very meaning of occult cinema:

> My publisher deigned to assign me an editorial on the occult, I said to myself. A command is a command, and every assignment must be carried out (my intuition has preserved this attitude from my bygone days in the military). It was, however, much easier said than done. When I asked my publisher what the general content of the editorial should be, he replied, "Write about occult films and such, you know what I mean."
>
> When someone says to me, "You know what I mean," then I am totally disarmed, as nothing in the world could make me ask further in order not to embarrass myself or to ruin the good reputation others have of me. Now good advice was at a premium and I didn't have the slightest clue as to what an occult film is. What could I do? Admit my ignorance openly? Never!
>
> ... I had a good idea. From my time in grammar school, I still had a Latin dictionary that might be able to help me. And I really found one aid there: "occultus," secret, hidden, dark. This was at least *something*, but at the moment, I could not imagine a "secret film" or a hidden one let alone a dark film, but why had one seen so many detective films? A veritable treasure-trove of films like those of Joe Deebs one had to have under one's belt! "Hidden secretively" put me on the trail of "backstair novels" [i.e. "whodunits"] for which our "hired girl" is responsible. So, I asked her what an occult film could be. She looked at me surprised and said she didn't know. I was shocked at her lack of knowledge and decided at that moment that she be fired as quickly as possible, as I cannot stand such uninformed hired help. When I told her she was fired, she began to cry and stammered and sobbed as she told me about her last time in a movie theater. It was a sing-song film with scenes, and she could not understand a single word of it, but she thought that might have been an occult film. "You dumb thing," I said to her, "what you saw was also a somewhat dark film, but we call such a thing *film operetta*."
>
> After this unsuccessful attempt, I decided to go on the search for an occult film myself.

In a suburban movie theater I was familiar with ... where I was once a regular customer. A film starring Bruno Kastner was announced with great fanfare. The film posters were appropriately terrifying. I went to the film, hoping I would find there what I was looking for. Bruno Kastner had nothing but problems with his gang of roguish criminals for 5 reels and the whole time he wore an imposing armadillo coat. After the fourth reel, I asked the usher as politely and shyly as I could if this was an occult film. The gentleman evidently misunderstood my question, because he pointed to a location with his finger and said, "Over there in the corner to the left, the small door."

I was desperate. Finally, I found the courage to telephone my small, blonde, sweetheart on Flimmer Street, with whom I had been arguing continually for the last 3 weeks, but she let me know through her maid that until I had paid her beauty parlor bill, she would not speak with me. On the corner of Flimmer Street I literally ran into a colleague of mine from the trade press, and I asked him, because he of all people must know what occultism in film is. I also told him what I had found out from my Latin dictionary. He told me right away, that it has something to do with Decla, the term is probably connected with that film company, because they do all sorts of "dark" films [such as *The Cabinet of Dr. Caligari*]. No sooner had he said this than he left me standing there. I noticed that he probably wanted to make a fool out of me.

Totally desperate, I even wanted to send my publisher a registered letter (our correspondence was always conducted by registered letter) and ask him to fire me immediately without notice, since I was not up to such exotic topics as an editorial about occultism in films. My eyes landed quite by accident on an edition of *Film Tribune* that I had always wanted to read. There I found an announcement in giant letters: "*Nosferatu*, the great occult film." Reconciled with my skill, I dashed for a telephone, called Studio Director, Mr. Enrico Dieckmann [who produced *Nosferatu*], and I knew immediately that I would finally understand what an occult film is.

But if you believe, dear readers, that I will now disclose to you what it is, you are mistaken, because now I am just as nasty as those who were nasty to me. Find out for yourselves![3]

Yes, we needed to find out for ourselves, his advice deserving its exclamation point. We needed to attend the Festival of Nosferatu, to join the cult of the occult, to see the dark film in the darkness of a theater.

Figure 6.2 Published in *8 Uhr-Abendblatt* on February 28, 1922.

As we awaited the premiere, another writer helped us prepare for it, a writer who did not withhold his knowledge. A journalist for *Der Neue Film* provided something of a codex for understanding *Nosferatu*:

> We lose all sense of destiny in the horrors of everyday life, because it dissipates in the innumerable details like daily life itself. Insignificant and often irrelevant events determine our lives, and, when we are confronted with such things, we say helplessly: "Coincidence." We label everything "coincidences" that remain inexplicable in the mechanical course of our destinies. We make do with this inexplicability, because we do not dare to give into the hidden connections that in a moment of distress flare up at a moment's notice. What forces are at work below the surface [of our consciousness] – virtually an underworld of our physical life that we can only suspect with terror – we sense this as something hostile. This causes the belief in the occult to appear in reality to humans who believe in destiny. Hidden powers rule over our lives against our free will, and mirror our sins that we commit daily and repeatedly. Whether this "coincidence" is a symbol of this power, which reveals itself in the most banal of personal experiences that we do not sense; whether this is a symbol of a truly existent power; or whether it is only a torturous, fear-mongering fantasy lodged in our subconscious, it exists almost beyond the avowal of the occult.
>
> For a grand, general search takes place in humanity and each human being contributes to this search in most cases subconsciously: We feel with outstretched hands as if we were blind for a goal through the labyrinth of our individual destinies. We sense that there must be something that will transport us out of our daily suffering and bring us to a higher level of life.
>
> What was handed down by the mountain dwellers of the Carpathians as the saga of *Nosferatu* represented the symbol of terror and the cause of their numbing horror. This was surely no localized phenomenon. The Vampire Nosferatu, a blood-sucker, was born of the original sin of mankind, cannot just be the personification of terror in the wild mountain terrain and was not conjured up by the thousands of primitive ethnic groups living there. The terrifying aspect in the form of this vampire is that it is too generally applicable and too rooted in folk traditions to be a creation of primitive, superstitious peasants. Here we experience as a single destiny and as the apparently indigenous saga of Nosferatu the nightmare, the perpetual torture of our existence, and leads to the battle for resolution [of the problem] of *Nosferatu*, the deepest, most religious purity of humanity which is at once loaded with feelings of guilt but also ready for revenge.[4]

The article continued by suggesting that we perceive "the saga of *Nosferatu* in the framework of a single destiny, [and] the film interprets this for us as a contemporary mode of expression." Rather than seeming so very old, *Nosferatu* was indeed a contemporary film, a new movie for those who attended its premiere. Let us now attempt to recreate that special event.

As Berliners living in 1922, we might or might not have understood the meaning of the term "Nosferatu," but we could well have grasped the story's source material. Advance publicity made no secret that writer Henrik Galeen adapted Stoker's *Dracula*, a fact that several journalists reported.

"It is said that the film is based on 'motifs' from the novel *Dracula*," one of them observed.[5] Another reported, "The film *Nosferatu* has been freely adapted by Henrik Galeen from elements in the novel *Dracula*."[6] Yet a third added, "Galeen was inspired by the English occultist novel *Dracula*."[7] Here was a vampire film, a supernatural vampire film, unlike the vamps or vampiric criminals we had seen in prior years, one that was based on a novel well-known in Berlin, one featuring a character long understood in Germany, including in Marschner's opera *Der Vampyr*.

Figure 6.3 Published in *BZ am Mittag* on March 3, 1922.

If we had not known the term "Nosferatu," we knew it now. We read it repeatedly in the days leading to the premiere. The Berlin correspondent for *Variety* described the ballyhoo as "one of the most expensive publicity campaigns yet waged in Berlin for the showing of a single feature."[8] Prana-Film even hired airships to promote *Nosferatu*. Advertisements were everywhere, it seemed, not just in film trades, but also in newspapers. On February 27, 1922, *BZ am Mittag* featured several ads for the film on the same page, their content ranging from "The Prana and the Festival" to "The party will be big!"[9]

Another ad told us to obtain tickets to the Festival, worded as an order rather than a request, one punctuated with an exclamation point. To obtain tickets was possible, but perhaps not easy or cheap. As of March 1, the *Berliner Börsen-Zeitung* informed readers that the event was "still accessible to the public, although the demand for entry tickets is immensely strong."[10] Of course important persons in the film business and in the press received complimentary tickets. When Prana-Film sent invitations to reporters asking them to visit the set of *Nosferatu* in 1921, the envelopes featured "crooked" Expressionist handwriting.[11] Perhaps complimentary tickets to the Festival did as well.

Figure 6.4 The cover of *Tanz und Welt* celebrated the Berlin premiere of *Nosferatu*. (Courtesy of Kantonsbibliothek Appenzell Ausserrhoden Ausserrhoden (CH), CMO-59-01-D-17-01-03-02.)

In celebration of the premiere, the publication *Tanz und Welt* featured pages of publicity, its cover photo depicting Hutter (Gustav von Wangenheim) and Ellen (Greta Schröder). Interior text provided more information than probably any other publication:

One of the most well-known film companies, Prana, has earned recognition for having brought *Nosferatu* to the screen. It is the first film production of this company. The assignment to accommodate the public's desire for films dealing with the theme of occultism has been magnificently accomplished. To create the fantastic film *Nosferatu* required the cumulative energy of the General Director of Prana, Enrico Dieckmann, and set designer Albin Grau. Enrico Dieckmann is German and was born in the country, where oranges grow, with that instinct for beauty and understanding of art that is the heritage of one with an Italian heritage. He brought these to the collaborative artistic creativity to the competence and technical skills of Albin Grau to create the film *Nosferatu*. But both of them knew that even the finest film can only be crowned with success, when the appropriate marketing is in place: true American film marketing verifies the magnificent organizational talents of both of these men . . . In spite of the ominous theme that extends through the entire film, we also see a series of serene scenes. The audience feels no trepidation or anxiety when the curtain falls after the final reel.[12]

Tanz und Welt concluded with a discussion of the film's purpose and artistic value. While the article's author is unknown, it is possible Albin Grau wrote these words:

> The work of art always remains as the completed film viewed in this entirety. As is the case in every art form, the film demands techniques without which there is no work of art. Every work of art requires a form that is unthinkable without the mastery of specific techniques.
>
> The cinematographer is the inspired "scribe of life." Where the embryos of life become apparent, his mission begins, and where life is extinguished, the expressions of his characters are lost.
>
> Usually we understand life as movement: the movement of the masses, of atoms, of the earth, of the universe. The cinematographer realistically reflects our existence. We recognize ourselves, nature, everything that lives around us in the photography that pleases us in this game. There can be no doubt that German film art took a massive step forward with the Prana film *Nosferatu* and at the same time could meet the highest [artistic] demands, when [these demands] are mastered by skillful hands that have all necessary materials at their disposal appropriate for the film they are to serve.
>
> What is singularly sensational about this film is the successful attempt to project outwards an internal, formless event that comes with daring to give effective, gigantic expression to a dream deeply rooted in folk tradition and life itself – so deep in fact that it can exist as a reflection of our childhood imagination. This film is life materialized from our subconscious. It will start a triumphal march through the entire world.[13]

The march began at the Festival of Nosferatu on March 4, 1922, and so with our tickets, at long last we set out for the Marmorsaal Theater at the Zoological Garden. *Der Kinematograph* told readers the Festival represented the "grandest style."[14]

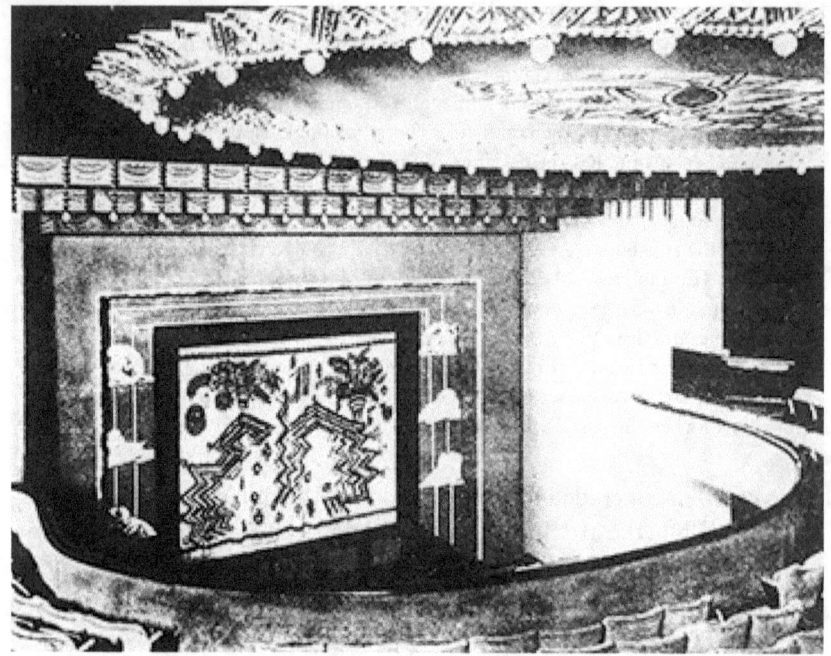

Figure 6.5 The Marmorsaal Theater in Berlin, as photographed c.1910. (Courtesy of the Deutsche Kinemathek.)

Why the Marmorsaal? It featured beautiful, elaborate, modernist architecture, with a white-grey Silesian marble facade covering its five floors. The theater inside the complex – the "Marmorhaus" – included a ticket booth made from mahogany. The theater's foyer and auditorium showcased César Klein's Expressionist paintings on the wall and ceiling; Klein also designed colored glass that formed part of the foyer's ceiling.[15] The theater's ground floor held 400 "comfortable lounge chairs." Four staircases led to the balcony, which held another 200 seats. The Marmorhaus was certainly not the largest theater in Berlin, but the somewhat limited seating would make the premiere simultaneously exclusive and easy to sell out. The location in Kurfürstendamm was easy to reach from the road and the U-Bahn subway.[16] Perhaps there were other reasons as well. The *Vossische Zeitung* reported, presumably in jest, "Because no theater-owner would allow [Orlok] in his theater, they introduced him in the Marmorsaal at the Zoological Garden."[17]

And so, we eagerly welcomed the weekend that began March 3, if only to have a break from Berlin's troubles. The increasing price of

Figure 6.6 The program for Das Fest des Nosferatu. (Courtesy of Kantonsbibliothek Appenzell Ausserrhoden Ausserrhoden (CH), CMO-59-01-D-17-01-03-02.)

bread and coal strained many family budgets. The population of undernourished children in the city was growing. Some of them had to seek work at construction sites to augment their parents' income. Communist members of the City Council protested the use of police as a protective measure against planned strikes. Various city managers took steps to ensure that emergency services would continue, including those vital for the Festival, meaning power and public transportation.[18] On March 4, the subway and street cars could still transport those who wished to get to the Marmorhaus.

Entertainment continued throughout the city, thanks in part to two new film theaters, the Alhambra and the Primus-Palast (where *Nosferatu* would play not long after its premiere). There was also live theater: Puccini's *La Bohème* at the Deutsches Operahaus, Rostand's *Cyrano de Bergerac* at the Deutsches Theater, and a play entitled *Die Ratten/The Rats* at the Volksbühne. Here was indoor respite not just from the city's woes, for those who could afford it, but also from the weather. Berlin's temperature was in the mid-fifties, cloudy with occasional rain.[19] Despite the approach of spring, the sky spelled enough of the wintry to greet the vampire's arrival appropriately.

Crowds began to gather at the Marmorsaal, some perhaps early, others fashionably late. Doors opened at 7 p.m. Special decorations of yellow, blue, and violet draped the interior, as did many posters for *Nosferatu*.[20] Well-dressed attendees exchanged pleasantries. Invitations had described the festival as a "Biedermeier Event," and so a number of women chose to dress in that style.[21] Some were likely excited about seeing the film, others more in the thrall of themselves and their sense of superiority. Perhaps there was champagne and other liquor, high spirits to prepare for the unearthly spirits. Whatever our level of fascination and sobriety, though, ushers finally had to begin their work, auditorium doors opening to allow everyone to take their seats, a process that involved numerous ticketholders begging the pardons of others. After all, according to the *Berliner Börsen-Zeitung*, the Marmorhaus "was full to bursting and literally not a single empty seat could be found."[22] Another article described the audience as "overabundant."[23] One or more would-be viewers were likely turned away.

We were part of an elite group, to be in attendance. Here were "artists, diplomats, government officials, and the press."[24] Perhaps Emma Stropp – who had just been named the first woman to sit on the Court of Honor of the National Press Association – was among them.[25] Perhaps some of the very city council members arguing over labor unions were present. Film industry elite definitely appeared. One newspaper reported that directors Ernst Lubitsch and Richard Oswald seemed to be surveying the crowds "on the lookout for new stars."[26] Another reporter spotted director Johannes Rieman, writer Hanns Kräly, distributor Heinz Schall, as well as other unnamed "film stars and those who fashioned themselves as such."[27] Presumably Murnau, Galeen, Grau, and some of *Nosferatu*'s actors were present as well. Hands were shaken; autographs were signed.

And then, finally, the house lights dimmed, save for those onstage. The Festival of Nosferatu commenced with Hans Erdmann conducting Marschner's *Vampire Overture*, from *Der Vampyr*, which "put the nerves of the audience into just the right mood."[28] The sounds of an old vampire welcomed the sights of the new. Then came a prelude, "a three-way conversation of actor, director and female dancer," the director being Leopold von Ledebur. According to the *Berliner Lokal-Anzeiger*, "Ledebur explained a few things in his prologue, which were partly conceptual, but also partly unintelligible due to the manner of their presentation. Then there was a prelude at the theater by Mr. [Max] Schreck in which he claimed he could do anything. This was unnecessary using the tone he did. . . ."[29] It would seem this "conversation" preceded a "prelude" written by Kurt Alexander. Details of these live performances are difficult to reconstruct, but they were met with condemnation by critics. The *Berliner Börsen-Zeitung* wrote, "As openers a prologue as well as a prelude scripted by Kurt Alexander missed the mark, because the unanimous verdict of those who should know was that both were mediocre at best."[30] *Der Film* also called Alexander's work "mediocre."[31] *Vossische Zeitung* condemned it as "inappropriate."[32]

Once the live performances ended, the entire auditorium was plunged into darkness. As *Berliner Lokal-Anzeiger* observed:

> Once upon a time there was someone, who didn't want to be horrified. Actually, he just wanted to go dancing with his wife. He attended a celebration thrown by Nosferatu. He was surprised that following a short prologue, the theater darkened, and the movie projector began to hum. A film title announced that a *Symphony of Horror* was appearing on the movie screen.[33]

The hum of the projector was probably heard by few, if any, of those in attendance. Instead, the sound of music boomed throughout the hall. Erdmann had composed an original score for *Nosferatu*. One critic called it a:

> sophisticated reflection of the feature film. The orchestra sounded fluid and sweet when unrequited love was in play in the film. The drums sounded a note of doom when emotional turbulence occurred and built to a crescendo when the ominous sailor, the man-eating Flying Dutchman, moved through the wildly foaming sea.[34]

Erdmann's music was an aptly "strange combination of full orchestration with a large organ that M. Schmidt played with virtuosity." Another critic later said, "Erdmann set the varied moods of the film to music with artistic sensibility."[35]

However important its music, though, *Nosferatu* appeared before us as a set of visions on the screen, its light reflecting on our faces and on our eyes. How did we react? Some might have been bored or unimpressed, just as others might have been deeply affected, frightened, and disturbed. *Vorwärts* noted, "Because rational people do not let themselves be duped by unearthly creatures very long, the audience quickly preferred to move from the poisoned atmosphere of slavish submission (to horror) to the clean air of a carefully considered chuckle."[36] The newspaper *8 Uhr-Abendblatt* interrogated the laughter, explaining:

> Naturally one will notice occasionally that laughter is just one step away from being terrified. But that occurs rarely – for example when a hearse races around or Nosferatu runs around with his coffins as if he were in a cartoon. Otherwise the atmosphere is uniform and the impact strong, even though this is achieved with the most ill of materials.[37]

Another review added, "When [terror] succeeds, [viewers] are happy with it, but they resist the attempt . . . by laughing if that is required. And every theater-owner knows that laughing is first and foremost a recoverable mishap."[38]

It is safe to presume that the film generated much nightmare fuel. According to *Lichtbild-Bühne*, "One can be assured that a few women who

Figure 6.7 Artwork of Das Fest des Nosferatu, as published in *Berliner Lokal-Anzeiger* on March 6, 1922.

attended the premiere of *Nosferatu* had a bad night."[39] And a newspaper review believed that some viewers "shudder[ed]" and later experienced "bad dreams."[40] In less than ninety minutes, both Orlok's undead existence and Murnau's film ended. When the projector dimmed, "The applause was lively and well deserved."[41] Unlike the less-than-successful prelude, *Nosferatu* succeeded with many viewers. We no longer needed a journalist to describe what an occult film was. We had seen it, we had experienced it, we had lived it.

Praise for Murnau and his film did not conclude the festivities. Though a planned "interlude" was cut at the last minute, presumably because of the response given to the prelude, stage lights illuminated for another act, which was apparently designed to restore calm to frightened viewers. Elizabeth Grube of the State Ballet Company appeared in a "Serenade" dance number, "which hit a high note as the result of the musical accompaniment of the Musical Society 'Dominator' of the Schiedmeyer-Pianoforte Company."[42] *Vossische Zeitung* called her performance "graceful."[43] At least a few of us at the Marmorhaus recognized Grube from her appearance in Willy Zeyn's film *Der Tanz um Liebe und Glück/The Dance of Love and Happiness* (Ostdeutsches Lichtspielhaus, 1921).

The Festival then moved out of the auditorium in the style of a polonaise. We proceeded slowly, in a kind of celebratory danse macabre, eventually passing a cinematographer who filmed us. Some of our faces still bore *Nosferatu*'s emotional imprint. The "procession ... caused a surge in the crowd, because every 'beauty' wanted to be seen as a budding movie starlet."[44] Our faces would later be seen by someone, perhaps even by a film audience in a long-forgotten and long-lost newsreel. For those of us who wished to continue the evening, our mood quickly "soared from the symphony of terror into a symphony of merriment."[45]

Shuttles took the throng to the Riemann School of Art and Design, "for those who had still not had their fill of the terrifying *Nosferatu*," so that we "could get a layer of goose pimples from viewing the most modern forms of art."[46] Perhaps one of Alfred Kubin's eerie vampire artworks hung on exhibit. But such edification was of little interest to most of us, hurrying as we did to the gala ball in order to drink and dance to the jazzy sounds of Otto Kermbach's orchestra.[47] As *Deutsche allgemeine Zeitung* reported:

> There the elegant women put on a show and the gruesomeness was forgotten. They danced, egged on by surprises provided by [Kermbach] and his superb orchestra until the wee hours of the morning. [T]he most extravagantly dressed women in gowns of all imaginable styles, ranging from Biedermeier-style to Sioux women's costumes, observed the festivities with amazement from the quieter loges.[48]

The party continued, to the delight of many of us, with sobriety becoming scarcer than the supernatural. Ecstasy with paramours overtook fear from vampires, save for those who pretended to bite their dates. What lovely necks some of them had, we joked. The party lasted until at least 4 a.m.[49] As expected, though, not everyone was pleased. Lubitsch danced with "amazing energy and stamina," but Oswald "left the festivities early on."[50] One reporter was so fed up with the post-screening fun that he wrote, "Praise God, it is over, and we survived."[51]

It was time to go home. Viewers returned to their beds, or to the beds of their lovers. Some dreamt of *Nosferatu*, perhaps even awakening with Orlok's memory fresh on their minds, both the vampire and the drink causing them to sweat. The Marmorhaus projectionist might have been among them, but more likely he simply fell asleep from fatigue, having to break down the film into its constituent reels following the exodus. A few critics had an even longer night, returning to their offices to type their responses to this new film.

But then there was another group, as tired as they were excited, as happy as they were worried. Here was Murnau, Grau, and Dieckmann, perhaps together, probably separate. They slept, whether passing out from alcohol or from sheer exhaustion, but the next few days beckoned their attentions. Newspapers meant news meant reviews. What did they say, to us and to the film industry, to those who comprised the audience and to those who could not be part of the same, those who would have to wait to experience *Nosferatu*? Collectively, the reviews were more positive than negative. Let us first open the pages of *Berliner Lokal-Anzeiger*:

> I have seldom seen a work in which the atmosphere of the screenplay is so sublimely reflected in the scenery, the interaction of the actors is so seamless, and where figures that walk a tightrope between comedy and tragedy for five acts, succeed in overcoming this treacherous chasm . . . Visibly invisible F. W. Murnau prevails over the production. He is one of those who will have a lot to say about the future development of pure film styles.[52]

From there, another of us can fold the first two pages of *Vossische Zeitung* until our eyes fall on the review:

> The sympathetic author Henrik Galeen is an understudy from the school of Wegener. His vampire "Nosferatu" could have come from the workshop of Wegener: non-speaking and unread – a style of film for itself. Murnau, the arbiter of scenes in the film, arranges each and every carefully edited scene into a harmonized composition. The castle of horror, the house of Nosferatu, are masterful accomplishments – a veritable museum of scenic themes.[53]

To smile and toast, even if alone that morning, raising a glass of coffee instead of champagne, that was easy to do, especially after reading *Berliner Börsen-Zeitung*:

> One point is clear: an artistic victory has been won here. And the victor is F. W. Murnau. His production is exemplary. He completed each and every scene with "film eyes," whether it was to portray an imposingly sinister castle on the movie screen, or the zigzagging streets and small alleys where the pest is breeding. His main strength is visually capturing dead objects and he has shown his ability to incorporate especially breathtaking and atmospheric landscapes into the plot.[54]

Murnau was fast being considered a major force in German cinema, a master filmmaker, as *Lichtbild-Bühne* told us:

> The film *Nosferatu* is a thriller, because it departs radically from the overworked love stories and mechanical adventure films. It creates elements of the fantastic without presuppositions, whose source is the chilling superstition of a vampire that sucks human blood ... Max Schreck's Nosferatu – [was] brilliant in makeup and pantomime, although at times he could have acted more transcendental and more unearthly in the role. Henrik Galeen's screenplay could not be more completely effective, nor could it be more beautifully balanced. The direction of F. W. Murnau was a stroke of genius. The photography of F. A. Wagner was of the highest artistic quality. The sets of Albin Grau cannot remain unmentioned as a generator of moods.[55]

The critic concluded by declaring that *Nosferatu* "must go into general release in the movie theaters! One does not have the right to keep such an interesting (not to mention thrilling) film in its totality from general audiences."

Other critics tempered their enthusiasm, which caused some of us reading their reviews to do the same. Witness *BZ am Mittag*:

> Credit goes to the director F. W. Murnau in first order for succeeding in making incorporeal terror visible, making ghostly apparitions credible, and to transform the spiritual into sensually perceptible reality.
>
> Only the special effects sequences were not entirely successful in my opinion. When the hearse jolts through the remote ravines of the Carpathian Mountains or when the vampire scurries about, stacking up one coffin on another, the technical film effects become apparent, thus destroying the illusion to a certain extent. In general, the uncanny atmosphere is made to feel terrifyingly realistic.[56]

The *Berliner Tageblatt* also praised Murnau and the film, likening it to the works of Edgar Allan Poe, but thought Schreck's performance was lacking, effective only due to his makeup and costume.[57]

Almost as quickly as these reviews appeared, they disappeared, being discarded into trash bins throughout Berlin. Thus, the festival was over, with the correspondent for *Variety* left to report in the days ahead that "expenses were about cleared, which is pretty good when one considers the amount of publicity they raked in."[58] Orlok had been here with us, then he departed to other theaters, including in other cities and other countries. As *Berliner Börsen-Zeitung* told readers, "It is not immediately apparent whether this film is something for the broad masses of our movie-going audiences, but perhaps in this regard we will be surprised. One never knows."[59]

The Festival of Nosferatu became forgotten, save for the fleeting memories of attendees long since dead, and for the record preserved by contemporary journalists. But of course, the film *Nosferatu* remains ever with us, so much so that it now seems as old as Orlok himself. Here memory does not fail us. A botched prologue at the festival could not dispel him, nor could daylight entering Ellen's bedside window. It has often been remarked that *Nosferatu* survived a court edict that demanded all film prints be destroyed. *Nosferatu* survives, even though, ironically, the court records that condemned the film do not.[60] While we are sleeping, Orlok comes creeping, again and again. We have not forgotten him, nor has he forgotten us.

Notes

1. "*Der Vampir*: Heinrich August Ossenfelder," FusionTheme, December 17, 2014, accessed July 17, 2022, https://www.firbolgpublishing.com/der-vampir-heinrich-august-ossenfelder/.
2. Heinrich Marschner, *Der Vampyr*, 1828. Libretto translated by Jutta Romero in 1997, accessed October 5, 2022, http://opera.stanford.edu/iu/libretti/vampyr.html.
3. "Der okkulte Leitartikel," *Film-Tribüne*, no. 34/35, October 30, 1921, 1–2.
4. "*Nosferatu Eine Symphonie des Grauens*," *Der Neue Film*, no. 3, 1922, 1.
5. "*Nosferatu*," *Film-Kurier*, no. 52, March 6, 1922.
6. "*Nosferatu*," *Tanz und Welt*, nos 3–4, early March 1922, 15.
7. "Occultismus und 'Shimmy,'" *BZ am Mittag* (Berlin), March 6, 1922.
8. C. Cooper Trask, "Berlin Film News," *Variety*, April 21, 1922, 43.
9. Advertisements, *BZ am Mittag*, February 27, 1922, 6.
10. "Das Fest des *Nosferatu*," *Berliner Börsen-Zeitung*, March 1, 1922, 8.
11. "Aus der Welt des Films," *Deutsche allgemeine Zeitung* (Berlin), October 16, 1921, 8.
12. "*Nosferatu*," *Tanz und Welt*, 17.
13. Ibid., 17.
14. "Brief aus Berlin," *Der Kinematograph*, March 12, 1922, 3.
15. "Marmorhaus," *Allekinos*, August 19, 2022, accessed October 4, 2022, http://allekinos.com/BERLINMarmorhaus.html.
16. I am very grateful to Lisa Roth of the Deutsche-Kinemathek for information regarding the Marmorhaus. Lisa Roth, email to Gary D. Rhodes, September 27, 2022.
17. "*Nosferatu*," *Vossische Zeitung* (Berlin), March 7, 1922, 4.
18. I am deeply grateful to Robert Cremer for kindly examining Berlin newspapers for March 3 and 4, 1922, and providing these details.
19. Ibid.
20. "Das Fest des Nosferatu," *Deutsche allgemeine Zeitung* (Berlin), March 6, 1922, 3.
21. "Das Fest des Nosferatu," *Berliner Börsen-Zeitung*, March 7, 1922, 8.
22. Ibid., 8.
23. "*Nosferatu*," *Film-Kurier*, Number 52, March 6, 1922.

24. "Das Fest des Nosferatu," *Deutsche allgemeine Zeitung*, 3.
25. Here again I would acknowledge Robert Cremer, who shared this information after his examination of Berlin newspapers for March 3 and 4, 1922.
26. "Das Fest des Nosferatu," *Deutsche allgemeine Zeitung*, 3.
27. "Film-Echo," *Berliner Lokal-Anzeiger*, March 6, 1922, 1.
28. "Das Fest des Nosferatu," *Deutsche allgemeine Zeitung*, 3.
29. "Film-Echo," 1.
30. "Das Fest des Nosferatu," *Berliner Börsen-Zeitung*, 8.
31. "Die neuesten Filme," *Der Film*, March 12, 1922, 45.
32. "*Nosferatu,*" *Vossische Zeitung*, 4.
33. "Film-Echo," 1.
34. Ibid., 1.
35. "Occultismus und 'Shimmy,'" *BZ am Mittag* (Berlin), March 6, 1922.
36. "Filmschau," *Vorwärts* (Berlin), March 21, 1922, 6.
37. "*Nosferatu,*" *8 Uhr-Abendblatt* (Berlin), March 6, 1922, 5.
38. "Das Nosferatufest," *Berliner Börsen-Courier*, March 6, 1922, 5.
39. "*Nosferatu,*" *Lichtbild-Bühne*, no. 11, March 11, 1922, 49.
40. "*Nosferatu,*" *8 Uhr-Abendblatt*, 5.
41. "*Nosferatu,*" *Der Tag*, March 17, 1922.
42. "Die neuesten Filme," 45.
43. "*Nosferatu,*" *Vossische Zeitung*, 4.
44. "Das Fest des Nosferatu," *Deutsche allgemeine Zeitung*, 3.
45. "*Nosferatu,*" *Film-Kurier*, no. 52, March 6, 1922.
46. "Film-Echo," 1.
47. Ibid., 1.
48. "Das Fest des Nosferatu," *Deutsche allgemeine Zeitung*, 3.
49. "Das Fest des Nosferatu," *Berliner Börsen-Zeitung*, 8.
50. Ibid., 8.
51. "Occultismus und 'Shimmy.'"
52. "Film-Echo," 1.
53. "*Nosferatu,*" *Vossische Zeitung*, 4.
54. "*Nosferatu,*" *Berliner Börsen-Zeitung*, March 6, 1922, 2.
55. "*Nosferatu,*" *Lichtbild-Bühne*, 49.
56. "Occultismus und 'Shimmy.'"
57. "Das Fest des Nosferatu," *Berliner Tageblatt*, March 7, 1922, 16.
58. Trask, 43.
59. "Das Fest des Nosferatu," *Berliner Börsen-Zeitung*, 8.
60. I am deeply grateful to Anika Goetz for searching for the court records and sharing her determination that they had been discarded.

CHAPTER 7

London after Midnight

"I've solved this mystery. You're at the bottom of it."
– Hibbs (Conrad Nagel)
London after Midnight, 1927

Tod Browning's *London after Midnight*, released by MGM in 1927, represents America's first supernatural vampire feature film. Except that it isn't. It does not depict a supernatural vampire, not really. Its story features Lon Chaney as a detective, Inspector Burke, who costumes as a supernatural vampire ("The Man in the Beaver Hat") as part of an elaborate ruse to catch a murderer. The detective also enlists an actress (Edna Tichenor) to costume as a vampire known as the "Bat Girl." Here is thus a supernatural vampire film without a supernatural vampire, a paradox, one perhaps well suited to the subject matter.

During its running time, *London after Midnight* included an insert shot of a "vignetted passage of the printed page of an old book, the paper of a parchment-like quality, aged, the print in an Old English type." According to the script, the page read as follows: "– the undead, the vampyrs [*sic*]: dead bodies which leave their graves at night to suck the blood of the living."[1] Here was a definition, one that made vampires synonymous with the "undead," a term that Bram Stoker's *Dracula* (1897) rendered with uppercase letters and hyphenated as "Un-Dead." In the novel, Dr. Van Helsing explains that the Un-Dead are "desperate," "strong," and are distinctly different than the "common dead." In response, Arthur Holmwood exclaims, "Un-Dead! Not alive! What do you mean? Is this all a nightmare, or what is it?"[2]

The questions are hardly unexpected. The term undead was little-known in English prior to Stoker, not appearing in such nineteenth-century literature as John Polidori's *The Vampyre* (1819), James Malcolm Rymer's *Varney the Vampire* (1845–7), and J. Sheridan Le Fanu's *Carmilla* (1872).

Figure 7.1 The Man in the Beaver Hat (Lon Chaney) in Tod Browning's *London after Midnight* (MGM, 1927). (Courtesy of Daniel Titley.)

True, the concept was present in those tales, as well as those published after Stoker's *Dracula*. F. Marion Crawford's short story *For the Blood Is the Life* (1911) describes "a woman's shriek, the unearthly scream of a woman neither dead nor alive, but buried deep for many days." Nevertheless, the concept remained difficult to fathom, to understand, and the term was rarely used during the silent film era.³ To be undead is paradoxical, far more so than Browning's equation in *London after Midnight*, "Vampire/ Not a Vampire." Here is a liminal, threshold space between life and death, not inscrutable, but more complicated to grasp than, say, purgatory.

London after Midnight regularly appears on lists of the most sought-after lost films, the last known copy having burned in an MGM vault fire in 1965. Efforts to reconstruct it and to rediscover it are legion, ranging from the sincere and earnest to the faulty and fraudulent. No known print of *London after Midnight* exists. The film is not alive, but it is not dead, given the ongoing interest in it, as well as its cultural influence, whether rematerializing in the form of Sean Brennan's band London After Midnight or as the title monster in Jennifer Kent's film *The Babadook* (Umbrella Entertainment, 2014).⁴ *London after Midnight* now belongs more to the imagination than to the projection booth. Here then is the ghostly, gossamer narrative. Here is undead cinema.

Afterimages

In the era before television and home video, most viewers were unable to see films once their theatrical runs ended. Reissues occurred on occasion, but never for *London after Midnight*. As a late silent film, the talking picture era prevented it from returning to theaters. Indeed, Lon Chaney died in 1930, having made only one talkie, Jack Conway's *The Unholy Three* (1930). Chaney's fame continued, but his films did not, at least not during the thirties and forties. Silent films largely disappeared from the American screen.

One of the last published exhibitor reports on *London after Midnight* came in April 1929, with a theater manager calling it, "A good picture and one that brings in the business. Showed it in a snow storm [*sic*], with the roads in bad shape. Too spooky to please many of the fans, but Chaney's acting is admired."⁵ A final report printed in June 1929 explained, "Pretty good picture, but bad print from New Orleans."⁶ By mid-1929, most prints of *London after Midnight* would have been worn, from use, reuse, and abuse. But even seeing a scratchy and stained print meant seeing the film, experiencing it directly. As of 1930 and thereafter, such an experience became increasingly rare.

At least a few viewers who saw *London after Midnight* in 1927, 1928, and 1929 remembered it years later. Bob Kane once compared Chaney's vampire to Danny DeVito's Penguin character in Tim Burton's *Batman Returns* (Warner Bros., 1992).⁷ Some years ago, I spoke with William K. Everson, Robert Bloch, and Forrest J Ackerman about the film, hoping to learn more about it, even experience it vicariously through their smiling, happy memories. Ackerman specifically recalled Chaney's crouched stance and walk while in the vampire guise, which he described as similar to Groucho Marx's onscreen gait, though performed in a serious, uncanny manner. I particularly remember interviewing Margaret Brannan, a family friend, about *London after Midnight* for my hometown newspaper when I was a teenager. Unlike Ackerman, she had no particular interest in horror cinema, but she had watched the film on its original release when she was a child. She never forgot another important detail: Chaney rolled his eyes around their sockets when guised as the vampire, creating for her – and presumably many viewers – an eerie effect.[8]

Memories have always been one way to preserve films, or at least particular scenes and images from them. But memories fade, sometimes rapidly. Henry James Forman's book *Our Movie Made Children* (1935) included a quotation from a "youth of twenty-four under sentence for burglary":

> A picture I consider very interesting and inspiring to the criminal in the line of his profession is *London after Midnight*. This picture has a cast of daring gangsters and murderers. I took a great liking to this picture as it was very exciting. This picture kept the law on the go, as there were daring crimes throughout. Like every other crook picture, the criminal is caught and punished.[9]

The memory is important for many reasons, ranging from the sociological to the historiographical. But the "youth" misremembered. The plot details he cites are not from *London after Midnight*. He was recalling another film, perhaps another Chaney film, such as Jack Conway's *While the City Sleeps* (1928).

Period materials are arguably more reliable than aging memories, whether shooting scripts, plot synopses in period magazines and newspapers, or book-of-the-film novelizations that were popular before the age of home video. Marie Coolidge-Rask's *London after Midnight*, published by Grosset & Dunlap in 1928, represents such a book. Couch Pumpkin Press published a new edition, edited by Niels W. Erickson, in 2010. An introductory note rightly explains, "the tale . . . is even more intriguingly complex than the one which made it to the screen."[10] And yet, books of films are not films, nor are plot synopses, no matter how faithful they attempt to be. There is a limit to how well words can describe images and editing, just as there is a limit to how much memories can capture experiences.

For that matter, there is a limit to how much still pictures can capture moving pictures. Unknown to most filmgoers, the images they have historically seen from films are usually not from films. Rather than frame blow-ups taken from film prints, the images published in movie magazines and promoted on advertising materials were publicity stills, taken not by a cinematographer, but by a still photographer. They generally attempted to approximate scenes from the film, though there are exceptions, as well as overall variations, specifically a different aspect ratio during the classical Hollywood era, meaning a 5:4 photograph (or 4:5, if vertical rather than horizontal) instead of a 4:3 film frame. Describing Wallace Chewning's work as still photographer for *London after Midnight*, *American Cinematographer* wrote in 1927:

> he passed weeks of study, using the script and light effects to devise methods of translating fear to terms of photography. Chaney's picture was a thriller, with the star as a detective in a strange mystery in a haunted house. It naturally lent itself to fantastic shadows and weird effects, and with Chaney's strange makeup and the photographer's uncanny lighting, some really remarkable effects were produced.[11]

Remarkable effects, indeed, with the large number of extant *London after Midnight* publicity stills giving us access to how the costumes and makeup and sets appeared. While they are certainly not frames from the film, they provide far more insight into how it looked than mere memories and text. They are the key reason why the film is remembered by those who never saw it.

Reanimations

Remembering *London after Midnight* through paracinema has not been the only means of revivifying it. Exploring film history through making new films has been another approach. Max and Dave Fleischer's animated cartoon *Swing You Sinners!* (Paramount, 1930) features a ghost that clearly resembles Chaney's Man in the Beaver Hat. His faux-vampire was also reborn in Joseph Pevney's *The Man of a Thousand Faces* (Universal, 1957), thanks to poster artwork depicting James Cagney in Chaney's makeup.

Figure 7.2 Max and Dave Fleischer's *Swing You Sinners!* (Paramount, 1930).

Tod Browning undertook the most notable reimagining of *London after Midnight*, remaking it as *Mark of the Vampire* (MGM, 1935). The new film simultaneously is and is not *London after Midnight*. In large measure, save for splitting the detective and Man in the Beaver Hat into two different characters, the plots are very similar. That said, to an extent *Mark of the Vampire* also reimagines Browning's *Dracula* (Universal, 1931), the vampires in both played by Bela Lugosi in comparable costume and makeup, eschewing the appearance of Chaney's character. Even actor Michael Visaroff's role as an innkeeper in *Mark of the Vampire* evokes his earlier performance in *Dracula*.

Of particular importance to later generations was Basil Gogos's painting of the Man in the Beaver Hat, which first appeared on the cover of *Famous Monsters of Filmland* in November 1962. While the fan magazine was aimed at children, it was also crucial in bringing renewed attention to classic horror movies, including those of the silent film era that were no longer receiving much attention. Here was Chaney's faux-vampire, with his jagged teeth crooked into an evil smile, his dark eyes staring out directly at a new generation who eagerly looked to the past of horror cinema. In 1962, popular culture had forgotten most silent films of 1927. By contrast, *London after Midnight* was prominently displayed on most American newsstands. This was an important step in the film becoming a "famous monster" to a new generation.[12]

Famous Monsters continued to levy attention on *London after Midnight*, with the Gogos artwork – in slightly altered form – reprinted on the cover in September 1970. The interior included a "filmbook" of *London after Midnight*, recreating its plotline with a number of still photographs and text that relied heavily on Coolidge-Rask.[13] Since the earlier Gogos cover, the MGM vault fire had occurred, leading *Famous Monsters* to note correctly in 1970 that it was chronicling a "lost" film.[14]

Relying on a similar but far more expansive approach, Philip J. Riley compiled a book-length reconstruction of *London after Midnight* in 1985, reproducing the full script, as well as a separate compilation of onscreen intertitle text and over 150 photographs that told the story in words and images. However, as Riley noted in the book, his project was incomplete:

> In comparing the script to the cutting continuity, I found that the final screen version was very different from the original scenario. And, to top it off, stills were shot to match the script, which meant that they could not be used in the film portion of this book.
> ... When all the stills were together, I found that ... they did not shoot any stills of many important scenes, nor did they have any stills of the ending, where the hypnotist captures the real murderer.[15]

Figure 7.3 The November 1962 issue of *Famous Monsters of Filmland*. (Courtesy of George Chastain.)

Nevertheless, the Riley book was a major accomplishment. The film seemed somewhat alive, even if the only movement resulted from one's fingers turning the pages.

In 2002, writer and filmmaker Paul Davis presented his own version of *London after Midnight* on the website *Celluloid Shockers*. Relying on text and photos, Davis promoted it as being "the most comprehensive reconstruction." That might have been true, given that he covered some narrative details that Riley did not, his work becoming something of an amalgam of the shooting script and cutting continuity. Nevertheless, the photo quality on his site did not equal Riley's.[16] Worse still is that its internet publication has since disappeared from the web. It now represents a lost reconstruction of a lost film.

Then, in 2016, Thomas Mann published his narrative reconstruction of *London after Midnight*.[17] He approached the project differently than Riley, the result meaningfully augmenting its predecessor. Relying on less than ten still photographs, Mann concentrated on the sheer variety of text-based sources, including the script and the Coolidge-Rask book, as well as the original music cues, pressbook, and a narrative adaptation published in *Boy's Cinema* in 1928. In his introduction, Mann importantly explains the value as well as the limitation of such sources in reconstructing films.[18]

Between Riley and Mann came the most substantial reconstruction, one undertaken by film restorationist Rick Schmidlin. Rather than being present in the form of a book or magazine, Schmidlin's *London after Midnight* was on film, or at least digital video. It premiered on Turner Classic Movies in 2002 before being released the following year on DVD.[19] Running forty-eight minutes, the reconstruction relies on hundreds of publicity stills presented in a sequence based on the cutting continuity and the intertitle continuity. In one respect, the film moves, from its overall time-based presentation to Ken Burns-style movement added to given photos, including zooms, a camera effect that would not have been used in *London after Midnight*. Some photos are repeated, while other extant photos were not used. And then there are narrative elements for which publicity stills either do not exist or were never even taken. Thus, the result is best understood as a photo film (or "photofilm," as it is sometimes spelled), a tradition that has merit, but also has limitations.

Reaction to Schmidlin's reconstruction varied from the extremely positive to the greatly disappointed. As Chaney biographer Michael F. Blake noted, "The *biggest* limitation is that the project does *not* move. No matter how much panning, zooming, etc. you do [to a still photograph], it can never recreate a moving image."[20] There is no crouched gait to observe; there are no rolling eyes to see. To be sure, film restorationists had relied on still photographs to replace lost footage since at least 1984, in the case of Giorgio Moroder's reconstruction of Fritz Lang's *Metropolis* (UFA, 1927). But Schmidlin's *London after Midnight* marked the first use of publicity stills to recreate an entire feature film.[21] Hence the mixed reactions. One post on the Internet Movie Database claimed, "It just isn't the original film nor is it even a truncated version – it's a bizarre attempt to recreate the film from nothing."²² While that comment represents an overstatement, the reconstruction is arguably as much Schmidlin's film as it is Browning's. The result is and is not *London after Midnight*.

After all, none of these reconstructions rely on a single frame from Browning's film, a vampire movie about a hoax vampire.

Folklore

"*London after Midnight* – Found!" So read the headline of an Associated Press article published on Joseph K. Meadows's website *Horror-Wood* in 1999:

> Clyde McGuffin, 82, one-time Metro-Goldwyn Mayer film archivist and now the owner of a chicken ranch in El Segundo, California, found a valuable "nest egg" – in an actual chicken's nest. An old film canister used as the base of one of his chicken nests proved to contain a print of MGM's silent thriller *London after Midnight* . . .
>
> "After I left old MGM with 'leather goods' – a belt in the mouth and a boot in the butt – I started up my chicken ranch. I needed a good, strong base for the nests that wouldn't get ate up by chicken droppings," McGuffin explained at a press conference at the MGM Grand Hotel in Los Vegas, Nevada. "Well, we had a bunch of old silent films lying around in their cans waiting to be 'archived' – that meant tossed in the crapper," he added with a chuckle. "So I took some of them home and put 'em to good use–providing firm support to my layers."
>
> However, one old hen named Henrietta wasn't fond of her nest's hard bottom. She pecked at the film can beneath the straw until it popped open, McGuffin explained.
>
> "Me and my old lady, Muriel, looked at that there film and saw it had that old funny-face actor, Chaney, wearing pointy teeth and a top hat. I mentioned it to my son, who works for MGM now too, in their casino as a pit boss, and he said that film had to be valuable. So I took it to my old employers and they nearly fainted."
>
> According to MGM executives, the print is badly deteriorated and smells rather bad ("Henrietta's droppings didn't do it any good," one admitted). But it is watchable . . .
>
> "I got to watch it," McGuffin said. "It was pretty silly, and kind of reminded me of that other film MGM made with that Bela fella, with him wearing his black cape and walking around with a bullet hole in his head. Can't see what all the fuss is about, myself. Now if it was a Tom Mix film . . ."
>
> Screenings of the film will be delayed until MGM's lawyers sort through a sea of lawsuits from over 25 foreign countries claiming a copyright on the film. When asked about McGuffin's observations concerning MGM's treatment of its film achieves, studio executives refused comment.²³

Meadows clearly labeled the article, "A Horror Hoax." Nevertheless, some horror fans believed his prank, one that speaks to the sheer desire for the film's rediscovery. Actress Ingrid Pitt, famed for her appearances in Hammer vampire films, wrote, "I was a little surprised at not having heard about the

[*London after Midnight*] discovery before, but swallowed the whole story till I logged off. A box came up explaining it was all a spoof – but wasn't it fun?"[24]

Meadows was not the first to create such a prank, however creative his was. That distinction probably goes to a New England-based film service, which listed *London after Midnight* as a forthcoming title in the early 1970s, not too long after the film burned at MGM. Pranks of this type continued after Meadows as well, including at least one that claimed that Turner Classic Movies would broadcast a print of the film in December 2013.[25]

Figure 7.4 Fake film frame created by Jack Theakston. (Courtesy of Jack Theakston.)

Film restorationist Jack Theakston concocted his own prank by recreating the title frame for *London after Midnight*. He recalled:

> I'm afraid a little prank of mine has gotten a little out of control. No footage has been found from the film – it's a joke I concocted for some friends. I was going to say something about it when people were starting to think it was legitimate. For a little image, I put a lot of work into it to the point of anal-retentive detail. I threw some things into the frame that people who were truly experts would know it wasn't real, but I was shocked how many people thought it was real.[26]

Theakston's faked frame was extremely well produced, hence the belief it was authentic, his hoax described (and appropriately identified for what it is) in Dennis Bartok and Jeff Joseph's book *A Thousand Cuts: The Bizarre Underground World of Collectors and Dealers Who Saved the Movies* (University Press of Mississippi, 2016).[27]

Probably the most elaborate prank appears on Michael Gebert's website, *Mike's London after Midnight Myths Page*.[28] Here one can see a flyer for a 1975 screening of the movie and a 1998 advertisement for a VHS release, indications that the film cannot really be lost. Gebert also includes a frame grab from a TV broadcast of *London after Midnight* and artwork for a pending DVD. Only when the reader reaches the end of the text does Gebert reveal what many would already have guessed, his *Myths Page* is itself a myth, a "prank site," as he calls it.[29]

The fact that MGM conducted a worldwide search for *London after Midnight* during the 1970s has not tempered gossip or rumors about its ongoing existence. Most discussion about the film's current whereabouts has fallen into two other categories, one being led by sincere hopes and earnest searches. For example, in 1985, Forrest J Ackerman wrote:

> It was said to have resurfaced several years ago, been seen in San Francisco. In fact, I know the young chap who said he saw it. I have no reason to doubt his word – but on the other hand, I could never find anyone to corroborate his story. It was at an annual Ann Radcliffe awards banquet of the Count Dracula Society, being held in Hollywood . . .
> And suddenly the word reached my table like wildfire: "A young fellow over at that table said he saw *London after Midnight* last week."
> Fleet as the wind, in my Dracula cape, I whisked over to the indicated youngster. Put my arm around him. Said, 'What's this I hear about you seeing *London after Midnight*?'
> 'Oh yes, Mr. Ackerman. Last week.' And he named the little theater, which unfortunately I've since forgotten, but I know it exists – I went there subsequently. "Why, is there something unusual about it? Everybody seems to be getting very excited."[30]

Ackerman concluded his tale by mentioning that none of his friends in San Francisco were aware of said screening, even though they were "old-time movie buffs." The event almost certainly did not occur. The bigger question is whether the "young fellow" was lying or honestly mistaken.

Ackerman's story would not be unique. Decades later, the rumors continued. In 2017, film producer Robert Parigi noted:

> I'm noticing chatter that a 7-reel print of long-lost Tod Browning/Lon Chaney film *London after Midnight* (featuring Chaney's iconic "Man in the Beaver Hat" Vampire) has been discovered in Spain! I had long heard rumors of a print in Cuba. Is this perhaps that print, now sent to Spain? Twenty years ago, I had rumors of a print in the U.S., and contacted the supposed owner offering to transfer it to (then state-of-the-art) D1, but when it came time to produce the print, he backed out.[31]

To these stories, I can add various occasions from the 1980s to the present when collectors and historians have personally told me rumors of prints, tucked inside an American refrigerator, or perhaps stored in an old building in Korea. It survived in the form of footage from a coming attraction trailer, or as a fragment, or in an abbreviated 9.5mm format, or even in complete 35mm form, with one person confidently assuring me that Stanley Kubrick kept a copy in his personal vault. A few of these tales revolved around issues of copyright. In the nineties, I heard that a collector was supposed to emerge with a print once it went public domain in 2003. He didn't, allegedly because the United States Congress extended copyright from seventy-five to ninety-five years.

Tales of lost films are rife. In the 1970s, Hollywood agent Don Marlowe ran advertisements offering the lost print of Bela Lugosi's test footage for *Frankenstein* (1931) for sale. In the twenty-first century, more than one story has been told about the rediscovery of F. W. Murnau's *4 Devils* (Fox, 1928). Neither film is known to exist. And yet many of us retain hope that they might, in part because we are optimists, and in part because major rediscoveries continue to be made around the world. Much may still be found, whether improperly labeled, or perhaps archived in Cuba or Russia, or buried in forgotten attics and basements. Consider the 1988 rediscovery of the Georges Méliès's *Le Manoir du diable/The Devil's Castle* (1896), the print being found not in France, its country of origin, or even the United States, where it played to some degree of popularity, but instead in New Zealand.

And yet clearly fraudulent stories require us to temper our optimism. Immediately after *London after Midnight*, Tod Browning directed Lon Chaney in the crime movie *The Big City* (MGM, 1928). It is lost, the last known copy having burned in the same 1965 MGM vault fire that destroyed *London after Midnight*. But F. Gwynplaine MacIntyre claimed to have seen a copy in the modern era. His rationale is unknown. Perhaps he was playing a prank that he did not reveal. Perhaps he was lying to achieve credibility amongst historians. Whatever his reason, MacIntyre probably ranks as the most infamous purveyor of myths about lost films, which he had allegedly seen in a secret European collection. He managed not only to post such falsehoods on the Internet Movie Database, but he also published a chapter on *The Big City* in *The Cinema of Tod Browning* (McFarland, 2008), thus giving potentially unintended meaning to its subtitle, *Essays of the Macabre and Grotesque*.[32]

On July 23, 2008, someone calling himself "Sid Terror" published an online article at the Horror Drunx website that became the most dubious of *London after Midnight* "rediscovery" stories. Advance publicity claimed, "Within 48 hours the biggest news story in horror will be revealed." Two days later, the headline read, "*London after Midnight* Found." In it, Terror proclaimed:

> Yes. It is true. For those who scoff and doubt (I'm sure you will be legion) that the most notorious lost film of all times was located, I will say it again with authority and conviction ... I, Sid Terror, saw Lon Chaney's lost classic *London after Midnight* with my own eyes. Without a doubt. No, I am not talking about a recreation made completely from still photos, I'm talking about the entire long-lost motion-picture![33]

Terror wrote that in 1988, he worked for a cinema delivery service in Los Angeles. While at a "massive film storage facility" owned by Turner (who had acquired MGM's catalog), he asked a worker about *London after Midnight*, referencing its original title, *The Hypnotist*. The worker gave him the "section, row, and shelf number" of its location. While the nitrate print was incomplete, it was indeed *London after Midnight*, Terror insisted. Once he examined the reels, Terror was "positive." He "may have even wept a little." But nothing happened. The worker told him that Turner didn't wish to release the film until the missing footage was located. Terror used a magic marker to write *London after Midnight* on the film canisters, given that they were labeled *The Hypnotist*. Two decades later, he published his story.[34]

Websites like *Ain't It Cool News* and *What Culture* heralded the story. Others were immediately skeptical. A post on the silent film board *Nitrateville* announced, "The annual 'sighting' of a print of *London after Midnight* is on again."[35] Another asked if Sid Terror and F. Gwynplaine MacIntyre were the same person.[36] Most discussion unfolded at the Classic Horror Film Board, resulting in approximately seventy-two pages of posts.[37] Some questioned Sid Terror's biography, including his claim to be the great-grandson of Max Schreck, who portrayed Graf Orlok in F. W. Murnau's *Nosferatu* (1922). After all, Schreck did not have children.[38]

Of Terror's story about *London after Midnight*, Chaney biographer Michael F. Blake wrote, "The facts do *not* add up here people. Stop drinking the Kool-Aid and realize the Emperor doesn't have a new suit of clothes."[39] David Colton, longtime journalist at *USA Today*, concluded, "This was a tall tale of wishful thinking (and that's putting a positive spin on it) that yes, had some threads of truth throughout, but made no sense when examined."[40] Horror film historian Tom Weaver remarked, "Hoaxes can be fun; this one was a bore."[41]

Figure 7.5 Faked footage of *London after Midnight* featuring the Man in the Beaver Hat doll produced by Sideshow Toys.

In 2009, a brief clip from *London after Midnight* appeared online, including at YouTube. It was in fact modern footage featuring a twelve inch doll of Chaney's Man in the Beaver Hat released by Sideshow Toys in 2001, the clip relying on stop-motion effects and digitally added "film damage."[42] The following year, the website *Harpodeon* unleashed its own monster of a prank. This story was about a South American film collector, who in the 1920s made an illegal bootleg copy of a 35mm.[43] Its perpetrator recalled:

> It was a joke made around the same time another person claimed to have found a print of *London after Midnight* . . . With each update, his tale grew more fantastic and less believable. It ended, as most of these stories do, with him simply disappearing.
>
> Our joke story started out being just within the realm of possibility – that a projectionist moonlighting as a film pirate secretly made a 16mm dupe of the negative of *London*. It also grew more incredible as it went on, eventually descending into total madness by the end. I remember it had time travel, references to timecube.com, and somehow involved a 19th century opera singer (I think it was Nellie Melba). There were pictures of the reels of 16mm film and the VHS copy supposedly made from them. The centerpiece was the video clip. It was made from a couple of stills copied from a book, crudely animated, with a real talking mouth superimposed over Polly Moran's. The whole thing was so blurry and dark that it masked how fake looking it was. The joke was only posted on film forums where everyone already knew it wasn't real. Unfortunately, the video clip took on a life of its own and spread without the accompanying story. Many people who saw it didn't realize it was only poking fun at the other fellow's so-called discovery.[44]

In 1965, the South American collector "had no reason not to return the film, which he did in Culver City in 1965, surreptitiously depositing the film in MGM vault #7." The article ended by telling readers, "Expect to see *London after Midnight* on DVD and Blu-Ray sometime next month."[45] Here was another fun joke, rather than a serious announcement of a fake discovery.

In Stoker's *Dracula*, Harker notes, "I went down even into the vaults, where the dim light struggled, although to do so was a dread to my very soul. Into two of these I went, but saw nothing except fragments of old coffins and piles of dust; in the third, however, I made a discovery." Unlike film historians and collectors in search of *London after Midnight*, Harker actually finds a vampire.

The Undead

In *London after Midnight*, when Hibbs announces that he's solved the mystery, he declares that Inspector Burke is "at the bottom of it." But he is incorrect. The real culprit is Sir James Hamlin (Henry B. Walthall), as Burke proves through hypnosis. The murderer is real, but the vampire is not. And Hibbs has solved nothing, in spite of his confidence, in spite of his optimism. *London after Midnight* has not been found. The day before he committed suicide by setting his apartment on fire, F. Gwynplaine MacIntyre posted his final review on the Internet Movie Database. He wrote, "Nitrate film stock doesn't last forever, and all good things come to a happy ending."[46]

However, to be undead is not an ending, happy or sad; it is to be neither alive nor dead. For Halloween of 2019, the website *Old Hollywood in Color* posted a tribute video to Lon Chaney, featuring colorized versions of black-and-white photos with the illusion of movement added thanks to Motion Portrait software.[47] The Man in the Beaver Hat blinks and turns his head slightly, the eleven-second simulation seeming more alive than the entirety of Schmidlin's restoration. But it is a simulation. It is not the Man in the Beaver Hat moving, even if it is. He is alive, even though he is not alive. He is a faux, faux-vampire.

Figure 7.6 Film frame discovered in the Canary Islands.

Perhaps there are reasons beyond the flames of a fire that *London after Midnight* resides not in a vault. It stalks our imaginations, and with increasing verve. In 2017, the website *Dread Central* published two rediscovered film frames from *London after Midnight*. An archive in the Canary Islands had discovered them approximately five years earlier.[48] These frames are authentic, as are the nineteen amazing frames that Daniel Titley published in his book *London after Midnight: The Lost Film* (Keyreads, 2022).[49] Titley's discoveries – some of them featuring Chaney as the Man in the Beaver Hat – are revelations, their images spanning the overall film narrative. They take us closer to *London after Midnight* than we have ever been, even though they are static. They cannot move. But they are real frames from a reel film of a fake vampire. They now exist outside of any vault, burial or archival, for all to see, for all to believe.

Figure 7.7 Daniel Titley's book featuring the film frames that he rediscovered.

In *Reading the Vampire*, Ken Gelder provides the formulation "I know there are no vampires ... but I believe in them."[50] We believe in *London after Midnight*, even if do not we believe a print of it survives. The film exists, even if it does not. It is undead, as much as any vampire that ever has or has not come back from the grave.

Notes

1. Quoted in Philip J. Riley, *London after Midnight* (New York: Cornwall Books, 1985), 49.
2. Along with being mentioned in the film *London after Midnight*, the term "undead" (rendered as "un-dead") also appeared in at least one article about it. See "Haunted Castles to Feature [in] New Chaney Picture," *Los Angeles Times*, October 2, 1927, C10.
3. While the term "undead" was rarely used in the United States prior to *London after Midnight*, it was not unknown. One prominent example of its usage appears in Gorman M. Hendricks, "Haunted Houses and 'Undead' Found Here," *Washington Post*, September 30, 1923, 75.
4. Other examples would include the 1990 model kit of *London after Midnight*, as well as the twenty-first-century horror host "Lon Madnight."
5. "*London after Midnight*," *Exhibitors Herald-World*, April 27, 1929, 60.
6. "*London after Midnight*," *Exhibitors Herald-World*, June 15, 1929, 156.
7. Taylor L. White, "*Batman Returns*: Director Tim Burton Wins the Creative Control to do the Dark Knight Justice," *Cinefantastique* 21, no. 1 (August 1992): 9.
8. Gary D. Rhodes and Ryan Baker, "In Search of *London after Midnight*," *Video Watch*dog 99, September 2003, 27.
9. Henry James Forman, *Our Movie Made Children* (New York: Macmillan Company, 1935), 243.

10. Margali, "'Oly 'enry! The Bloomin' 'Ouse Is 'Aunted," in Marie Coolidge-Rask, *London after Midnight*, edited by Niels W. Erickson (United States: Couch Pumpkin Press, 2010), 7.
11. Joseph Stillman, "The Stills Move the Movies," *American Cinematographer*, November 1927, 7.
12. Later artists also depicted the Man in the Beaver Hat. For example, he appears on the February 1980 and December 1982 covers of *Cracked Collector's Edition*.
13. Ronald V. Borst with Norris Chapnick, "London after Midnight," *Famous Monsters of Filmland* 69, September 1970, 26–39. Part 2 of this "filmbook" appeared in *Famous Monsters of Filmland* 80, October 1970, 6–12. Strangely, the issue immediately after 69 was numbered 80, rather than 70.
14. "Contents," *Famous Monsters of Filmland* 69, September 1970, 5.
15. Philip J. Riley, *London After Midnight* (New York: Cornwall Books, 1985), 19–20.
16. Rhodes and Baker, 26.
17. Thomas Mann, *London after Midnight: A New Reconstruction Based on Contemporary Sources, with a Transcription of a Newly-Discovered Magazine Fictionalization of the Lost Film* (Albany, GA: BearManor Media, 2016).
18. Mann, 1–4.
19. *The Lon Chaney Collection*, DVD (Warner Bros./TCM Archives, 2003).
20. Rhodes and Baker, 25.
21. Photos had been earlier used to construct restorations of short films. See Daniel Woodruff, "Recreating Motion Pictures from Visual Artifacts," *Journal of Film Preservation* 58/59, October 1999, 63–6.
22. Martin Hafer, "Restored Intertitle Cards and Still[s] Do Not Make a Movie," user review, *Internet Movie Database*, April 7, 2012, accessed March 19, 2022, https://www.imdb.com/title/tt0018097/reviews?ref_=tt_urv.
23. Joseph K. Meadows, "*London after Midnight* – Found!," accessed March 18, 2022, https://web.archive.org/web/19990221214023/http://www.horrorwood.com/london.htm.
24. Ingrid Pitt, "The Ingrid Pitt Column: *London after Midnight*," *Den of Geek*, April 8, 2008, accessed March 18, 2022, https://www.denofgeek.com/culture/the-ingrid-pitt-column-london-after-midnight/.
25. "Happy Birthday, Lon Chaney! *London after Midnight* Found at Last!", *Dr. Film's Blog*, April 1, 2013, accessed March 19, 2022, http://www.drfilm.net/blog/?p=419.
26. Quoted in *A Thousand Cuts: The Underground World of Collectors Who Saved the Movies*, Facebook group, May 7, 2020, accessed March 19, 2022, https://www.facebook.com/aThousandCutsBook.
27. Dennis Bartok and Jeff Joseph, *A Thousand Cuts: The Bizarre Underground World of Collectors and Dealers Who Saved the Movies* (Jackson, MS: University Press of Mississippi, 2016), 177–8.
28. Michael Gebert, *London after Midnight* myths page, accessed March 18, 2022, https://www.michaelgebert.com/lam/lam1.html.
29. Ibid, https://www.michaelgebert.com/lam/lam8.html.

30. Forrest J Ackerman, "Foreword," in Riley, 15–16.
31. John Squires, "Rumor Spreading That Long-Lost *London after Midnight* Has Been Found," *Bloody Disgusting*, February 14, 2017, accessed March 12, 2022, https://bloody-disgusting.com/movie/3424566/rumor-spreading-long-lost-london-midnight-found/.
32. F. Gwynplaine MacIntyre, "*The Big City*: All of Browning's Universe in One Film," *The Cinema of Tod Browning: Essays of the Macabre and Grotesque*, edited by Bernd Herzogenrath (Jefferson, NC: McFarland, 2008), 116–31.
33. Quoted in Matt Holmes, "*London after Midnight* Is Out There . . . Somewhere!", *What Culture*, July 24, 2008, accessed March 5, 2022, https://whatculture.com/film/warner-bros-have-found-the-most-famous-lost-film-in-cinema-history-london-after-midnight.
34. Ibid.
35. Scoundrel, "*London after Midnight* . . . Lost Again . . .?", user post, *Nitrateville*, July 24, 2008, accessed March 15, 2022, https://www.nitrateville.com/viewtopic.php?p=5630&sid=00171b9f58f773de8814fc184d8b78f9.
36. Robb Farr, "*London after Midnight* . . . Lost Again . . . ?", user post, *Nitrateville*, July 25, 2008, accessed March 15, 2022, https://www.nitrateville.com/viewtopic.php?p=5630&sid=00171b9f58f773de8814fc184d8b78f9.
37. "*London after Midnight*: Amazing News or Same Old, Same Old?", *Classic Horror Film Board*, 2008, accessed March 10, 2022, https://www.tapatalk.com/groups/monsterkidclassichorrorforum/london-after-midnight-amazing-news-or-same-old-sam-t17841.html.
38. See Stefan Eickhoff, *Max Schreck: Gespenstertheater* (Munich: Belleville, 2009).
39. Michael Blake, *The Classic Horror Film Board*, July 24, 2008, accessed March 14, 2022, https://www.tapatalk.com/groups/monsterkidclassichorrorforum/london-after-midnight-amazing-news-or-same-old-sam-t17841.html.
40. Taraco (David Colton), *The Classic Horror Film Board*, October 17, 2008, accessed March 14, 2022, https://www.tapatalk.com/groups/monsterkidclassichorrorforum/london-after-midnight-amazing-news-or-same-old-sam-t17841.html.
41. TomWeaver999 (Tom Weaver), *The Classic Horror Film Board*, July 28, 2008, accessed March 14, 2022, https://www.tapatalk.com/groups/monsterkidclassichorrorforum/london-after-midnight-amazing-news-or-same-old-sam-t17841.html.
42. *London after Midnight*, March 13, 2009, accessed March 12, 2022, https://www.youtube.com/watch?v=aFk36pizlcM.
43. "*London after Midnight* Recovered," *Harpodeon*. This article was posted in 2009 at the following website, which is no longer available: http://www.harpodeon.com/london_after_midnight/.
44. Quoted in Daniel Titley, email to Gary D. Rhodes, January 18, 2022.
45. "*London after Midnight* Recovered," *Harpodeon*.
46. F. Gwynplaine MacIntyre, "*Metropolis*: My Favorite Film, My Last Review," *Internet Movie Database*, June 25, 2010, accessed March 19, 2022, https://www.imdb.com/review/rw2268894/.

47. "Lon Chaney – Just in Time for Halloween 2019," *Old Hollywood in Color*, September 26, 2019, accessed March 7, 2022, https://oldhollywoodincolor.com/tag/london-after-midnight/.
48. Steve Barton, "Update: *London after Midnight* Found?", *Dread Central*, February 14, 2017, accessed March 20, 2022, https://www.dreadcentral.com/news/214519/london-midnight-finally-found/.
49. Daniel Titley, *London after Midnight: The Lost Film* (London: Keyreads, 2022).
50. Ken Gelder, *Reading the Vampire* (New York: Routledge, 1994), 53.

CHAPTER 8

Vampires at Home

"It would be a dreadful capture to make to seize a vampyre."
– James Malcolm Rymer
Varney the Vampire, 1845–7

"I pity ye and the guv'nor for havin' to live in the house with a wild beast like that."
– Bram Stoker
Dracula, 1897

Vampire hunters are necessarily brave. Their prey is powerful. Their prey is supernatural. And their prey sees them as prey, hence the need to be well prepared, mentally, spiritually, and practically. In 2022, a vampire-slayer kit from the nineteenth century auctioned for over $15,000, its contents including holy water and brass crucifixes.[1]

In the eighteenth century, Dom Antoine Augustin Calmet recorded the use of decapitation, impaling, burning, and staking to make dead the undead.[2] Nearly two centuries later, Montague Summers explained, "The only way to obtain deliverance from their molestations is by disinterring the dead body, by cutting off the head, by driving a stake through the breast, by transfixing the heart, or by burning the corpse to ashes."[3] In Stoker's *Dracula*, Van Helsing also keeps garlic close at hand.

The means of destroying a vampire are many, of course. In F. W. Murnau's *Nosferatu* (Prana-Film, 1922), Ellen Hutter (Greta Schröder) keeps Graf Orlok (Max Schreck) in her bed all night until the cock crows at dawn. She captures a dark entity long enough to expose him to the light, thus creating an unforgettable image, his disintegration. The process is not unlike the image capture intrinsic to filmmaking. In 1928, the book *Amateur Movie Making* instructed readers that the filmmaker "must capture spirit and emotion and imprison them upon his celluloid ribbon, and for this purpose, nothing is more efficient than the lamp."[4] Artificial light or real, supernatural vampire or reel, professional vampire hunter or hobbyist, fiat lux are words to the wise. Light dispels the dark, even as it produces new images, new shades, new shadows.

Amateur filmmaking, the production of "home movies," became a somewhat popular pursuit in the mid- to late twenties, particularly for the wealthy, being spurred by cameras and projectors that used smaller gauges than 35mm. In late 1926, an editorial in the *New York Herald-Tribune* informed readers:

> When a pastime has become so popular as to warrant the publication of a magazine devoted solely to its interests, it must be recognized as a factor in the life of the people . . . Well, there is no stopping the spread of the new picture taking and no doubt it will do more good than harm.[5]

The magazine reference was to the Amateur Cinema League's official publication, *Amateur Movie Makers*. The first issue launched in December 1926, its editor predicting, "Amateur cinematography has a future that the most imaginative of us would be totally incapable of estimating."[6] Not only was this statement true in the general, it was also true in the vampiric.

In its second issue, the magazine recommended, "Make your movies move with interest. Put your family and friends in story form."[7] While shooting one's Christmas holiday and children rated as important, so too did the lure of fiction.[8] "Why not do a real photo-drama, just like they do in Hollywood?", one amateur filmmaker suggested to friends in New Jersey. All agreed, and they formed a club for that purpose, producing the five-reel "thriller" *Love by Proxy* (1926).[9] A New Yorker made *The Horsemen of Death* in circa 1926, a "super-melodrama dealing with the deeds of death and destruction of three masked riders."[10] Students at Yale produced a version of Henry Fielding's *Tom Jones* in 1927.[11] *Amateur Movie Makers* also covered the three-reeler *Fly Low Jack and the Game* (1927) and the six-reel feature *The Thrillproof Age* (1927), which included a "vamping scene."[12] The following year, another amateur shot *The Sign of the Vampire* (1928), a 400-foot "racing detective tale" featuring a "murderous maniac."[13]

As of June 1928, the Amateur Cinema League changed the name of its publication to *Movie Makers*, perhaps seeing their enterprise as being more important than merely capturing the family pet or beachside frolics, more ambitious even than films like *The Sign of the Vampire*. As the publication recommended, "For this delightful and exciting sport, a carefully prepared outfit [of 'cine equipment'] is highly desirable," meaning a great camera, panchromatic film, and a light meter.[14] Here were hunters in search of greater respect, and they considered American avant-garde filmmakers to be their colleagues. *Movie Makers* repeatedly extolled the virtues of James

Sibley Watson and Melville Webber's *The Fall of the House of Usher* (1928), using it as evidence of their declaration, "Amateurs have . . . through new cinematic methods, reached new artistic heights."[15]

Watson and Webber hunted Edgar Allan Poe. Other amateur filmmakers hunted vampires. "You are hunters of [a] wild beast, and understand it so," Van Helsing warns his comrades in Stoker's *Dracula*. Their names are Jonathan Harker, John Seward, Quincey Morris, and Lord Godalming. As for the makers of two important but largely unknown American vampire home movies of the mid- to late twenties, their names are sadly lost to time. So too are the exact dates on which they shot their films, as well as the names of their onscreen talent. Neither film has a formal title. Both are brief narratives, embedded on surviving reels that feature other images, simultaneously distinct from the vampire tales and yet connected to them, being that the entire reels could be read as stories of the lives of people who had the desire and time and money to shoot film, to capture images.

After having initially appeared on a Something Weird DVD entitled *Monsters Crash the Pajama Party Spook Show Spectacular* (2001), both films are currently preserved by Historic Films, Inc. in New York, a for-profit stock footage house.[16] Their exact journey over the decades is unknown. As Paolo Cherchi Usai has written, "In qualitative terms, the analysis of provenance in film relies on a clear understanding of both the profound connections and the equally significant differences between the image carrier and the work it represents."[17] At times, regrettably, image carriers during the life of a film become forgotten. In terms of the two vampire home movies, neither has a formal title, and so their current library numbers must serve as identifiers, as latter-day titles, however nondescriptive they are. Nevertheless, these two home movies are essential, more than might at first be expected. As Patricia R. Zimmermann has observed, "Amateur film provides a vital access point for academic historiography in its trajectory from official history to the more variegated and multiple practices of popular memory, a concretization of memory into artifacts that can be remobilized, recontextualized, and reanimated."[18]

The first of the two films to consider is *F-0343*.[19] Its overall running time is approximately ten minutes. While the Amateur Cinema League touted various post-production methods of editing home movies, the editing in *F-0343* occurs in-camera, the result of the camera operator starting and stopping the film to shoot different images at different locations. Exactly where the film was shot is unknown, but at one point we see a sign on a building that reads "Richmond Furnace." It is very likely the train depot for Richmond Iron Works in Richmond Furnace, Massachusetts.[20]

The final seven minutes includes handheld footage of three men and three women dancing and playing music, a man shooting a rifle, a dog prancing, a child playing, a man and woman horseback riding, a monkey swinging in a cage, squirrels running up a tree and across the ground, cows standing in a field, and people posing for the camera. The reel ends with various images, including a man and woman kissing, then two men talking, then an abrupt cut to black. Here are indeed home movies, the in-camera edits producing jump cuts, with the pacing of shots seeming random. The cinematography is led by the onscreen action, with not-unexpected pans to catch the action. Here are real lives preserved thanks to the motion picture. Here is amateur filmmaking of a type that the Amateur Cinema League would have approved, even while hoping for greater professionalism.

By contrast, other elements of *F-0343* speak to a degree of knowledge of film language and special effects. In one scene, a man sits in a chair on screen left, facing screen right. He stands and flaps his arms, then a match-on-action cut completes the action of his arm flapping while he and his chair have "magically" moved to the middle of the frame. He repeats the action, with a jump cutting moving him back to his original location; two more jump cuts move him to the middle and finally to the right of the frame. The trick relies on substitution splices of the type associated with Georges Méliès's creative ethos, a sensational, visually indebted aesthetic. The following scene repeats the same idea, but with far fewer frames devoted to each shot, the result making it seem as if the chair is moving somewhat rapidly, all thanks to stop-motion. The person behind the camera had some knowledge of how to make a film, knowledge of the type that *Amateur Movie Makers* shared.

Figure 8.1 Film frame from *F-0343*.

VAMPIRES AT HOME 179

Figure 8.2 Film frame from *F-0343*.

In its most well planned and realized segment, *F-0343* features a vampire story, running approximately three minutes in length, comprising six shots, with one edit meant to be invisible. The first shot lasts approximately fifty-six seconds; it is a long shot with proscenium-arch framing. It is tripod bound rather than handheld, its mise-en-scène cleverly making an outdoor setting appear to be indoors, presumably because the filmmaker was shooting stock rated for daylight. The back of the set is the side of a house with a window; thanks to having moved a sofa, chair, and lamp outside, as well as hanging a painting, the side of the house becomes a living room, albeit with a grass floor.

A male and female sit on the sofa and kiss, then the man departs. She lies down, perhaps going to sleep. The vampire soon enters through the window. Dressed in black, he wears a top hat and a sheer, bat-like cape. He has long black hair, black circles around his eyes, and sharp protruding fangs. Much care has gone into his makeup and costume, the result intentionally mimicking the appearance of Lon Chaney in Tod Browning's *London after Midnight* (MGM, 1927). Hunched over slightly, he shuffles towards the camera and then back to the sofa, his blocking creating a sense of depth. At times he looks into the camera, something the man and woman do not do. Then his hand gestures hypnotize the sleeping woman. She stands and approaches him. He embraces her and bends his head towards her neck, apparently biting her.

The second shot lasts approximately eight seconds. It is a medium shot, one that crosses the 180-degree line while still maintaining the continuity of the action, the vampire still biting the victim, then lifting his head, and then biting her and looking upwards a second time. The third shot is a long shot, the vampire holding the victim. In a minor continuity error, the shot begins with him biting her, his head thus in a notably different position than where the prior shot ended. The vampire returns the victim to the sofa before witnessing the arrival of the male hero. The vampire stretches his arms upwards and disappears into thin air. The hero seems baffled by the vampire's exit and looks out the window (which is really into the house) before rushing to the sofa and holding the woman's hand. When he releases it, her hand falls limply. She is unconscious, perhaps deceased. This shot appears to last approximately twenty-two seconds, though there is a substitution splice after ten seconds that creates the illusion of the vampire's disappearance.

F-0343 continues, its fifth shot showing the vampire standing, flanked by the male and female leads. The trio acknowledges the camera and takes a bow. The vampire story seems to have concluded in the manner of a stage play, but the filmmaker has one more image for us to experience. The sixth and final shot lasts approximately fifteen seconds. In it, we see a field, with the vampire approaching the camera, his legs somewhat crouched, his gait reminiscent of Chaney's in *London after Midnight*. The vampire stares at us as he outstretches his arms, flapping them like bat wings. His stare continues as he walks away from the camera.

Unlike the bulk of *F-0343*, the vampire story unfolds with cinematic language that illustrates careful planning and competent execution, self-contained within the larger whole of the home movie. It constitutes a recreation as well as a variation of *London after Midnight*. The Browning film and Chaney's makeup are clearly the inspiration, with *F-0343* apparently made in the days, weeks, or months following *London after Midnight*'s release in December of 1927. But while the Browning film featured a fake vampire, a detective in disguise, *F-0343* presents a startlingly different character. Its vampire is not unmasked; its vampire is not debunked. Instead, *F-0343* features a supernatural vampire, one who bites his victim, apparently to suck her blood, and one who disappears magically. The onscreen hero is unable to slay the undead, but the filmmaker behind the scenes captured him, exposing his darkness to light. The vampire hunter's shutter shuddered, all for a bit of cinematic fun.

Far more enigmatic, even if less polished, is *F-0332*, a different American home movie created by different filmmakers. It is also approximately ten minutes in length. *F-0343* begins with the vampire story. Perhaps its filmmaker believed the project would take the entire reel; perhaps not. But the filmmaker began with that story, filling out the rest of the reel with the ostensibly unrelated images. By contrast, *F-0332* does not begin its shorter and less complex vampire story until approximately six minutes into the ten-minute reel. While details about the making of *F-0332* are few, locations seen throughout the entire reel include Westhampton, New York; Patterson, New York; the Tuttle House in Oneida County, New York; and the beach at East Moriches, Long Island.

Images external to *F-0332*'s vampire story both precede and follow it. The reel begins with a hand drawing a man's portrait on a canvas. For approximately six minutes, we see quick shots of a dog panting, a man and woman sitting outside, two men dancing, friends playing games at the beach, the same people at a swimming pool, then some of them playing and dancing outside, and then a few of them boating. Their clothing, their automobiles, and their leisure activities suggest wealth. The final few minutes of the reel depict similar activities. There are also several shots of a train wreck. Every image on the reel is handheld. At times the camera operator begins to pan one direction only to change his or her mind and pan the opposite direction. These are very much home movies, wonderful home movies from the Roaring Twenties.

The vampire story in *F-0332* unfolds in approximately seven handheld shots over approximately thirty-four seconds. It begins with uncertainty, as it is difficult to discern exactly where the filmmaker intended for the vampire story to begin. He or she likely believed it started with a shot that depicts trees in the distance as a tree limb in the foreground takes up half

Figure 8.3 Film frame from *F-0332*.

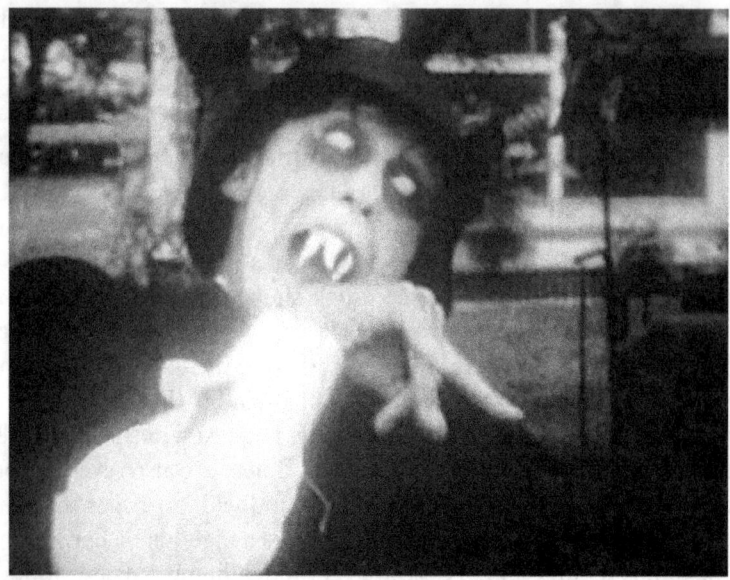

Figure 8.4 Film frame from *F-0332*.

of the frame. The image has the appearance of a filmmaker attempting to instill a sense of depth, as if someone had read a manual on photography or cinematography.

The second shot pans from left to right, showing two young women dressed in white who are walking outdoors.[21] The third shot begins with a jump cut, showing the two women seated in lawn chairs. In the upper left corner of the frame, we see part of a man's body. He is dressed in black. It would be easy for him to go unnoticed. Shot 3 continues, with the two women frightened at the sight of the offscreen vampire. Shot 4 depicts a medium long shot of the vampire, dressed in black save for a white shirt, his upper body uncannily arched backwards. His right hand makes a hypnotic gesture. Being able to examine his face for the first time, we notice two large fangs descending from the middle of his mouth. Dark makeup encircles his eyes. He wears some type of black material on his head. It is perhaps a hat, or meant to be a hat, or perhaps it is fabric to make his hair appear darker. The camera pans to follow his advance towards the offscreen women.

Shot 5 cuts inward to a medium closeup of the vampire, who moves his right hand and arm dramatically, as if he is intensifying his effort to hypnotize the offscreen women. Shot 6 shows the woman on screen right falling back into her lawn chair, as if she has been put to sleep. The camera pans to reveal the other woman doing the same, though she visibly smiles, breaking character. The camera then tilts upward to the vampire, his right hand continuing to make the same gesture. Shot 7 jump cuts to a medium long shot, the vampire standing behind a victim, one of his hands on her throat and the other holding the top of her head. He quickly steps back from her as a new character, the male hero, enters the frame. We do not initially see his face, his back being to the camera as he confronts the villain. The hero grabs the vampire by the throat and pushes him to the ground. The hero then sits on the vampire and smiles, having vanquished the undead. One of the women enters the frame to kneel and hug the hero. The camera then pans to reveal a second hero, one whom we have not seen till now, trying to bring the other woman back to consciousness. Her recovery is not depicted. The vampire tale ends abruptly, the film cutting to an image of the family dog, unless that shot, however unlikely, was also meant to be part of the story.

The vampire is not unmasked, and so we are left to believe that he is indeed supernatural, much like the vampire in *F-0343*. What the filmmakers of both stories intended is as unknown as their identities, but their narratives as realized strongly suggest that both characters are actually undead. Here then are likely the first two supernatural vampires in American film history, appearing some three years prior to the release of Tod Browning's *Dracula* (1931) with Bela Lugosi as the titular character.

While *F-0343* represents an adaptation of Browning's *London after Midnight*, the vampire of *F-0332* is far less scrutable.[22] His origins are indeterminant. At first, he too seems inspired by *London after Midnight*, including in his dark attire and makeup. The same might be true of his fangs, even though they are fewer in number and far larger than Chaney's vampire; as mentioned, he is wearing some type of hat or fabric on his head, even though it is not a top hat and quite different than Chaney's. It is understandable that an amateur filmmaker quickly shooting a simple parody in a single morning or afternoon would not necessarily have bothered to procure faithful wardrobe. And then there is *F-0332*'s emphasis on hypnotism, which also reminds us of *London after Midnight*'s story.

But *F-0332* remains enigmatic, unwilling to give up all of its secrets. Historical Films, Inc. records the reel as being from 1926, meaning at least one year prior to *London after Midnight*'s December 1927 premiere. Perhaps that is an error, or – we might consider – perhaps even if some of the initial footage on the reel dates to 1926, subsequent shots were taken weeks or months later, the partially exposed film carefully residing inside the camera until its operator decided to shoot more. Such would make sense until we revisit the reel's footage of a train wreck. That footage without doubt chronicles the train wreck at Calverton, New York, as close comparison to other surviving footage and photographs of the disaster makes certain. The train wreck occurred on August 13, 1926.[23] Perhaps the filmmaker of *F-0332* shot his train footage a day or two after the disaster, upon learning of the event and traveling to the aftermath, but a few days in August do not change matters as regards the vampire story, as it was filmed *prior* to the train wreck. It appears *earlier* on the same reel, with its only edits being in-camera. And so, the vampire story presumably cannot be a parody of *London after Midnight*.

Might the filmmaker have instead been parodying Murnau's *Nosferatu*? The dark clothing and eye makeup also evoke Count Orlok, as do the two protruding fangs, which are not canine teeth, as described in Stoker, but in the middle of the mouth, as in *Nosferatu*. And the hat worn by *F-0332*'s vampire might have been to conceal the fact he was not bald like Orlok. Perhaps it was also meant to represent Orlok's hat, which he wears during his initial meeting with Hutter. But would the apparently wealthy American filmmaker(s) of *F-0332* or, for that matter, *F-0343*, have been aware of cinema beyond mainstream Hollywood?

It is certainly possible, not just because they were interested enough in film to shoot home movies, and not just because they might have lived near New York City and its theaters, but also from reading reviews. At roughly the same time that *F-0332* and *F-0343* were produced, *Amateur Movie Makers* critiqued such films as Leopold Jessner's *Hintertreppe/Backstairs* (UFA, 1921), G. W. Pabst's *Geheimnisse einer Seele/Secrets of a Soul* (UFA, 1926), Murnau's *Tartüffe/Tartuff* (UFA, 1926), Walter Ruttmann's *Berlin: Die Sinfonias der Großstadt/Berlin: Symphony of a Great City* (Fox-Europa-Film, 1927), Fritz Lang's *Metropolis* (UFA, 1927), Murnau's *Sunrise: A Song of Two Humans* (Fox, 1927), and Carl Theodor Dreyer's *La Passion de Jeanne d'Arc/The Passion of Joan of Arc* (Société Générale des Films, 1928).[24] The publication even coined the term "Cintelligenzia" to describe those readers who attended "intellectual pictures."[25]

Even if the filmmaker(s) of *F-0332* enjoyed such films, could he or she have seen *Nosferatu* before or during the year 1926? The answer is yes. The American representative for Russian Artfilm had offered *Nosferatu* for rental in 1924, though to be sure *Nosferatu*'s publicized screenings in the New York area did not occur until 1929.[26] But *Nosferatu* had been screened in major European countries prior to 1926, including Germany and England in 1922. The film also appeared onscreen in France in 1925. Might the wealthy filmmaker making *F-0332* have traveled to Europe during or prior to 1926? It is certainly possible. *F-0332* includes footage of what appears to be a circa 1926 Crossley automobile in New York, and yet Crossley automobiles were never marketed in North America.[27] The owner would likely have purchased it in England and had it shipped it to the United States.

To be sure, the filmmaker of *F-0332* would not have needed to have watched *Nosferatu* to have been inspired by it, as photographs of the film appeared in various period publications, not just in Germany, but also in

Figure 8.5 The cover of *Le Film Complet* for December 3, 1925.

France, including in two issues of *Le Film Complet* in 1925, one of them featuring the hat-wearing Orlok on its cover.[28] But such possibilities do not unravel the mysteries of *F-0332*. In *Nosferatu*, Orlok is not a hypnotist, and that is central to the brief narrative of *F-0332*.

Might the filmmaker have taken inspiration from *Dracula* onstage? Here is another possibility, though Hamilton Deane and John L. Balderston's *Dracula – The Vampire Play* did not open on Broadway until October of 1927. For that matter, Deane's version (prior to Balderston's involvement) did not play in London's West End until July of 1927. However, Deane had staged *Dracula* in the British provinces from August 1924, and it had received much publicity, including in America. Seeing the play in England would explain the hypnotism, the dark clothing, and perhaps the dark eye makeup. Perhaps the hat in *F-0332* – given that Dracula does not wear one in the stage play – was indeed meant less to be a hat than an improvised way to darken one's hair, presuming the actor had light-colored hair. The owner of a Crossley returned to America with an automobile on a ship and a vampire in his nightmares.

Or not. Perhaps the filmmaker of *F-0332* had read Stoker's *Dracula* but had not seen *Nosferatu* or *Dracula – The Vampire Play*. Perhaps the costuming was nothing more than the filmmaker's personal visualization of Stoker's written descriptions. Stoker also invokes hypnotism repeatedly, though he concentrates largely on Van Helsing hypnotizing Mina. For that matter, the filmmaker might have been aware of other nineteenth-century vampire literature. Indeed, the filmmaker might have, even within mere seconds or minutes of thought, combined elements from various literature and/or theater and/or cinema, the resultant vampire thus becoming an amalgam, a witch's brew. Or the filmmaker might have relied less on previous vampires and more on his or her own imagination than it would seem. We do not know. *F-0332* is a vampire film that was apparently made in America in 1926. From there, fog rolls in, leaving us with nothing more than – as Dr. Seward says in Stoker's novel – "a view to making [ourselves] master of the facts of his hallucination."

In *Varney the Vampire*, we read, "all these dreams began to vanish into thin air, and, like the unsubstantial fabric of a vision, to leave no trace behind them." In *Dracula*, Stoker writes, "before our very eyes, and almost in the drawing of a breath, the whole body crumbled into dust and passed from our sight." Such seems to be true of the filmmakers of *F-0332* and *F-0343* and their rationale for shooting these home movies, which together probably do constitute the first supernatural vampires in American cinema.

While the filmmakers have faded to dust, their visions were not unsubstantial. The vampires they hunted, the vampires they captured and exposed, those remain. As a filmmaker excitedly announced in the December 1926 issue of *Amateur Movie Makers*:

> We had been successful in the most difficult of all hunting – where all the conditions for shooting must be present as well as many others, such as direction of light, background for the picture, time enough to get action on the screen and proximity to get a reasonably large picture. Now I can bring back the scene at will both for myself and my friends. If you don't believe such hunting is both difficult and exciting, try it for yourself.[29]

Notes

1. Isobel Whitcomb, "Mysterious Vampire-Slayer Kit Sells at Auction for $15,600," *Live Science*, July 8, 2022, accessed August 2, 2022, https://www.livescience.com/vampire-slaying-kit-sold-auction.
2. Augustine [sic] Calmet, *The Phantom World: or, The Philosophy of Spirits, Apparitions, &c., Volume I* (London: Richard Bentley, 1850), 300.
3. Montague Summers, *The Vampire, His Kith and Kin* (London: Kegan Paul, Trench, Trubner, 1928), 29.
4. Herbert C. McKay, *Amateur Movie Making* (New York: Falk Publishing Company, Inc., 1928), 112.
5. Quoted in "They Tell the Story," *Amateur Movie Makers*, January 1927, 21.
6. "Amateur Cinema League: A Close Up," *Amateur Movie Makers*, December 1926, 7.
7. Kenneth E. Nettleton, "Stories – Not Specimens," *Amateur Movie Makers*, January 1927, 11.
8. C. W. Gibbs, "Vacation Filming," *Movie Makers*, July 1930, 420–1; West Holbrook, "A Cinemerry Christmas," *Amateur Movie Makers*, December 1927, 18–19.
9. Frederick T. Hollowell, "*Love by Proxy*," *Amateur Movie Makers*, December 1926, 10.
10. "Swaps," *Amateur Movie Makers*, March 1927, 34.
11. "Hollywood at Harkness," *Amateur Movie Makers*, August 1927, 28.
12. "Actors as Amateurs," *Amateur Movie Makers*, October 1927, 26; Kenneth E. Nettleton, "*The Thrillproof Age*: An Amateur Presentation at New Haven," *Amateur Movie Makers*, January 1927, 17.
13. "Poulson Thrillers," *Movie Makers*, August 1928, 519.
14. W. E. Kidder, "Hints for Cine Hunters," *Movie Makers*, September 1930, 537.
15. Arthur L. Gale, "The March of the Clubs," *Movie Makers*, December 1928, 774.
16. *Monsters Crash the Pajama Party Spook Show Spectacular*, DVD (Seattle, WA: Something Weird Video, 2001). This DVD does not feature the entirety of *F-0343* and *F-0332*, just the vampire-specific scenes.
17. Paolo Cherchi Usai, "Film Provenance: A Framework for Analysis," in *Provenance and Early Cinema*, edited by Joanne Bernardi, Paolo Cherchi Usai, Tami Williams, and Joshua Yumibe (Bloomington, IN: Indiana University Press, 2020), 23.
18. Patricia R. Zimmermann, "Introduction, The Home Movie Movement: Excavations, Artifacts, Minings," in *Mining the Home Movie: Excavations in Histories and Memories*, edited by Karen L. Ishizuka and Patricia R. Zimmermann (Berkeley, CA: University of California Press, 2007), 1.
19. *F-0343*, accessed July 7, 2022, https://www.historicfilms.com/search/?q=F-0343#p1.
20. Erin Hunt (Curator, Berkshire County Historical Society), email to Gary D. Rhodes, July 5, 2022.
21. It is evident that the transfer of *F-0332* is backwards, given an onscreen number visible during the train wreck. Thus, as I refer to screen left and right, I am using

the terms as they would be properly applied to the film, not as they appear in the backwards transfer.

22. *F-0332*, accessed June 3, 2022, https://www.historicfilms.com/share/deda5cdc20e924d3a1d9bf9a950f92a81f84e1c5#sc_66ce70978da5fac2568bb110eaee02d5c6f05b1f_.
23. "Train Wreck is Laid to Lost Switch Pin," *New York Times*, August 15, 1926, 3.
24. "*Backstairs*," *Amateur Movie Makers*, July 1927, 23; "*Secrets of a Soul*," *Amateur Movie Makers*, June 1927, 22; "*Tartuffe*," *Amateur Movie Makers*, September 1927, 22; "*Berlin*," 464; "*Metropolis*," *Amateur Movie Makers*, May 1927, 45; "*Sunrise*," *Amateur Movie Makers*, November 1927, 20; "*The Passion of Joan of Arc*," *Movie Makers*, April 1929, 232.
25. See, for example, Gilbert Seldes, "The Intellectual Film," *Amateur Movie Makers*, March 1927, 15, 38.
26. Advertisement, *Film Daily*, February 7, 1924, 4; "Foreign Films Here," *The Film Daily*, February 10, 1924, 10.
27. Malcolm Asquith (Crossley Motors Automobile Club, Inc.), email to Gary D. Rhodes, June 21, 2022.
28. The two issues of *Le Film Complet* to which I refer were no. 195 (March 12, 1925), and no. 196 (June 12, 1925). Issue 195 featured images of Orlok wearing his hat on the cover as well as in an interior photograph.
29. C. E. Skinner, "Moose Ahead – Camera!", *Amateur Movie Makers*, December 1926, 31.

CHAPTER 9

Transformations

"Le vamp est mort, vive la vamp."
— Dorothy Dalton, 1917[1]

"The word vamp was so misused
that it died a natural death"
— Margaret Livingston, 1927[2]

"[H]e might creep again about the ship, like
Dracula, gorging himself with blood."
— John W. Lind, 1924[3]

Victims of vampires do not immediately become vampires. A period of transition occurs, whether it unfolds over minutes, days, or weeks. In Bram Stoker's *Dracula* (1897), the Count not only drinks Mina's blood, but also shares his own, making her sup from an open wound on his chest. During a slow transformation, Mina can feel what Dracula feels, see what Dracula sees, and hear what Dracula hears, even though vast geography separates them. She is a "poor soul in worse than mortal peril." The process of becoming is underway, for her character in the fin de siècle, just as it would be for the screen vampire during the Roaring Twenties.

In 1921, *The Nation* pointedly asked readers, "What shall be done with the vampires?":

> Do they not obviously corrupt the morals of the young – or have the young of today morals? And if they have no morals – as more than one passionate preacher has hinted – will not the vampires, those black-gowned, sylph-like, cigarette-smoking, eye-rolling enemies of their own sex, keep them from ever acquiring any.[4]

Here the question had to do with the negative effect that screen vamps could have on American youth. As Reverend William F. Crafts preached that same year, "I would rather have my son stand at a bar and drink two glasses of beer that have him see that [movie] vampire woman . . . he could not forget that vampire woman until he was 80 years old."[5]

These sentiments were not new. In 1916, a newspaper editorial declared that it was "time for movies to move" beyond the vamp era.[6] The following year, *Motion Picture News* published the following "sage" advice from the public to the producers: "we don't approve of vampire women nor of vampire men either."[7] Then, in 1918, another writer demanded that Hollywood "bury in oblivion the superfluous screen 'he vampire.'"[8] Women's organizations condemned vamps during the late teens, even as one company manufactured vampire dolls with "roguish eyes."[9]

Others also questioned the value of screen vampires, but for very different reasons, including their cultural currency and box-office appeal. As early as 1920, *Picture-Play Magazine* quoted a "solon of the studio" who stated the "vampire is dead."[10] In 1921, a newspaper journalist told readers, "It is well to note the characteristics of the Vampire, for the species is about to die out."[11] That same year, May Allison wrote an article called "Style Changes in Vamps," in which she recounted:

> the passing of the brunette vampire a few years ago (and really, the development of the cinema has been so rapid that a matter of several years seems ages), the dark creatures of somber moods that loved to drape themselves in fantastic funeral gowns, glide sinuously about exotic rooms, or recline languorously on divans, and shower burning glances on some weakly adoring male of the species.
>
> And where are the vamps of yesteryear?
>
> Gone, they have gone the way of all flesh, and what a cause for genuine joy that gives me! For the whole thing was silly – grotesquely untrue to life and accordingly untrue to the art of the motion picture. Instead, the pendulum has swung to the extreme opposite and now in the hearts of the great picture-going public is enshrined the more feminine, more artless blonde beauty.
>
> And with the blonde type has come the baby pout, deliciously supplanting the hypnotic blank stare; the tender mild request succeeding the imperious gesture of command; the winsomeness and simplicity replacing the gloomy tragedy, and best of all, the happy ending with the marriage and the little home for two, instead of the wretched suicide and shrug of disgust at the comedy of life.[12]

Some thought the vamp had become old-fashioned. Others believed the flapper had usurped her.[13] In 1920, Marion Harris recorded the song *I'm a Jazz Vampire* for Columbia Records, which combined elements of the two.[14] By contrast, ads for Harry Lehman's *Reported Missing* (Select Pictures, 1922) proclaimed the film pitted "Flapper Vs. Vampire," with the two types of women portrayed by Pauline Garon and Nita Naldi.[15]

In 1922, Emmet J. Flynn directed a remake of *A Fool There Was*, with Estelle Taylor portraying what had once been Theda Bara's character. *Photoplay* condemned Taylor for being a "feeble vampire," adding that the overall film had clearly been produced with an "eye to the censor."[16] *The Film Daily* surmised that producer William Fox was "trying to renew interest in vampire pictures which the public has apparently become

Figure 9.1 The title lobby card for *Exit the Vamp* (Paramount, 1921). (Courtesy of Heritage Auctions.)

disinterested in [during] the past few years."[17] Perhaps another film showed greater cultural awareness, at least in terms of its title: *Exit the Vamp* (Paramount, 1921).[18]

The obituaries continued. In 1922, producer Winfield R. Sheehan affirmed that vamps were doomed.[19] In 1923, actress Virginia Pearson observed, "The straight vamp type has just about passed out of the pictures, as well as the stage."[20] In 1925, the *Los Angeles Times* published a cartoon entitled *In the Days Beyond Recall: The Vampire*.[21] That same year, the *Washington Post* published an article called "Farewell to the Vamp," which explained that audiences had:

> turned thumbs down on the vamp and her younger sister, the flapper. It's the nice girl type that is bringing home the box-office bacon . . . [Vamp] films had a run for a while, but at no time had they the box-office drawing power of the romantic drama. Vamps blossomed and died on the stem.
>
> . . . The stars don't have to visit any of the numerology experts or horoscope casters to tell them what their best year is likely to be. They know it is the year in which they give up vamping and flapping and substitute heart appeal for sex appeal.[22]

In 1926, Philip Burne-Jones – whose painting (and its accompanying poem by Rudyard Kipling) spurred the vamp into popularity – died.[23] The same seemed to be happening to his creation. As actress Barbara La Marr appropriately asked in the mid-twenties, "In the final analysis, what is a vampire?"[24]

Shadowy Figures

Stage magician Howard Thurston presented a show that, like so many of his forerunners, featured spooky and occult elements, all clearly publicized as being illusions rather than reality. Along with broaching spiritualism and sorcery, Thurston offered a unique trick in 1920, one he called "The Vampire":

> Thurston has a wax face and bust of a woman brought out and placed on a pedestal. He paints in eyes, mouth, eyebrows, etc., finishing with a powder puff. His assistants then dress the image, and, when wheeled around before the electrified gaze of the audience, the figure comes to life, and, after being "wound up" by the tireless Thurston, does a mechanical dance.[25]

For many audiences, the trick was thrilling, its character being as much a supernatural vampire as natural vamp.

During the early twenties in America, the supernatural vampire became increasingly visible. In 1921, *American Cinematographer* defined the term "vamp" as "Short for bloodsucking vampire. The villainess in a picture play who steals a man willing to be stolen, or that some other woman is trying to steal."[26] Surprisingly, perhaps, the folkloric character came before the cinematic. Then, in 1923, the *Washington Post* published a story about haunted houses. It began:

> Shadowy figures in the garb of years gone by flitting from room to room. Eerie cries sounding in the dead of night. The white-clad figure of a beautiful girl, her face distorted by a pair of wolflike fangs, "undead" as the result of her own death at the hands of a dread "vampire" more than 70 years ago, leaving her vault at midnight and, herself turned "vampire," preying on the surrounding neighborhood.[27]

One witness claimed that the vampire possessed the "gleam of hell fire" in its eyes and reeked with the "foul odor of the charnel house." Days after encountering it, the man died.[28] Allegedly.

Figure 9.2 Published in the New Orleans *Times-Picayune* on December 7, 1924.

Bloodthirsty vampires continued to appear in print. In 1924, the American press told readers about German serial killer Fritz Haarmann, who was "accused of cutting his victims' throats and drinking their blood."[29] "I smashed their skulls in and sawed their bodies to pieces after biting their throats," he confessed.[30] In 1925, the *New York Times* published reports from Mexico about "winged vampires [that were] making savage attacks on inhabitants."[31] Other writers of the period discussed supernatural vampires in relation to vampire bats.[32]

The world of fiction also embraced the supernatural vampire. Published first in *The Strand* in Great Britain and then *Hearst's International* in America, Arthur Conan Doyle's *The Adventures of the Sussex Vampire* (1924) became the most famous vampire short story of the decade.[33] Holmes belittles the vampire superstition as "pure lunacy" before proving that such a creature does not exist. But supernatural vampires did exist, at least in literature. *Weird Tales* published approximately eight vampire stories between January 1925 and September 1928, including Victor Rowan's *Four Wooden Stakes* in February 1925, Arthur Leeds's *Return of the Undead* in November 1925, August Derleth's *Bat's Belfry* in May 1926, and Seabury Quinn's *The Man Who Cast No Shadow* in March 1927.[34]

THE STORY OF SUPERSTITIONS

NOWADAYS the word "vampire" has lost all the terrifying significance it had in olden times. It has been shortened to the colloquial "vamp," and in the movies it is used to designate a special type of beautiful, dark-haired young woman possessing decided sex appeal.

BUT to say "vampire" in medieval times called up a picture of a ravishingly beautiful woman who preyed on men and, by her physical allurements, drew them on to ruin and death. The good wives of those days feared the mythical vampires and believed them to be real creatures.

Figure 9.3 Published in the *Detroit Times* on May 18, 1927.

The arrival of these new supernatural vampires did not displace Dracula as being the most notable. In 1921, a journalist at the *Baltimore Sun* wrote, "I suppose there is not reader of these musings who does not know Bram Stoker's *Dracula*. In that cheap and flashy book, the terrible soon degenerates into the grotesque, and the reader ends it in weary disgust."[35] As an actress explained in 1924, "A vampire is a horrible creature that stalks from the grave at midnight, eyes blazing and wolfish teeth champing – but read *Dracula* by Bram Stoker (no ad intended) if you want to get the lowdown on vampires and were-wolves and such like demoniacal beings."[36] As of 1929, *Dracula* had sold an average of 30,000 copies per year since its publication.[37]

And Dracula – as if repeating his movements in Stoker's novel – began to move from the east, making "silent and ghostly way to the west," specifically into new entertainment terrain. In 1924, *Variety* described Hamilton Deane's British stage adaptation, claiming "Women fainted and men urged the actors to desist from their blood-thirsty conduct," before adding, "The future fate of the dramatization of *Dracula* is not known."[38] In 1927, after so many successful appearances in the provinces, *Dracula* debuted in London's West End. Even though he complained the play was badly written, the critic at London's *Graphic* confessed that his heart had leapt a half dozen times while watching it.[39] As the *London Daily News* advised, "For those who like horrors, *Dracula* can be thoroughly recommended."[40]

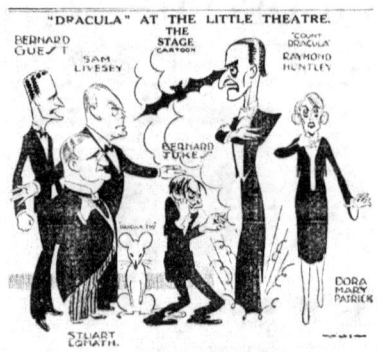

Figure 9.4 Artwork depicting Hamilton Deane's adaptation of *Dracula* during its successful run in London.

After seeing *Dracula* in England, Horace Liveright purchased the rights for the United States and hired writer John L. Balderston to "Americanize" the story.[41] *Dracula – The Vampire Play* starred Bela Lugosi in the title role when it opened on Broadway in October 1927. One newspaper felt obliged to explain that the play's title character was not the vamp of the "modern vernacular," but rather a "supernatural demon or ghost who sucks the blood of persons asleep."[42]

The Billboard suggested, "Perhaps werewolf would be a clearer description, the real meaning of vampire having been so confused in common misusage."[43] *Variety*'s critic relied on both terms for clarity when recounting, "Once Dracula is proven to be the werewolf or vampire, the battle between him and the professor wages."[44]

Werewolves and vampires had long been considered analogous creatures.[45] As early as 1865, Sabine Baring-Gould had written about their similarities.[46] In Stoker's novel, Jonathan Harker does not know whether to translate a given word as "were-wolf or vampire." Dracula himself boasts that some people compared the warlike Szekelys to "were-wolves." And in the Deane-Balderston play, the term "werewolf" is heard four times. In it, Van Helsing asks, "You have both heard the legends of Central Europe, about the Were-wolf, the Vampires?" Later, he inquires, "You think the Werewolf has done this too?" Harker adopts the term as well, fearing "the Werewolf is about."

But twentieth century attempts to replace the word "vampire" with "werewolf" were fraught with difficulties. To begin, the term werewolf refers to a lycanthrope and does not fully encapsulate what a supernatural vampire is. To add to the confusion, wolf-like terminology had already been applied to vamps. For example, Louise Glaum appeared in Raymond B. West's *The Wolf Woman* (Triangle, 1916), a film that supposedly featured "the vampire supreme."[47] *Motion Picture Mail* told readers:

> So we suppose we shall have to forgive Mr. [C. Gardner] Sullivan for writing *The Wolf Woman*, and granting that the picture public wants photoplays in which a "wolf woman," or a "moth," or a "spider," or some such vampires through five reels of celluloid, ruins men, "weaves webs," and all the rest of it, and that [the producing company] Triangle thought its duty to supply the public's demands.[48]

And then there was Rudolf Lothar's play *Der Werwolf*, which opened in Berlin in 1921. Gladys Unger adapted into it English. Premiering on Broadway in 1924, *The Werewolf* was a sex comedy about an amorous butler who is mistakenly believed to be Don Juan's ghost. The title character – initially portrayed in America by Bela Lugosi – was a male vamp.[49]

As the *New York American* grumbled in 1927, "The average New Yorker, asked to define a vampire, would say 'Theda Bara.' And that is as far as his lore goes."[50] The *Boston Transcript* added:

> Ever since somebody – they do say Burne-Jones, but it's beyond believing – painted that screaming potboiler of a Theda Bara sitting on the end of Mr. Kipling's bedside, the word "vampire" can be bought for two cents in the Hollywood coinage. *Dracula* . . . will at least remind us of that the original vampires buried their fangs into better things than heavy sugar daddies.[51]

To provide clarity, *Vanity Fair* informed readers that Dracula was a "vampire of the old school."[52] The Cleveland *Plain Dealer* called Dracula a "classic type of fictional human vampire."[53] And the *San Francisco Examiner* explained that the play dealt with "vampires of old," rather than of the "Hollywood variety."[54]

Within two weeks of *Dracula*'s Broadway premiere, news of a nearby supernatural vampire appeared in the press:

> Belief in the vampire, most gruesome of ghosts, apparently still lives. Within the last 10 days an effort seems to have been made to [slay] a vampire by the time-honored method of sinking a spike through the heart of his corpse.
>
> On one lonely farm in a wild portion of Long Island, eight miles south of the village of Huntington, lies a small graveyard overrun with weeds and screened from passersby by a cluster of gnarled scrub pines.
>
> Here in August, 70 years ago, they buried Francis Sands, a young farmer of the neighborhood. His wife Phebe was laid to rest at his side in 1874. Since that time no burials have been made. The weeds have grown high around the headstones.
>
> The tract on which the cemetery lies was bought four years ago by Ernest A. Bigelow of New York as a part of a large block of farmland. It is a lonely place.
>
> ... [The new owner and a friend] wandered about, inspected a deserted farmhouse and came at last to the little cemetery with its twenty-odd graves. To their amazement they found that the grave of Francis Sands had been recently opened.
>
> Fresh earth was piled on either side of the grave and a hole three feet deep had been made. But what startled them most was that into the earth at the bottom of the hole, exactly where the heart of the dead man would be, had been driven a hardwood stake.
>
> A superstition centuries old has stalked into the graveyard and left its mark.[55]

The story's publication and likely even its origin stemmed from *Dracula*'s success on Broadway.

Interest in the supernatural creature not only continued, but also grew measurably. A 1928 newspaper report described a Baltimore boy's "vampire complex," his obsession being to bite others. "I did it because I liked to see the warm blood flow," he admitted.[56] Montague Summers's nonfiction books *The Vampire, His Kith and Kin* and *The Vampire in Europe* were published in America in 1929.[57] As an advertisement for one of them heralded, "The Blood Suckers Are in the Cemetery Again!"[58]

Nevertheless, in 1929, Bela Lugosi discussed that a degree of cultural "confusion" continued to exist over the "exact meaning" of the term vampire:

> The word has generally been associated with motion picture stars whose so-called "sex-appeal" is often more obvious than convincing. According to Webster, "In the superstition of Eastern Europe, a vampire is a ghost which sucks the blood of its sleeping victim. One who lives upon others."[59]

A journalist in November 1929 agreed that the two vampires remained in competition with one another:

A vampire to the average reader in this part of the world means a type of motion picture actress. And the announcement of a vampire plays leads one to expect a Theda Bara character with dark-circled eyes, a feline expression and long claw-like finger nails, luring a man on to destruction.[60]

By contrast, only days later, another writer claimed, "the word 'vampire' [meaning the screen vamp], which came so much into vogue, has all but slipped from usage."[61]

What was actually happening? It is evident that the vamp became important in the construction of the supernatural vampire of the twenties, much as the reverse had happened in the fin de siècle. As portrayed by Edna Tichenor, the "Bat Girl" in Tod Browning's *London after Midnight* (MGM, 1927) featured dark hair, dark eyes, dark makeup, and a funereal gown not dissimilar to Theda Bara's appearance during the previous decade. Then, in 1929, *Motion Picture Classic* published a full-page photograph of Lugosi as Dracula that illuminated only his face and claw-like hands, the rest of his body engulfed by darkness. Its caption read, "The Kiss that Kills." Here was the male vamp, with dark hair and makeup, relying on his sexual power. Here was also the supernatural vampire who consumed blood to sustain his undead existence. The two types of vampires had merged, rather than one completely replacing the other.

The Strangest Passion

As early as 1915, Universal Pictures contemplated a film adaption of Stoker's *Dracula*.[62] Five years later, the *Oakland Tribune* published this announcement:

> Will Tod Browning's [sic] attempt to Little-Theaterize the screen? That's what Hollywood is asking since the rumor spread that this courageous young director wants to produce *Dracula* as a motion picture. *Dracula* is a daring novel that shocked even New York.
>
> They say that if [studio mogul] Carl Laemmle tells Browning to go ahead, Universal will probably start advertising, "He's going to shock you if it takes a million of our dollars to do it!"[63]

Laemmle was not swayed. In 1923, he wrote, "We have considered *Dracula* by Bram Stoker a little too gruesome to screen."[64] Nevertheless, in 1925, newspaper readers learned:

> Mr. Laemmle may present Bram Stoker's great thriller *Dracula* and that Arthur Edmund Carewe, who plays the mysterious, intriguing Persian in *The Phantom [of the Opera* (Universal, 1925)] and who was Svengali in *Trilby* [First National, 1923], may play the title role."[65]

Once again, Laemmle decided against the project. But the success of the Broadway version convinced his son, Carl Laemmle, Jr. ("Junior Laemmle"), to proceed, with trade publications mentioning his intention as early as 1928.[66]

In 1930, Universal Pictures acquired the rights to Stoker's novel and the Broadway play, famously producing *Dracula* as a talking picture. Tod Browning directed; Bela Lugosi starred. The industry press reported that Junior Laemmle and Tod Browning pondered whether the film "should be a thriller or romance" before deciding "to make it both."[67] Decades later, Laemmle recalled much the same: "We decided to hype it as both, and I've never regretted it."[68]

Figure 9.5 This artwork, published on the cover of *The Film Daily* on November 9, 1930, uses the tagline, "The Story of the Strangest Passion the World Has Ever Known."

For Laemmle, the "romance" angle had three possible benefits. For one, it might temper the story's gruesome aspects. Secondly, it might appeal to female moviegoers. Thirdly, it could incorporate the screen vamp tradition even as it reclaimed the vampire terminology for the supernatural. Consider the advance ads for Dracula in *The Film Daily* during November 1930:

> What is a Vampire Kiss? Only *Dracula* knows![69]
> Do human vampires actually exist? See *Dracula*.
> Was it a blessing or a curse? The kiss of *Dracula*.
> *Dracula* will get you if you don't watch out![70]

Such language drew upon the popularity of the novel and stage play while emphasizing Dracula's romantic and sexual prowess.

That same month, *The Film Daily* published an advertisement for *Dracula* on its cover, offering a tagline that relied on the vamp tradition: "The Story of the Strangest Passion the World Has Ever Known."[71] The ad depicted a woman who is fast asleep in her bed. Her gown is low-cut.

Her right nipple is erect. Descending from above is Dracula, his face staring down at her. His hand approaches her body.

Another ad proclaimed, "He Lived on the Kisses of Youth!" In it, Dracula looms over Mina (Helen Chandler) and Lucy (Frances Dade), his hands poised to grab both of them.[72] The image is much less one of romance than of unbridled sexual passion. A more daring exploration of the same idea appeared in an advertisement published in *Motion Picture Herald* on January 31, 1931. Dracula stands with his arm extended, as if to hypnotize nine women on the opposite page. They stand in elegant poses, none of them appearing frightened. One of them even applies makeup, apparently eager to impress the vampire.

The month before *Dracula*'s premiere, *Motion Picture Classic* published an interview with Lugosi, in which he recalled:

> When I was playing *Dracula* on the stage, my audiences were women. *Women*. There were men, too. Escorts the women *had brought with them*. For reasons only their dark subconscious knew. In order to establish a subtle sex intimacy. Contact. In order to cling and to feel the sensuous thrill of protection. Men did not come of their own volition. *Women did*. Came – and knew an ecstasy dragged from the depths of unspeakable things. Came – *and then came back again*. And *again*.[73]

Whether Lugosi said or believed these words is not as important as what they help to explain, meaning Universal's conscious publicity effort to merge vamps and vampires into the same character.

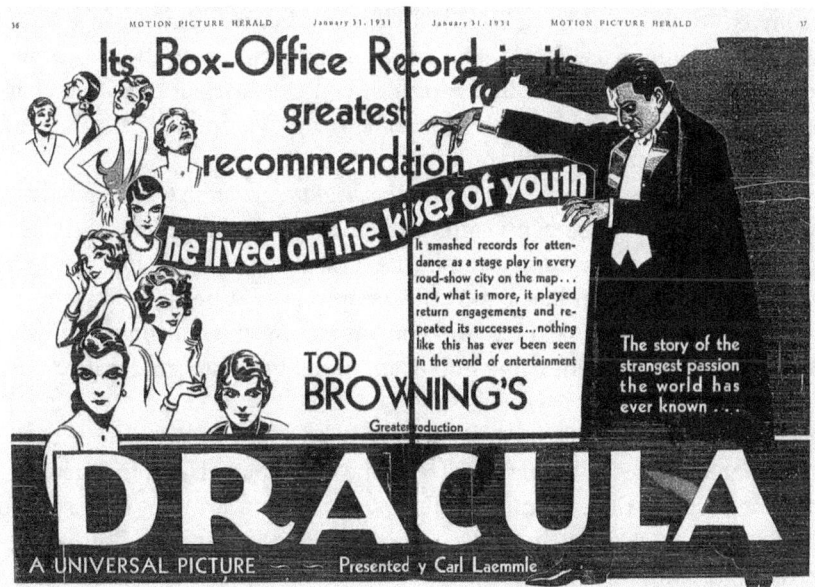

Figure 9.6 Published in *Motion Picture Herald* on January 31, 1931.

Consummation

In 1929, a journalist declared, "The vampire of the screen is gone, forgotten, dead and buried without the glory of a tombstone to designate her resting place."[74] Another writer that year believed:

> The stage revival of *Dracula*, Bram Stoker's veteran literary thriller (and it is!), may have aroused interest in the legendary figure of the vampire, that phantom of horror supposed to perpetuate its life in the grave by sallying forth to draw blood from some hapless human victim.[75]

But even if the vamp was largely "dead and buried," it didn't necessarily need the "glory of a tombstone," because it rose again, in undead style, and not just in the form of Lugosi's Dracula, but also his three wives in Browning's 1931 film, their make-up and gowns as evocative of Theda Bara as they were of Bram Stoker. The same was true of Luna (Carroll Borland) in Browning's *Mark of the Vampire* (MGM, 1935), of the title character in Lambert Hillyer's *Dracula's Daughter* (Universal, 1936), of Katherine Caldwell (Louise Allbritton) in Robert Siodmak's *Son of Dracula* (Universal, 1943), and of Dr. Sandra Mornay (Lenore Aubert) in Charles Barton's *Abbott and Costello Meet Frankenstein* (Universal, 1948).

In varying degrees, the same could be said of the vampire films produced from the fifties to the present day, whether the sexualized Draculas played by Christopher Lee and Frank Langella, or the vampire women of Hammer Film Productions, Ltd. Later vampires like those seen in Tony Scott's *The Hunger* (MGM, 1983), in Michael Almereyda's *Nadja* (Michael Almereyda, 1994), and in so many other movies have drawn upon the vamp tradition, directly or indirectly, as have such cartoon characters as Morticia Addams and horror hosts as Vampira (Maila Nurmi) and Elvira (Cassandra Peterson).

In 1931, Ernest Jones's book *On the Nightmare* rightly connected the "sexual charms" of screen vamps with the "particularly perversely sexual" attributes of folkloric vampires.[76] The vamp did not die. And the flapper did not usurp her. It was the vampire, the supernatural vampire, who undertook that role. Here was consummation and consumption, with the natural partner remaining important even as the supernatural partner became dominant.

The resultant vampires speak. Vampires had talked for centuries, but the resultant vampires could be heard audibly, with great clarity, in a new era, the era of sound film. From Browning's *Dracula* onward, they have spoken loudly. Nonetheless, their forebears in silent cinema remain with us, quietly, importantly, and immortally. And they thirst for us. They shall always thirst for us, just as we thirst for them. Let us conclude with a memory of Stoker's novel, one of Harker's diary entries, one in which Dracula does not speak. Instead, Harker tells us that he noticed the vampire's "quiet smile, with the sharp, canine teeth lying over the red underlip," adding "I understood as well as if he had spoken."

Figure 9.7 Dracula (Bela Lugosi) and Mina (Helen Chandler) in a publicity still for Tod Browning's *Dracula* (Universal, 1931).

Notes

1. Quoted in "The Vampire Role a Thing of the Past," *Montgomery Advertiser* (Montgomery, AL), November 18, 1917, 29.
2. "Day of Old Style 'Vamp' Is Passed," *Los Angeles Times*, November 13, 1927, C18.
3. John E. Lind, "The Book of the Month: Studies in Murder," *The Bookman: A Review of Books and Life*, September 1924, 88.
4. Quoted in "Revamping the Vamp," *The Billboard*, August 20, 1921, 17.
5. Marguerite Dean, "What Sort of 'Vampire' Really Vamps?," *Buffalo Times*, January 2, 1921, 1
6. "Time for Movies to Move," *Washington Post*, September 30, 1916, 6.
7. "The Public Speaks," *Motion Picture News*, February 24, 1917, 1196.
8. "Film Villains Imaginary," *The Billboard*, July 10, 1918, 49.
9. See, for example: "Bar Vampire Films, Club Women's Plea," *Jackson Citizen Patriot* (Jackson, MI), April 6, 1918, 11; "Death to the Vampire," *Wid's Daily*, October 30, 1920, 1. With regard to vampire dolls, see advertisement in *The Plain Dealer* (Cleveland, OH), November 30, 1919, 49.
10. Herbert Howe, "Viva La Vampire," *Picture-Play Magazine*, July 1920, 67.
11. "The Vampire," *New Britain Herald*, February 14, 1921, 10.
12. May Allison, "Styles Change in Vamps," *Washington Post*, July 24, 1921, 42.
13. "The Vampire and the Flapper," *Motion Picture Magazine*, April 1923, 90.
14. For information on the song's origin, see "Jazz Vampire," *The Billboard*, July 24, 1920, 29.
15. Advertisement, *Tuscaloosa News* (Tuscaloosa, AL), June 26, 1922, 3.
16. "*A Fool There Was* – Fox," *Photoplay*, October 1922, 60.
17. "Will Please Those Who Liked the Old Vampire Pictures," *The Film Daily*, July 23, 1922, 3.
18. "Pleasing Entertainment Made More So by a Pleasing Star," *The Film Daily*, February 5, 1922, 17.
19. "'Vampire' Films Are Doomed, Says Director Sheehan," *Kalamazoo Gazette* (Kalamazoo, MI), November 17, 1922, 26.
20. "Blond Vampire Most Dangerous Serpent Type," *Los Angeles Times*, May 13, 1923, III41.
21. "In the Days Beyond Recall: The Vampire," *Los Angeles Times*, July 5, 1925, C2.
22. Doris Blake, "Farewell to the Vamp," *Washington Post*, November 15, 1925, SM5.
23. "Sir P. Burne-Jones, Painter, Dies at 64," *New York Times*, June 22, 1926, 23.
24. Barbara La Marr, "This Business of Being a Vampire," *Motion Picture*, March 1925, 43.
25. "Thurston's Show," *The Billboard*, December 11, 1920, 12.
26. "Film Lingo," *American Cinematographer*, December 15, 1921, 7.
27. Gorman M. Hendricks, "Haunted Houses and 'Undead' Found Here," *Washington Post*, September 30, 1923, 75.
28. Ibid., 75.

29. "Vampire Admits Sucking Blood of 14 Youths," *Chicago Tribune*, July 12, 1924, 5.
30. "'Vampire Butcher' Describes Murders," *The Times-Picayune* (New Orleans, LA), December 7, 1924, 1.
31. "Vampires Reported in Oaxaca, Mex.," *New York Times*, February 18, 1925, 21.
32. "New Discoveries about the Deadly Vampire," *Hamilton Evening Journal* (Hamilton, OH), January 10, 1925, 18.
33. Arthur Conan Doyle, "*The Adventure of the Sussex Vampire*," *Hearst's International*, January 1924, 31–6.
34. For more information, see Jeremy Brett and Candace R. Benefiel's *Weird Fangs: The Vampire Story in Weird Tales* from 1920–39, a conference paper presented at the Pulp Studies Symposium in 2016, accessed April 12, 2022, https://oaktrust.library.tamu.edu/bitstream/handle/1969.1/195018/2016PSSWeird%20Fangs.pdf?sequence=1.
35. Prospero's Musings," *Baltimore Sun*, June 20, 1921, 4.
36. "Wonder What a Movie Vamp Thinks About," *Davenport Democrat and Leader* (Davenport, IA) 27 July 1924.
37. "*Dracula* Popular for Thirty Years," *Seattle Times*, June 20, 1929, 17.
38. "English Audience Is Horrified by Drama," *Variety*, June 18, 1924, 2.
39. Herbert Farjeon, *The Graphic* (London), February 26, 1927, 320.
40. "A Play of Horrors," *The Daily News* (London), February 16, 1927, 3.
41. "Digging into Dracula," *New York Times*, December 25, 1927, X3.
42. "*Dracula* A Play of Intense Moments," *New Haven Journal-Courier*, September 20, 1927.
43. Gordon M. Leland, "Fulton," *Billboard*, October 15, 1927, 87.
44. "*Dracula*," *Variety*, October 12, 1927, 50.
45. For an example, see "Lycanthropy," *The Evening Post* (New York City, NY), October 23, 1849, 1.
46. Sabine Baring-Gould, *The Book of Werewolves* (London: Studio Editions, 1995), 114, 115, 253.
47. Thomas C. Kennedy, "*The Wolf Woman*," *Motography*, September 9, 1916, 610.
48. "What Our Critics Thought of Them," *Motion Picture Mail*, September 2, 1916, 14.
49. Gary D. Rhodes and Bill Kaffenberger, *Becoming Dracula: The Early Years of Bela Lugosi, Volume 2* (Orlando, FL: BearManor Media, 2021), 108–9.
50. Alan Dale, "Dale Finds Stoker Story Well Done in Stage Version," *New York American*, October 6, 1927.
51. "Vampires All," *Boston Transcript*, October 29, 1927, quoted in Rhodes and Kaffenberger.
52. Photo caption, *Vanity Fair*, December 1927.
53. "Facts about Vampires, Winged and Human," *Cleveland Plain Dealer Magazine* (Cleveland, OH), December 4, 1927, 12–13.
54. "Plays Based Upon Belief of Ancients," *San Francisco Examiner*, August 12, 1928, 8E.

55. "Stake Driven into Heart of Long-Buried Body in Long Island Grave Lay 'Vampire Ghost,'" *Milwaukee Journal*, October 15, 1927, 20.
56. "Science Baffled by This Boy's 'Vampire Complex,'" *New Britain Herald* (New Britain, CT), September 15, 1928, 22.
57. Milton Whitney Schlutter, "Plumbing the Vampire Family History," *Baltimore Sun*, April 28, 1929, 114; "Dr. Summers' *Vampire in Europe* a Structure of Gothic Horror," *Philadelphia Inquirer*, December 7, 1929, 12.
58. Advertisement, *The Bookman: A Review of Books and Life*, November 1929, XXIII.
59. "*Dracula* Comes to Music Box," *Los Angeles Record*, May 18, 1929.
60. "Anent the Vampire Play," *Brooklyn Times-Union*, November 3, 1929, 29.
61. "Theda Bara Seeks Fame She Once Had," *Olean Evening Times* (Olean, NY), December 6, 1929, 14.
62. Richard Koszarski, email to Gary D. Rhodes, April 26, 2012. Koszarski made this discovery in the 1970s while researching Universal's legal files.
63. "Little Theatre Film?," *Oakland Tribune*, December 19, 1920, 43.
64. Quoted in "Inside Stuff – Pictures," *Variety*, April 25, 1951, 14.
65. "Behind the Screen in Movies," *Indiana Evening Gazette* (Indiana, PA), February 18, 1925, 4.
66. "*Dracula* Bought by 'U' for Talkie," *Exhibitors Daily Review*, October 22, 1928, 1.
67. "Universal's *Dracula* to Have Romance and Thrills," *Exhibitors Herald-World*, October 4, 1930, 58.
68. Atkins, 18.
69. These quotations appeared in advertisements in *The Film Daily* on November 10, 1930.
70. These quotations appeared in advertisements in *The Film Daily* on November 12, 1930.
71. Advertisement, *Film Daily*, November 9, 1930, 1.
72. Advertisement, *Variety*, December 31, 1930, 279.
73. Gladys Hall, "The Feminine Love of Horror," *Motion Picture Classic*, January 1931, 33, 86. Emphases in original.
74. "Vampire of Screen Yields to Flappers," *The Evening Repository* (Canton, OH), October 10, 1929, 24.
75. "Tracing Vampire Tradition," *Dallas Morning News*, June 23, 1929, 3.
76. Ernest Jones, *On the Nightmare* (London: Hogarth Press, 1931), 118, 130.

Index

Abbott, Stacey, 11, 16
Abbott and Costello Meet Frankenstein (1948), 200
Acid Thrower, The (1894) see *Vitrioleuse*
Ackerman, Forrest J, 85, 103, 158, 159, 166
Adams, Morticia (character), 200
Adventures of the Sussex Vampire, The (1924), 193
Afterlife Wanderer, The (1915) see *Zagrobnaia skitalitsa*
Allbritton, Louise, 200
Alexander, Kurt, 148
Alexander, Louise, 25
Alexandrovna, Ekaterina, 85
Alibi (1929), 72
Alighieri, Dante, 18, 19
Allianz–Film, 107
Allison, May, 190
Almereyda, Michael, 200
Alraune (1918), 106
Amateur Cinema League, 176, 178
Amateur Movie Makers, 176, 178, 184, 186
American Film Manufacturing, 94
American Mutoscope and Biograph, 1, 9
Ancient Mariner, The (1925), 94, *95*
Anderson, Hans Christian, 34
Anna Boleyn (1920), 104
Apachenrache (1920), 67, 78
Apakyna/Dracula (c. 2021), *87*, 88, 97
Arrival of a Train (1895) see *L'Arrivée d'un train en gare de La Ciotat* 1

Ashes of Embers (1916), 47
Askonas, Paul, *106*, 107, *108*, *109*, 110, *111*, 112, 114, 117, 137
Astronomer's Dream, The (1898) see *L'Lune à un mètre*
Átok vára (1918), 104
Aubert, Lenore, 200
Auerbach, Nina, 63
Aylesworth, Thomas G., 16
Azagarov, Georgii, 43

Babadook, The (2014), 158
Baby Vampire (1917), 54
Backstairs (1921) see *Hintertreppe*
Baclanova, Olga, 4, 88, *90*
Baker, Leroy, 82
Balderston, John L., 186, 194, 195
Balogh, Gyöngyi, 101, 135, 136
Balshofer, Fred J., 110
Balzac, Honoré de, 55
Bara, Theda, *5*, 25, 44, *45*, *46*, 47, 50, 51, 53, 190, 195, 197, 200
Baring-Gould, Sabine, 195
Barlow, Joel, 61
Bartok, Dennis, 165
Barton, Charles, 200
Bat, The (1920), 71–2
Bat, The (1926), 4, 72, 73, *74*, 75
Bat, The (1959), 75
Batman Returns (1992), 158
Batman, The vs. Dracula, The (2005), 75
Bat-Woman, The (c. 1890) see *Le Femme Chauve-Souris*
Bat Whispers, The (1930), 74, 75

Bat's Belfry (1926), 193
Bava, Mario, 81
Beatrice Fairfax (1916), 62
Beck, Edward, 54
Beck, Elga, 91, 92, *93*
Beck, Lili, 43
Belle Dame sans Merci, La (1819), 37–8, 94
Belle dame sans Merci, La (1921), 94
Beloved Vampire, The (1917), 53
belva della mezzanotte, La (1913), 66, 75, 78
Bennett, Charles, 95
Berber, Anita, 110, 112
Berlin: Die Sinfonie der Großstadt (1927), 184
Berlin: Symphony of a Great City (1927) see *Berlin: Die Sinfonie der Großstadt*
Bierman, Robert, 75
Big City, The (1928), 167
Biller, Joe, 27
Billie Van Deusen and the Vampire (1914), 51
Black Pearl, The (1908) see *La Légende du fantôme*
Blake, Michael F., 163, 168
Blind Husbands (1919), 50
Bloch, Robert, 158
Blom, August, *26*
Blonde Vampire, The (1922), *53*, 54
Blood of a Vampire, The (1897), 38
Boleslavsky, Richard, 28
Borland, Carroll, 200
Borst, Ron, 16, 32, 83, 98, 99
Boucicault, Dion, 12
Bow, Clara, 95
Boyer, Maurice, 70
Braddon, Mary E., 41
Bram Stoker's Dracula (1992), 1, 16
Brannan, Margaret, 159

Brennan, Sean, 158
Brent, William, 2
Brockwell, Gladys, *95*
Brown, Clarence, 72
Browne, Porter Emerson, 22, 29, 40, 41, 42, 44, 52, 55
Browning, John Edgar, 10
Browning, Tod, ii, 2, 6, 82, 83, 84, 88, 97, 102, 109, 114, 156, 157, 158, 161, 164, 166, 167, 179, 180, 183, 197, 198, 200, 201
Burne-Jones, Philip, 4, 13, 15, 15, 22, 23, 28, 29, 37, 38, 39, 41, 42, 44, 47, 48, 62, 83, 191, 195
Burns, Ken, 163
Burton, Charlotte, 45
Burton, Tim, 158
Büsche der Pandora, Die (1929), 107
Butterfly Man, The (1920), 51
Byron, Lord, 11

Cabinet of Dr. Caligari, The (1920) see *Das Cabinet des Dr. Caligari*
Cabinet des Dr. Caligari, Das (1920), 4, 103, 104, 105, 106, 114, 140, 141
Cagney, James, 160
Calico Vampire, The (1920), 48
Calmet, Dom Antoine Augustin, 39, 55, 97, 175
Captain Cutlass, the Ocean Spider; or, The Buccaneer's Girls Foe (1884), 62
Captain of the Vampire, The; or, The Smugglers of the Deep Sea (1904), 63
Carewe, Arthur Edmund, 197
Carl Harbaugh Productions, 51
Carmilla (1872), 38, 156
Casablanca (1942), 72
Cavalieri, Lina, 45, *46*
Celluloid Vampires: Life after Death in the Modern World (2007), 11

Cenere e vampe (1918), 84, 99
Chadwick, Arch, 82
Chandler, Helen, 199, *201*
Chaney, Lon, *ii*, 156, *157*, 158, 159, 160, 161, 163, 164, 166, 167, 168, 169, *170*, 179, 180, 183
Chaplin, Charlie, 114
Chastain, George, 106, 162
Chester, C. L., 99
Chevalier des Neiges, Le (1912), 18
Chewning, Wallace, 160
Chomón, Segundo de, 4, 19, 20
Christabel (1816), 1, 38
Christensen, Benjamin, 26
Cinematic Vampires (1992), 16
Circular Staircase, The (1908), 71
City Vampires, The; or, Red Rolfe's Pigeon (1888), 64
Clemenceau Case, The (1915), 44
Clifford, William, 64
Cody, Lew, *50*, 51
Coleridge, Samuel Taylor, 1, 38, 94, 95
Colton, David, 168
Colussi, Béla, 105
Comedy Vampire, A (1917), 48
Conspiracy of Kings, The (1792), 61
Conway, Jack, 158, 159
Coolidge-Rask, Marie, 159, 161, 163
Coppola, Francis Ford, 1, 3
Corpse Vanishes, The (1942), 75
Corvin Film Studio, 108, 109, 136
Count von Count, 80
Crafts, Reverend William F., 189
Crawford, F. Marion, 31, 157
Curious Indian Animals (1913), 99
Curtiz, Michael *see* Mihály Kertész

Dacia Films, 70
Dade, Frances, 199
Dafoe, Willem, 1, 138
Dale, Violet, 23
Dalton, Dorothy, 42, 45, *46*, 189

Dance of Death, The (1914), 27
Dances of Horror, Vices and Ecstasy (1923) *see Tänze des Grauens, des Lasters und der Extsase*
Dandy Dutch, the Decorator from Dead-Lift; or, Saul Sunday's Search for Glory (1889), 64
Danesi, Roberto, 84
Danske Filminstitut, Det, *26*, 35
Dauntless Dan, the Freelance; or Old Kit Bandy in Arcadia (1890), 64
Davis, Paul, 162
Day, Marceline, *ii*
Deception (1920) *see Anna Boleyn*
Dead Men of Pest, The: A Hungarian Legend (1807), 98
Dead Woman in Love, The (1836) *see Le Morte amoureuse*
Deane, Hamilton, 97, 186, 194
Death Tree, The, or Bloodthirsty Susanna (1915) *see Derevo Smerti, ili Krovozhadnaia Susanna*
Défaite de Satan, La (1910), 17
DeMille, William C., 91
Derleth, August, 193
Destruction (1915), 44
Deutsche Bioscop, 91, 140
Deverez, Mildred, 24
Derevo Smerti, ili Krovozhadnaia Susanna (1915), 95, *96*
Devil Bat, The (1940), 69
Devil in the Convent, The (1900) *see Le Diable au couvent*
Devil's Castle, The (1896) *see Le Manoir du diable*
Devil's Claim, The (1920), 50
Devil's Commandment, The (1957) *see I Vampiri*
Devil's Daughter, The (1915), 44
Devil's Playground, The (1894), 37
Devil's Playground, The (1918), 47
Diable au couvent, Le (1900), 18
Dickson, W. K. L., 88

Dieckmann, Enrico, 141, 145, 152
Doctor X (1932), 105
Doré, Gustave, 18
Dorian Grays Portræt (1910), 26
Doro, Grace, 54
Doyle, Arthur Conan, 38, 193
Dracula, the Frolicsome Demon, 176
Dracula (1897), 1, 8, 12, 39, 60, 80, 102, 138, 168, 175, 189
Dracula (1924), 194
Dracula (1927, American), 194–6
Dracula (1927, British), 194
Dracula (1931), 198–9, 200, *201*
Dracula Book, The (1975), 85
Dracula's Daughter (1936), 200
Drakula halála (1921), 4, 102–37
"*Drakula halála* (1921): The Cinema's First Dracula", 116
Drakula (1920), *86*, 87
Dread Central (website), 170
Dream Dance, The (1915), 35
Drew, Lillian, 45, 62
Dreyer, Carl Theodor, 184
Droste, Sebastian, 110, 112
du Maurier, Daphne, 68
Du Maurier, George, 38
Dua-Film, 67
Dulac, Germaine, 94
Dyer, Peter John, 83

Eagle, The (1925), 72
Edeson, Arthur, 72
Edison Manufacturing Company, 9, 15, 16, 18
Edwards, Amelia B., 2
Eis, Alice, 22–3, *27*, *43*
Eisner, Lotte, 91
Elsaesser, Thomas, 9, 10
Elvira (character), 200
Enchanted Well, The (1903) *see Le Puits fantastique*
Erdmann, Hans, 148, 149
Erickson, Niels W., 159

Essanay Film Manufacturing Company, 47, 62
Eternal City, The (1915), 47
Everson, William K., 158
Excursion dans la lune (1908), 19, 33
Excursion to the Moon, An (1908) *see Excursion dans la lune*
Exit the Vamp (1921), *191*
Exploits of Elaine, The (1915), 65, 72, 82

F-0332 (c. 1926), 180, *181*, *182*, 183, 184, 185, 186, 187–8
F-0343 (c. 1928), 177, *178*, *179*, 180, 183, 184, 186, 187
Falena, Ugo, 84
Fall of the House of Usher, The (1928), 177
Famous Hi Henry Minstrels, 22
Famous Monsters of Filmland, 85, 161, 162
Farkas, Jenő, 135
Fazenda, Louise, 74
Fejös, Pál, 103, 106
Female of the Species, The (1916), 47
Femme Chauve-Souris, La (c. 1890), 37
Fenton, Leslie, 95
Fest des Nosferatu, 140–53
Festival of Nosferatu *see* Fest des Nosferatu
Feuillade, Louis, 4, 28, 70, 71, 75
Féval, Paul, 68
FIAT-Film-Gesellschaft, 91, 92
Fielding, Henry, 176
Film Complet, Le, *185*, 188
Filmindustrie AG Wien, 106
Filmwerke, 112
Fils du diable, Le (1906), 17
Fischer, Margarita, 42
Fleck, Jacob and Luise, 106
Fleischer, Dave, 160

Fleischer, Max, 160
Flicker Alley, 15
Flirting Princess, The (1909), 23
Frederick, Pauline, 45, *46*
Florescu, Radu, 16, 99
Fly Low Jack and the Game (1927), 176
Flynn, Emmett J., 190
Flynn, John L., 16
Folies-Bergère, 20
Fool There Was, A (1909), 22, 29, *40*, 41, 44
Fool There Was, A (1914), 44
Fool There Was, A (1915), 44, 47
Fool There Was, A (1922), 190
For the Blood Is the Life (1911), 31, 157
Forbidden Path, The (1918), 50
Forbidden Way, The (1913), 47, 62
Ford, Francis, 50
Forest Vampires, The (1914), 64
Forman, Henry James, 159
4 Devils (1928), 167
Four Wooden Stakes (1925), 193
Fox Film Corporation, 44, 47, 48, 50, 51, 95, 167
Fox, Wallace, 75
Fox, William, 44, 190
Frampton, Daniel, 30
Frankenstein (1931), 72
Freaks (1932), 88
Freda, Riccardo, 75
Freeman, Mary Wilkins, 39
French, Burt, 22–3, *27*, *43*
Fritz, Edmund, 106
Fuji-ko, 22
Fuller, Loïe, 20

Galeen, Henrik, 91, 140, 142, 143, 148, 152, 153
Gambler and the Devil, The (1908), 17
Garon, Pauline, 190
Gasser, Lajos, 106
Gaudreault, André, 9
Gaumont, 28, 68, 69, 70, 71, 78, 106
Gautier, Théophile, 38
Gebert, Michael, 165–6
Gelder, Ken, 171
Genuine (1920), 84
George Kleine, 43, 47
Georges Méliès Encore (2010), 15
Gerard, Theodora, 24
Ghost, A (1797), 16
Ghost Train, The (1901), 1
Gifford, Denis, 16
Gildea and Phillips, 26
Gilling, John, 75
Glaum, Louise, 45, *46*, 48, 195
Gliese, Rochus, 91
Glut, Donald F., 85
Goetz, Carl *see* Karl Götz
Gogos, Basil, 161
Goguen, Michael, 75
Golem, Der (1915), 91, 140
Golem, Der, und die Tänzerin (1917), 91
Goncharov, Vasili, 87
Good Lady Ducayne (1896), 41
Gorky, Maxim, 3
Gosfilmofond, 85, 100
Götz, Karl, 107, 117
"Grand Vampire Transformation Dance" (1890), 22
Grasset, Eugène Samuel, 37
Grau, Albin, 6, 139, 145, 153
Great Train Robbery, The (1903), 18
Griffith, D. W., 10
Groom, Nick, 96
Grube, Elizabeth, 151
Gunning, Tom, 9–10, 20

Haarmann, Fritz, 193
Hadges, Hild, 27, 35
Hammer Film Productions, Ltd., 164, 200
Hands of Orlac, The (1924) *see Orlacs Hände*

Hansen, Kai, 83
Harbaugh, T. C., 62
Harris, Marion 190
Haunted Pajamas, The (1917), 110
Häxan (1922), 26
Hayakawa, Sessue, 50
He Male Vamp, A (1920), 50
Hegener, Anna Marie, 136
Henley, Hobart, 54
Heritage of Hate, The (1916), 50
Herzinger, Charles, 72
Hesperia, Maria, 45
Hiawatha (1855), 35
Hiawatha (1913), 27, 30, 35
Hilliard, Robert, 41, 55
Hillyer, Lambert, 200
Hintertreppe (1921), 184
His Vampy Ways (1919), 50
Historic Films, Inc., 177, 183
Hitchcock, Alfred, 68, 70
Hodder, Reginald, 2
Hoesch, Eduard, 106
Hoffmanns Erzählungen (1923), 106
Hollister, Alice, 4, 43–4, 53
Holmes, Stuart, 51
Homespun Vamp, A (1922), 53
Hopwood, Avery, 71, 75
Horror Studies, 116
Horsemen of Death, The (c. 1926), 176
Hossein, Robert, 75
House of the Vampire, The (1907), 49
Hunger, The (1983), 200
Huston, John, 72

I Am Legend (1954), 81, 97
Ihász, Aladár, 107, 117
I'll Be Your Baby Vamp If You'll Be the Fool There Was (1919), 54
In den Krallen von Gg. Corvin, dem Ausbrecher–König (1920), 67, 78

In the Grip of the Vampire (1912) see *Le mystère des roches de Kador*
In the Shadow of Dazaar, or, At the Mercy of Vampires (1904), 39–40
Ince, Thomas H., 47, 64
Infernal Palace, The (1896) see *Le Manoir du diable*
Ingraham, Prentiss, 62
Innocent Vampire, An (1916), 48
International Film Service, 62
Inventor's Secret, The (1912), 43
Invisible Man, The (1933), 72
Invisible Prince! Or, the Island of Tranquil Delights (1854), 61
Irma Vep (1996), 70
Ivanko, Ekaterina, 86
Ivarono, Yuri, 86

Jamaica Inn (1936), 68
Jamaica Inn (1939), 68
Jannings, Emil, 104
Jansen, Eulalie, 23
Jason, Eric, 85
Jerry and the Vampire (1917), *48*
Jessner, Leopold, 184
John Hopkins III (1920) see *Der Sklavenhalter von Kansas-City*
Johnson, Lee, 52
Jones, Ernest, 96, 200
Joseph, Jeff, 165
Júlia kisasszony (1919), 104, 106

Kaelred, Katharine, *40*, 41, 49
Kahn, Gus, 54
Kalem Company, The, 27, 30, 43, 44, 48, 53, 64
Kane, Bob, 75, 158
Kay-Bee Pictures, 47
Keats, John, 37, 38, 47, 84, 94
Kent, Jennifer, 158
Kermbach, Otto, 151
Kertész, Deszö, 106, 107, 117
Kertész, Mihály, 72, 105, 106
Keystone Film Company, 48, 50

Kid, The (1921), 114
Kind des Teufels, Das (1919), 92
King, Stephen, 97
Kingston, William H. G., 38
Kinkaid, Charles A., 60
Kipling, Rudyard, 4, 9, 14, 15, 22, 23, 24, 27, 28, 29, 37, 38, 39, 41, 42, 43, 44, 47, 48, 62, 83, 191, 195
Knight of the Snow, The (1912) see *Le Chevalier des Neiges*
Kober, Erich, 4, 91
Komet Films, 91
Königin Draga (1920), 107
Korda, Alexander see Sándor Korda
Korda, Sándor, 92, 98, 105
Koster and Bial's Music Hall, 8
Kräly, Hanns, 148
Kronegg, Paul, 110
Kubin, Alfred, 151
Kubrick, Stanley, 166

La Marr, Barbara, 62, 191
Laemmle, Carl, Jr., 198
Lammle, Carl, Sr., 197, 198
Laemmle, "Junior" see Carl Laemmle, Jr.
Lamia (1820), 47, 84
Lang, Fritz, 4, 70, 91, 163, 184
Langella, Frank, 200
Lapa Film Studio, 104, 110
L'Arrivée d'un train en gare de La Ciotat (1895), 1
Laskina, V., 28
Last Man on Earth, The (1964), 81
Latest in Vampires, The (1916), 48
Lathjay, Károly, *104*, 105, 110, 114, 136
Le Fanu, J. Sheridan, 38, 156
Ledebur, Leopold von, 148
Lederle, Charles see Károly Lathjay, 104
Lee, Christopher, 200
Lee, Walt, Jr., 83

Leeds, Arthur, 193
Legend of a Ghost (1908) see *La Légende du fantôme*
Légende du fantôme, La (1908), 4, 11, 19–20, 29, 97, 101
Lehman, Harry, 190
Lewis, Edgar, 35
Lewis, Sheldon, 65
Library of Congress, 30
Liddell, Henry, 38
Lidércnyomás (1920), *103*, 106
Lilith and Ly (1919) see *Lilith und Ly*
Lilith, des Mädchen vom See (1912), 91
Lilith, the Girl from the Lake (1912) see *Lilith, des Mädchen vom See*
Lilith und Ly (1919), xii, 4, *91*, 92, *93*, 96
Lind, John W., 189
Lines to a Mosquito upon My Wife's Bosom (1844), 61
Litván, Péter, 116
Living Pictures (1901), 39
Livingston, Margaret, 189
L'Lune à un mètre (1898), 15
Loïe Fuller (1905), 4, 11, 20, *21*, 28, 29, 81, 88, 90
L'Oiseau de Mort (1914), 69
London After Midnight (band), 158
London After Midnight (1927), ii, 2, 5, 156–74, 179, 180, 183, 184, 197
London After Midnight (1928, book), 159, 161, 163
London After Midnight (2002 restoration), 163–4, 170
Longfellow, Henry Wadsworth, 35
Lord Arthur Savil's Crime (1887), 103
Lothar, Rudolf, 195
Lotus Woman, The (1916), 47, 53
Louisa: A Fragment (1833), 38
Love and Hate (1916), 51
Love and Pain (c. 1895) see *Vampire* (c. 1895)

Love by Proxy (1926), 176
Love Will Conquer (1916), 48
Lu Synd-Wartan-Film GmbH, 83
Lubin Manufacturing Company, 15, 16, 17, 44, 93
Lubitsch, Ernst, 104, 114, 148, 151
Luella Miller (1902), 39
Lugosi, Bela, 68, 97, 102, 104, 105, 107, 114, 161, 167, 183, 194, 195, 196, 197, *198*, *199*, 200, *201*
Lumiere Brothers, 1, 3
Luna-Film-Gesellschaft, 67
Lupack, Barbara Tepa, 82
Lust of the Vampire (1957) *see I Vampiri*
Lux, Margit, 106, 107, *108*, *109*, 112, 117, 136
Lykke-Per (1870), 34

MacIntyre, F. Gwynplaine, 167, 168, 170
Mackie, John, 37
Madnight, Lon, 171
Mágia (1917), 92–3, 101
Magic (1917) *see Mágia*
Malkovich, John, 2
Mallo, Alexander, 86
Maltese Falcon, The (1941), 72
Man of a Thousand Faces, The (1957), 160
Man Who Cast No Shadow, The (1927), 193
Mann, Thomas, 163
Manoir du diable, Le (1896), 3, 11, 15, 16, *17*, 18, 20, 22, 32, 81, 97, 167
Mark of the Vampire (1935), 161, 200
Marmorhaus, 146, 148, 151, 152,
Marmorsaal, 145, *146*, 147
Marriage of the Vampire (1922) *see A vámpír násza*
Marryat, Florence, 38, 47

Marschall, Hans, 91, 92, *93*
Marschner, Heinrich, 138, 143, 148
Marlowe, Don, 167
Marx, Groucho, 159
Mathé, Édouard, 71
Matheson, Richard, 81, 97
Matos, Lajos, 92–3
Mazepa (1909), 87
McAvoy, May, 53
McGilligan, Patrick, 91
McKinley, President William, 64
McNally, Raymond T., 16, 99
Meadows, Joseph K., 184, 185
Méliès, Georges, 3, 11, 15, 16, 17, 18, 19, 81, 167, 178
Melton, J. Gordon, 16, 83, 85, 88
Menzies, William Cameron, 72
Mephisto's Son (1906) *see Le Fils du diable*
Merhige, E. Elias, xiii, 1, 80, 138
Merivale, John Herman, 97–98
Messters Projektion, 42
Metro-Goldwyn-Mayer (MGM), ii, 156, 157, 158, 161, 164, 165, 166, 167, 168, 169, 179, 197, 200
Metropolis (1927), 163, 184
Michelena, Vera, 23
Milk-Fed Vamp, A (1917), 48
Mr. Monster's Movie Gold (1981), 103
Mr. Vampire (1914), 50
Milton, John, 18
Mitchell, Julian, 24–5
Modern Husbands (1919), 50
Monster, The (1922), 72
Monster, The (1925), 72
Monsters Crash the Pajama Party Spook Show Spectacular (2001), 177
Moore, Tom, 35, 44
Moran, Polly, 169
Moroder, Giorgio, 163
Morphy, Michel, 68
Morris, Harry, 39
Morte amoureuse, Le (1836), 38

Mother Riley Meets the Vampire (1952), 75
Movie Makers, 176
Movie Monsters (1969), 16
Munch, Edvard, 3, 7
Murnau, F. W., xii, 2, 4, 6, 30, 103, 110, 113, 139, 140, 148, 150, 151, 152, 153, 167, 168, 175, 184
Musidora, 71
Musser, Charles, 9, 18
Myl, Lene, 107, 114, 117, 136
Mystère des roches de Kador, Le (1912), *68*, 69
Mystery of Ravenswald, The (1878), 60, 75
Mystery of the Wax Museum (1933), 105
Mysteries of Myra, The (1916), 82–3, 93, 98–9

Nächte des Grauens (1917), 83, 99
Nadja (1994), 200
Nagel, Conrad, 156
Naldi, Nita, 45, 190
Napierkowska, Stacia, *28*
Nászdal (1918), 104
National Film Corporation of America, 50
Navette, Nellie, 22
Nead, Lynda, 20
Nero-Film AG, 107
Neufeld, Max, 106
Newark Athlete, The (1891), 88
Newman, Frank, 84
Ngā Taonga Sound & Vision, 15
Niblo, Fred, 62
Night of Horror (1917) see *Nächte des Grauens*
Nightmare (1920) see *Lidércnyomás*
99-es számú bérkocsi (1918), 105, 107
Nosferatu, a Symphony of Horror (1922) see *Nosferatu, eine Symphonie des Grauens*

Nosferatu, eine Symphonie des Grauens (1922), *xii*, xiv, 2, 4–5, *6*, 30, 103, 110, 113, 138–54, 168, 175, 185, *185*, 186
Nurmi, Maila, 200

Occasionally Yours (1920), 51
Ocean Vampire, The; or, The Heiress of Castle Curse (1882), 62
Odd Fresh Water Creatures (1917), 96
Olalla (1885), 36
Oland, Warner, 50
Old Dark House, The (1932), 72
Oldman, Gary, 1
On the Nightmare (1931), 96, 200
Orlacs Hände (1924), 106
Ortner, Theo, 67
Ossenfelder, Heinrich August, 136
Österreichisch-ungarische Kino-Industrie, 106
Österreichisches Filmmuseum, 92
Oswald, Richard, 140, 148, 151
Other Man's Wife, The (1919), 51
Otto, Henry, 95
Our Movie Made Children (1935), 159

Pabst, G. W., 184
Pan-Film, 106
Pánczél, Lajos, 114, 115, 116, 137
Pandora's Box (1929) see *Die Büsche der Pandora*
Panteleev, Aleksandr, 95, 96
Paradise Lost (1667), 18
Parasite, The (1894), 38
Paramount Pictures, 45, 53, 91, 160, 191
Parigi, Robert, 166
Passion de Jeanne d'Arc, La (1928), 184
Passion of Joan of Arc, The (1928) see *La Passion de Jeanne d'Arc*
Pathé Frères, 4, 11, 17, 19, 20, 21
Pearson, Virginia, 41, *42*, *46*, 54, 191
Pénot, Albert Joseph, 37

Perret, Léonce, 68, 69
Peterson, Cassandra, 200
Petrova, Olga, 45, *46*
Pevney, Joseph 160
Phantom, The (1856), 12
Phantom Coach, The (1864), 2
Phantom of the Opera, The (1925), 197
Phantom World, The (1850), 39
Physioc, Wray, 54
Pianelli, Vittorio Rossi, 66
Picart, Karen, 10
Picture of Dorian Gray, The (1910) see *Dorian Grays Portræt*
Pirate, The (1819), 62
Pitt, Ingrid, 164
Planché, James Robinson, 12
Planet of the Vampires (1965), 81
Poe, Edgar Allan, 12, 37
Poet of the Peaks, The (1915), *94*
Polidori, John, 11, 39, 49, 156
Pontoppidian, Clara see Clara Wieth
Porter, Edwin, S. 18
Posner, Bruce, 9
Prana-Film, xiii, 6, 30, 103, 139, 143, 145, 175
Price Mark, The (1917), 47
Princess Ka, 25
Protazanov, Yakov, 28
Przybyszewski, Stanisław, 3
Puits fantastique, Le (1903), 18

Queen Draga (1920) see *Königin Draga*
Quinn, Seabury, 193

Radcliffe, Ann, 166
Ragona, Ubaldo, 81
Raven, The (1845), 37
Reading the Vampire (1994), 171
Rees, Felicia Blake, 48
Rental Car Number 99 (1918) see *99-es számú bérkocsi*
Reported Missing (1922), 190
Reputation (1917), 50
Réthey, Lajos, 107, 117

Return of the Undead (1925), 193
Reventlow, Count Ernst zu, 61
Rich, Vivian, 94
Rieman, Johannes, 148
Riley, Philip J., 161, 162, 163
Rime of the Ancient Mariner, The (1798), 94
Rinehart, Mary Roberts, 71
Roberti, Roberto, 65
Robertson-Cole Pictures, 51
Robison, Arthur, 83
Rogers, Dora, 45
Romero, George, 75
Ronzani, Domenico, 17
Rose of Blood, The (1917), 44
Rosen, Phil, 75
Ruthven, Lord (character), 11, 12, 39
Ruttmann, Walter, 184
Rye, Stellan, 140
Rymer, John Malcolm, 40, 156, 175

St. John, Adela Rogers, 51
Salkow, Sidney, 81
Sands, Francis, 196
Sands, Phebe 196
Satan Defeated (1910) see *La Défaite de Satan*
Satan, or, The Drama of Humanity (1912) see *Satana, ovvero il dramma dell'umanità*
Satana, ovvero il dramma dell'umanità (1912), 18
Saved from the Vampire (1915), 50
Savoia-Film, 84
Scenes from A Fool There Was (1911), 41
Schall, Heinz, 148
Schmidlin, Rick, 163–4, 170
Schwarzwald, Milton E., 54
Schreck, Max, *xiii*, 2, 138, 148, 153, 168, 173, 175
Scott, Tony, 200
Secret of House No. 5, The (1912), 83
Select Pictures, 190

Selig Polyscope, 42
Sesame Street, 80
Shadow of the Vampire (2000), xiv, 1–2, 80, 138
She Was Some Vampire (1916), 48
She-Devil, The (1918), 44
Sheehan, Winfield R., 191
Shepard, Iva, 45
Sherry, J. Barney, 64
Schröder, Greta, 30, *144*, 175
Sideshow Toys, 168–9
Sign of the Vampire, The (1928), 176
Siodmak, Robert, 200
Sjöström, Victor, 43
Skal, David J., 84, 99
Sklavenhalter von Kansas-City, Der (1920), 68, 78
Smith, Joseph C., 23
Société Générale des Films, 184
Something Weird Video, 177
Son of Dracula (1943), 200
Sonya, Magda, 136
Soul of Broadway, The (1915), 47
Spooks Run Wild (1941), 75
Sport-Film, 67
Staiger, Janet, 14, 40
Stedman, Eric, 82, 98
Stevenson, Robert Louis, 36
Stoker, Bram, 1, 3, 4, 6, 8, 12, 14, 15, 16, 23, 29, 30, 36, 39, 47, 54, 60, 71, 75, 80, 85, 86, 88, 97, 102, 103, 104, 105, 106, 110, 114, 115, 136, 138, 142, 156, 157, 169, 175, 177, 184, 186, 189, 194, 195, 198, 200, 201
Story of Vampires, The (1977), 16
Straight Way, The (1916), 47
Strangers of the Night (1923), 62
Stranz, Fred, 67
Strayer, Frank, 75
Stroheim, Erich von, 51
Stropp, Emma, 148
Strøm, Alex, 26
Student von Prag (1913), 140

Student of Prague, The (1913) see *Student von Prag*
Succube, Le (1837), 55
Succubus, The (1837) see *Le Succube*
Sull'orlo dei tetti (1908–1910), 93–4
Summers, Montague, 97, 175, 196
Sunrise: A Song of Two Humans (1927), 184
Suratt, Valeska, 45
Svengali (character) 38, 49, 106, 197
Swing You Sinners! (1930), *160*

Tales of Hoffmann (1923) see *Hoffmanns Erzählungen*
Tanets Vampira (1914), 28, 35
Tanner, Beatrice Rose Stella, 37
Tanz um Liebe und Glück, Der (1921), 151
Tänze des Grauens, des Lasters und der Extsase (1923), 112
Tarpley, Floyd, 45
Taylor, Estelle, 190
Terror, Sid, 167–8
Tespi-Film, 84
Terriss, Tom, 24
Theakston, Jack, 165
Thief of Bagdad, The (1924), 72
Thomas, Olive, 45, *46*
Thompson, Kristin, 9
Thousand Cuts, A (2016), 165
Three Vampires, The; or, Maids Beware of Moonshine (1823), 60–1
Thrillproof Age, The (1927), 176
Thury, Elemér, 107, 117
Thurston, Howard, 192
Tichenor, Edna, ii, 156, 197
Tiger Woman, The (1917), 44
Titley, Daniel, ii, 157, 170, 171
Tláni, az elvarázsolt hercegasszony (1920), 104
To Oblige a Vampire (1917), 48
Tom Jones (1927), 176
torre dei vampiri, La (1913), 84

Tourjansky, Viktor *see* Viacheslav Turzhanskii
Trail of the Vampire, The; or, The Mysterious Crimes of Prospect Park (1904), 64
Tree of Knowledge, The (1920), 91
Tricked by a Vampire (1914), 45, 49
Trilby (1894), 38, 49
Trilby (1912), 106
Trilby (1923), 197
Trip to the Moon, A (1902) *see Le Voyage dans la Lune*
Trovatore, Il (1909), 93
Trovatore, Il (1911), 93
Trovatore, Il (1914), 93
Tüchten, Jenő, 110, 112
Turner Classic Movies (TCM), 163, 165
Turzhanskii, Viacheslav, 4, 85, 87, 88, 89
Twentieth Century Maids (1898), 39
Twitchell, James B., 94

UFA GmbH, 163, 184
Umbrella Entertainment, 158
Unger, Gladys, 195
Unheimliche Geschichten (1919), 140
Unholy Three, The (1930), 158
United Artists, 71, 72, 74,
Universal Ike and the Vampire (1914), 47–8
Universal Pictures, 47, 48, 50, 64, 65, 72, 82, 102, 109, 160, 197, 198, 199, 200, 201
Unseen Cinema: Early American Avant-Garde Film, 1894–1941 (2005), 9
Uriella (1854), 17
Usai, Paolo Cherchi, 177
Usurer, The (1910), 64

Vamp, The (1918), 47
Vamp Cure, The (1918), 48
Vamp of the Camp, The (1917), 48

Vampe di gelosia (1913), 84, 99
Vamped (1923), 48
Vamping Babies (1926), 84, 99
Vamping Reuben's Millions (1917), 48
Vamping the Vamp (1918), 48
Vampir, Der (1748), 138
vámpír násza, A (1922), 110
Vampira (character), 200
vampira indiana, La (1913), 65–66
Vampire (c. 1895), 3, 7
Vampire, La (1855/1865), 68
Vampire, Le: les mystères du crime (1886), 68
Vampire, The (1826), 2
Vampire, The (1897), 9, *13*, 14, 23, 37, 39, 42, 48, 191
Vampire, The (1899), 62
Vampire, The (1909), 50
Vampire, The (1910), 42
Vampire, The (1913), 43–4
Vampire, The (1914) *see L'Oiseau de Mort*
Vampire, The (1915), 45
Vampire Almanac, The: The Complete History (2022), 88
Vampire Ambrose (1916), 50
Vampire Bat, The (1933), 75
Vampire Bat and Armadillo, The (1911), 84
Vampire Book, The: The Encyclopedia of the Undead (1965), 85
Vampire, The: His Kith and Kin (1929), 196
Vampire in Europe, The (1929), 196
Vampire Maid, The (1900), 39
Vampire of Düsseldorf, The (1965), 75
Vampire of Indiana, The (1913) *see La vampira indiana*
Vampire of the Continent, The (1916), 61
Vampire of the Desert, The (1913), 43
Vampire, The; or, Pedro Pacheco and the Bruxa (1862), 38
Vampire Bride, The (1833), 38

Vampire Dancer, The (1912) *see Vampyrdanserinden*
Vampire Dances, 22–9, 34, 42, 70, 81
Vampire Out of Work, A (1916), 48
"*Vampire," the Bravo; or, Man of Many Disguises* (1891), 64
Vampire Woman, The (1917) *see Zhenshchina vampir'*
Vampire's Dance (1914) *see Tanets Vampira*
Vampire's Kiss, The (1989), 75
Vampire's Prey, The; or, Nick Carter's Blow (1910), 64
Vampire's Tower, The (1913) *see La torre dei vampiri*
Vampire's Trail, The (1914), 44
Vampire's Treasure, The (1922), 60
Vampires, Les (1915–1916), 4, 28, 70–1
Vampires, The (1915–1916) *see Les Vampires*
Vampires and Vampirism (1914), 15
Vampires de la Côte, Les (1908), 68
Vampires of the Big City (1914) *see Vampyre der Großstadt*
Vampires of the Coast (1908) *see Les Vampires de la Côte*
Vampires of the Night (1913) *see La belva della mezzanotte*
vampiri, I (1957), 75
vampiro, Il (1914), 66
Vamps and Scamps (1923), 48
Vampyr, Der (1828), 138
Vampyr, Der (1911), 42
Vampyr, Der (1920), 67
Vampyr im Spiegel, Der (1921) 92
Vampyrdanserinden (1912), *26*, 29, 30, 35, 81, 88, 90
Vampyre, The (1819), 39, 49, 156
Vampyre, The (1837), 2
Vampyre, The (1858) 62
Vampyre, The; or, The Bride of the Isles (1820), 12
Vampyre der Großstadt (1914), 67

Vampyren (1910), 42
Varney the Vampire (1845–1847), 39, 166, 175, 186
Vasco the Vampire (1914), 39, 156, 175, 186
Veda the Vampire (1916), 45
Viereck, George S., 49
Ville-Vampire, La (1865), 68
Virtuous Vamp, The (1919), 53
Visaroff, Michael, 161
Vitagraph, 15, 17, 43, 48
Vitrioleuse (1894), 37
Vlad Dracula *see* Vlad III
Vlad Drăculea *see* Vlad III
Vlad Țepeș *see* Vlad III
Vlad III, 102, 105
Voyage dans la Lune, La (1902), 19

Wallack's Theatre, 12
Walsh, Raoul, 72
Walthall, Henry B., 169
Wandering Ghosts (1911), 31
Wangenheim, Gustav von, 144
Warner Bros., 72, 105, 158
Was She a Vampire? (1915), 45
Watson, James Sibley, 177
Watson, Michael, 63
Weaver, Tom, xii, 168
Webber, Melville, 177
Wedding Song (1918) *see Nászdal*
Wegener, Paul, 91, 140, 152
Weinstock, Jeffrey, 33
Weird Tales, 193
Wells, H. G., 103, 107
Werwolf, Der (1921), 195
Werewolf, The (1924), 195
West, Raymond B., 195
West, Roland, 71, 72, 74
Whale, James, 72, 82
Wharton, Leopold, 82
Wharton, Theodore, 82
When a Woman Loves (1913), 47
When That Vampire Rolled Her Vampy Eyes at Me (1917), *52*

While the City Sleeps (1928), 159
White, Pearl, 65
Wiene, Robert, 4, 84, 103, 106, 140
Wieth, Clara, 26
Wilbur, Crane, 72, 75
Wilde, Oscar, 103
Wolf Woman, The (1916), 195
Woman's Slave, A (1911), 42–3
Woolf, Edgar Allan, 49
Wright, Dudley, 15

Yarbrough, Jean, 69
Young, Clara Kimball, 45, *46*
Youngblood, Denise J., 83, 86

Zaccaria, Gino, 84
Zagrobnaia skitalitsa (1915), 4, 88, *89*, *90*, 96
Zeyn, Willy, 151
Zhenshchina vampir' (1917), 43, 56
Zimmermann, Patricia R., 177

EU representative:
Easy Access System Europe
Mustamäe tee 50, 10621 Tallinn, Estonia
Gpsr.requests@easproject.com